The Making of T.S. Eliot

The Making of T.S. Eliot

A Study of the Literary Influences

Joseph Maddrey

McFarland & Company, Inc., Publishers

Jefferson, North Carolina, and London

LIBRARY OF CONGRESS CATALOGUING-IN-PUBLICATION DATA

Maddrey, Joseph, 1979–
The making of T.S. Eliot : a study of the literary influences / Joseph Maddrey.
p. cm.
Includes bibliographical references and index.

ISBN 978-0-7864-4271-3
softcover : 50# alkaline paper ∞

1. Eliot, T. S. (Thomas Stearns), 1888–1965 — Sources. 2. Eliot, T. S. (Thomas Stearns), 1888–1965 — Childhood and youth. 3. Eliot, T. S. (Thomas Stearns), 1888–1965 — Knowledge — Literature. 4. Eliot, T. S. (Thomas Stearns), 1888–1965 — Philosophy. 5. Eliot, T. S. (Thomas Stearns), 1888–1965 — Religion. 6. Poets, American — 20th century — Biography. 7. Influence (Literary, artistic, etc.) I. Title.
PS3509.L43Z713 2009   821'.912 — dc22 [B]   2009012380

British Library cataloguing data are available

On the cover: Gerald Kelly. *Portrait of T.S. Eliot.* Oil on canvas, 114.6 × 94 cm., 1962 (National Portrait Gallery, Smithsonian Institution / Art Resource, New York)

Manufactured in the United States of America

McFarland & Company, Inc., Publishers
Box 611, Jefferson, North Carolina 28640
www.mcfarlandpub.com

Acknowledgments

No one who writes about T.S. Eliot in this day and age can do so without acknowledging a huge debt to those critics and teachers who have inevitably helped to shape their thoughts on the subject. I humbly acknowledge those writers whose influence will be obvious in these pages — particularly Lyndall Gordon, F.O. Mathiessen, Helen Gardner, Grover Smith, Bernard Bergonzi, Ronald Bush and Ronald Schuchard. What I have attempted here is not literary criticism, but a personal investigation and synthesis. I am aware of certain gross generalizations and oversimplifications in this text — the result of my own desire to produce a concise overview that will enhance enjoyment and understanding of Eliot's poetry. I have chosen — for the sake of my own clarity — to devote most of my investigation to poetry and criticism that Eliot himself wrote, and to works that influenced him, rather than on the intimidating wealth of criticism that has been written *about* Eliot. This seemed to me the most rewarding approach, particularly since Eliot refers to his own literary criticism as "a by-product of my private poetry-workshop; or a prolongation of the thinking that went into the formation of my own verse."[1]

For helping to shape my way of thinking about literature, I gratefully acknowledge the influence of two wonderful teachers: Lisa Marshall and Dr. Robert Geary. For editorial guidance, I am indebted to Liza Douglass and Dr. Laura Holt. Most of all, I am indebted to my parents, Tom and Renelle Maddrey, for a lifetime of support.

I am also extremely grateful for various public-access collections, including those of the Virginia Beach Public Library, the Association for Research and Enlightenment in Virginia Beach, the Los Angeles Public Library, the Charles Young Research Library at UCLA, as well as numerous public domain collections online.

Table of Contents

Part VI: Between Dying and Birth (1922–1930)

A Note on Translations

This seems as good a place as any to admit that my firsthand experience of all the non–English-language works discussed herein has been via English translation. That is how I discovered the classics of Western literature in high school and college, beginning with Robert Fitzgerald's translations of Homer and George Thompson's translations of Aeschylus. I discovered Augustine via R.S. Pine-Coffin, Goethe and Nietzsche via Walter Kaufmann, Dostoevsky via Constance Garnett. In rereading many of these pivotal works, I found that I was most comfortable with the translations that I'd studied previously and so I have used those editions for the purposes of quotation. In approaching works that I had not already studied in depth, I compared multiple editions in an effort to identify translations that seemed particularly alive to me — as, for example, Charles Martin's translation of Ovid's *Metamorphoses* and Mark Musa's translation of Dante's *Divine Comedy*.

T.S. Eliot read many of the classics in their original Greek and Latin, and discovered Dante "the Harvard way" — reading the original Italian, before he had a firm grasp of Italian grammar, with the help of an English prose translation for side-by-side comparison.[2] Likewise, he discovered a group of highly influential French poets — Baudelaire, Rimbaud, Laforgue, Valéry, et al. — by reading them in their original language. I, on the other hand, have relied largely on translations by Kendall Lappin, Wyatt Mason, William Jay Smith and James R. Lawler, respectively — not because I can affirm these translations to be the most authentic English translations, but because they have inspired me the most. The same holds true for Eastern texts: I have studied (and been moved by) Vedic texts in translations by Max Muller, Eknath Easwaran and A. Parsatharathy, so those are the editions that I've quoted from.

In other cases, where there was no distinct definitive English translation, I have chosen translations based on what was readily available — such is the case with many of the mystic writers as well as German novelist and essayist Herman Hesse. In general, I have tried to avoid translations that use archaic language. The major exception is the King James Version of the Bible, which I've used throughout because of Eliot's use of it in his own work, and his stated preference for it.[3]

1

Preface

To the best of my memory, I first saw the name T.S. Eliot in print when I was a freshman in high school. I was reading Stephen King's novel *The Stand*, which featured a haunting epigraph from "The Hollow Men." I had no idea who Eliot was, or what he was selling, but the incantation struck me. A year or two later, I ran across Eliot's name again when I read the third book in King's *Dark Tower* series, subtitled *The Waste Lands*. I understood that there was some loose connection between the story I was reading and Eliot's poetry, just as I understood that the first *Dark Tower* book had been loosely based on Robert Browning's poem "Childe Roland to the Dark Tower Came." Once again, I was haunted by an epigraph from Eliot, this one ending with the phrase "I will show you fear in a handful of dust."

Soon afterward, my father gave me a paperback edition of Eliot's *Selected Poems* that he had held onto since he was in high school. I began to read and became captivated with the cadences, the imagery, and the enigmatic quality of Eliot's first major poem, "The Love Song of J. Alfred Prufrock." I was convinced that I understood the hidden meaning of the poem, which the poet conveyed through tone rather than a straightforward narrative. In my mind, Prufrock's "insidious intent" was the dark matter of a Stephen King novel ... or worse. Shortly before I picked up "Prufrock," I had read a book on the Whitechapel murders. As a result, the setting of "Prufrock" conjured very specific images in my mind: the narrow, polluted lanes of East London at the end of the 19th century, where Jack the Ripper made his rounds. I began to think of Prufrock as what FBI profiler John Douglas might call a "thought-criminal."

In his book *Serial Killers: Death and Life in America's Wound Culture*, Mark Seltzer theorizes that serial killers are a product of industrialization: machines have replaced the human work force, and the consumer culture that stems from mass production has diminished the value of individuality. Men no longer feel like men in the most primal sense, because their life's work has become intellectual rather than physical. Overt physicality is unnecessary and must be repressed. Frustrated, the serial killer lashes out in a desperate attempt to assert himself. The thought-criminal — like Prufrock, or Dostoevsky's Underground Man — implodes.

I kept reading Eliot and, by the time I got to college, I had moved from "Prufrock" to *The Waste Land*, in which the poet's quest for meaning has driven him to near-schizophrenia. Unlike "Prufrock," *The Waste Land* ends with the hope of violent purgation. The poet demands action, but it is unclear whether he takes action and, if so, where this action leads him.

In the summer of 2000, I visited London — Eliot's chosen city — to study Shakespeare at the Globe Theatre. On my first trip to the Globe, I passed by a faded mural on an exterior wall of one of the older buildings in West Bank, just a few blocks from London Bridge. It was difficult to distinguish many of the figures in the painting, but one block of text was clear. It read: "the fear in a handful of dust." A few days later, I visited an exhibit at the British Library, where I heard an audio recording of Eliot reading "The Burial of the Dead," the first section of *The Waste Land*. It was the first time I had heard the poet's voice, and I was captivated by the way he spoke his words, matter-of-factly, "I will show you fear in a handful of dust." He sounded like a man who had lost hope. Later that week, I attended Sunday service at Westminster Abbey, where the priest gave a sermon based on a line from *East Coker*, the first of Eliot's *Four Quartets*: "In my end is my beginning." This reminded me of a favorite passage from Aldous Huxley's *The Doors of Perception* (1954): "Our goal is to discover that we have always been where we ought to be."[4] Had the seemingly hopeless poet eventually found himself where he "ought to be"? It seemed that I was not done with Eliot.

The following summer, I accepted an internship in London and spent several months living a few blocks from Eliot's one-time workplace in Russell Square. I read *Four Quartets* daily. They seemed to offer the solution that Eliot's earlier poetry had been pursuing. I knew that he had accepted Christianity later in his life, but I wondered how the young "thought-criminal" could have embraced any single philosophy or religion ... and whether Christianity had genuinely helped him to find peace of mind.

I began this study of Eliot's life and influences not simply with a desire to understand his poetry but — as most students of literature do — with the hope that literature will help me better understand the world, and my place in it. Since Eliot's poetry so effectively conveys the nagging fears, doubts and questions that have always been important to me, I decided to use his work as a guide.

I have spent four years examining Eliot's poetry within the context of his own studies and experiences simply because I enjoyed it. In one of his final essays, Eliot writes that "we must enjoy the poetry before we attempt to penetrate the poet's mind; we must enjoy it before we understand it, if the attempt to understand is to be worth the trouble."[5] I cannot imagine that any study of Eliot's poetry would be worthwhile to someone who has not first read and enjoyed the poetry itself. As it happens, there is no shortage of readers who have been affected by Eliot's work.

I am certainly not the first reader to be drawn in by Eliot's rhymes and cadences. We are intrigued by enigmatic imagery and phrases that stay with us for days or weeks afterward, haunting us like a musical melody. Some readers go back and tackle the poetry in scientific fashion — deconstructing it as if it were a clock, to see what makes it tick. Of course, it's not that easy. Mining Eliot's poetry for details may enhance the reader's knowledge, but can often muddle understanding. By focusing too much on concrete details, we sometimes forget our initial reaction to the poetry, which can be the clearest explanation of the nebulous whole. Eliot wanted us to analyze our reactions, not just his intentions. He felt convinced that the two would overlap — because he was, at the most basic level, writing about the human condition. Eliot spent his life studying and trying to create timeless art that would speak to all of us. Certain thoughts and ideas, he believed, affect all of us — they are universal.

Early 20th century readers regarded Eliot as the voice of the modern age. At the beginning of the 21st century, we are in a better position to understand the more timeless aspects of Eliot's art. Certainly, Eliot expressed the mindset of Europe through the course of two world wars by expressing his own personal anxieties, hopes and fears with unremitting honesty. But his poetry can also be said to illustrate the angst of the 21st-century Information

Age, in which there is more readily accessible information on any subject — including Eliot's poetry — than any individual could ever process, let alone assimilate. More than ever, the individual struggles to see the universals beyond so many details. It is enough to drive the seeker to madness.

In fact, that is more or less what happened to Eliot, who believed that the ultra-rational methodology of Western philosophy could not make sense of the world. Only through his own impressionistic art was he able to express honestly the chaos of the world in all its minutiae, as well as a reassuring sense of the whole. Through poetry, he found meaning in life and began to understand his place in the world. *The Waste Land* finds Eliot at a crisis point — seeking some kind of universal that exists outside of his own fractured perspective. Later, he would say that his search had always been a search for God. Until his conversion at age 38, however, the concept of "God" was a confusing one. Modern man found himself living in a global community populated by hundreds of gods, living and dead, in cultures around the world. How should one go about choosing between them? *Does one even have a choice?*

Doubts and anxieties colored the world of the young poet. In his studies, he gravitated toward those voices that intrigued him: the late Victorian poets of despair and the French Symbolists provided a point of departure and a template for his early poetry. Encouraged by college professors to study the Western classics, Eliot soon could place his favorite poets within the context of a vast, continuous literary tradition. One professor also encouraged him to study Eastern literature, which Eliot struggled to assimilate into a coherent modern worldview. So we see that Eliot's personal involvement with world literature began with vague impressions, just as everyone's does, and proceeded to critical analysis. In his best poetry, Eliot unites impression and analysis and makes the timeless questions at the heart of all world literature come alive in the contemporary world, and in the individual's imagination.

For the past few decades, literary critics have tended toward "biographical criticism," examining literature as a product of both literary tradition and personal history. Although Eliot was often associated with New Criticism, and once argued that "poetry is not the expression of personality, but an escape from personality,"[6] the biographical critic has a good chance of penetrating his personal beliefs by studying his works as, at least in part, a means of self-understanding. It is, of course, fair to suggest that different readers will attribute different meanings to a poem. Perhaps the same reader, at different times, will have multiple interpretations of the same poem. Eliot would not want us to insist that any particular meaning is "right" or "wrong" — only that a specific interpretation may be right for a specific person at a specific time. This is true of the poet himself: each poem was a product of time and place — a reflection of one stage in his intellectual and emotional development.

Poetry, Eliot believed, is a means to an end. Through the same means, individuals may reach different conclusions. This book is partly a means for me to reach my own conclusions, and partly a means toward understanding how Eliot reached his. I believe that I would not be drawn to Eliot's poetry if he and I did not have some things in common, so it is fair to assume that I may be able to learn something from his example. For me — and for many readers — Eliot's poetry provides a point of departure.

The main thrust of this study is simple: how did Eliot get from "Prufrock" to *Ash Wednesday*, from "thought-criminal" to outspoken advocate of the Christian faith? I tackle his spiritual and intellectual evolution in stages, by trying to see the world as Eliot did. In the first section, I examine his childhood influences as well as the literary influences that inspired him to write his earliest poetry. In the second section, I examine his years as an undergraduate at

Harvard University, where he focused his studies on the Western canon and came to understand his own writing as the product of a cumulative literary tradition. (The reader who has a thorough grounding in the classics might conceivably skip much of this section, which serves mainly as a reminder of the foundational ideas of Western literature — which are also, as will be demonstrated, the foundational ideas of Eliot's work.) The third section focuses on his postgraduate studies in Eastern philosophy and his attempt to construct a personal life philosophy based on the whole of his formal education. The second half of the book tracks Eliot's life as an American expatriate, living in London between the years 1915 and 1930. In the fourth section, I examine Eliot's ill-fated marriage and his intellectual engagement with the literary tradition of his new country. The fifth section finds the poet examining his identity as a European in the aftermath of the Great War — an examination which, coupled with personal crisis, produced his masterpiece *The Waste Land*. Finally, in the sixth section, I examine the way that Eliot's intellectual pursuits led him to a spiritual rebirth that simultaneously reflected his past and revealed his future. The end, as Eliot explains in *East Coker*, is implicit in the beginning — so we must start there.

PART I

A Point of Departure
(1905–1910)

Some are born to sweet delight
Some are born to endless night
— William Blake

Childhood

Thomas Stearns Eliot was born on September 26, 1888, in St. Louis, Missouri, two and a half miles west of the Mississippi River. He was the seventh child of Henry Ware Eliot, a painter turned businessman, and Charlotte Champe Stearns, a schoolteacher and amateur poet. Tom was the baby in the family; his parents were in their mid–forties when he was born, and his youngest brother, Henry, was almost nine years older.

The Eliot family lived in a section of town that Tom's grandfather had helped settle in the 1830s. William Greenleaf Eliot (1811–1887) was a descendant of Andrew Eliott (1627–1649), an Englishman who had come to America as a member of the Massachusetts Bay Colony. Like his parents and grandparents, William was raised in Boston, where he attended Harvard Divinity School and became an ordained Unitarian minister. Like his more distant ancestor, he had the pioneer spirit and quickly left his childhood home. In 1834 he headed west to found the first Unitarian church of St. Louis. He also contributed significantly to the founding of Washington University and served as its first president. William Greenleaf Eliot's mission was to build a healthy, conservative culture in one of America's newest and fastest-growing cities, so he was constantly fighting for better standards of education and sanitation, as well as lobbying on behalf of women's rights and prohibition and against the legalization of prostitution.[1]

In a reflection on his childhood, Eliot later wrote:

I was brought up to be very much aware of him. [...] The standard conduct was that which my grandfather had set; our moral judgments, our decisions between duty and self-indulgence, were taken as if, like Moses, he had brought down the tables of the Law, any deviation from which would be sinful.[2]

The Law, for William Greenleaf Eliot, was in large part Unitarianism, the religious movement that began in the middle of the eighteenth century and was championed by New England's intellectual elite: Thomas Paine, Benjamin Franklin, Ralph Waldo Emerson, Nathaniel Hawthorne and Herman Melville.

The name *Unitarianism* connoted a rejection of the Church of England's doctrine of the Trinity and comprised a distinctly American dismissal of traditional theology. Barrett Wendell, an early 20th century professor at Harvard, offers an explanation of the effect of Unitarianism on Christian belief:

> According to the old creed, which held salvation from Adam's fall to be attainable only through God's grace, won by the mediation of Jesus Christ, the divine character of Christ was essential to redemption; without his superhuman aid all human beings were irrevocably doomed. But the moment you assumed human nature to contain adequate seeds of good, the necessity for a divine Redeemer disappeared, and redemption became only a matter of divine convenience. The second person of the Trinity [the Son] having thus lost his mystic office, the third [the Holy Spirit] spread wing and vanished into the radiance of a new heaven.[3]

Echoing this perspective, biographer Peter Ackroyd refers to Unitarianism as "Puritanism drained of its theology."[4] Born into this legacy, T.S. Eliot found the religion to be as empty as this description suggests: it provided rules for what was "done and not done,"[5] but no metaphysical answers. He traced the origins of his own philosophical poetry back to his childhood — specifically, to what he later regarded as the shortcomings of his family's religious tradition. In a 1937 introduction to Djuna Barnes's novel *Nightwood*, he writes, "In the Puritan morality that I remember, it was tacitly assumed that if one was thrifty, enterprising, intelligent, practical and prudent in not violating social conventions, one ought to have a happy and 'successful' life. Failure was due to some weakness or perversity peculiar to the individual; but the decent man need have no nightmares."[6] One might conclude that Eliot's religious training transformed his fears of failure into feelings of guilt. Since his family regarded such feelings as "weak," he repressed them. In the following years, Eliot's nightmares began coming to life in his poetry.

In addition to being troubled by his intellectual environment, the poet was also troubled by his physical environment — or, at least, he unconsciously associated the latter with the former. In *Notes on Some Figures behind T.S. Eliot*, Herbert Howarth explains that during Eliot's childhood St. Louis was struggling to redefine itself as a city of the future, but visions of a great city on the hill were marred by public corruption. Despite the civic legacy of men like William Greenleaf Eliot, parts of turn-of-the-century St. Louis (including the neighborhood where Henry Ware Eliot and his family lived) slowly became portraits of urban blight — the type of portrait that would appear in Eliot's early poetry.

In the summers, the family was eager to escape St. Louis and head to their traditional vacation spot on the rocky seashore of Gloucester, Massachusetts. For the rest of his life, the poet would remember that setting with heartfelt nostalgia. In multiple works — his 1905 prose pieces "The Tale of a Whale" and "The Man Who Was King," his 1911 article "Gentleman and Seamen," his 1928 introduction to James B. Connolly's *Fisherman of the Banks* and appreciations of *Captains Courageous* by Rudyard Kipling — he revealed his fascination with the near-mythic life of seamen. Despite ancestral ties to New England, however, the family always returned to St. Louis in the autumn, to a dingy neighborhood with few children. In that solitary environment, T.S. Eliot became highly imaginative. He composed his first poem in 1897 — four verses about the sadness of having to start school again every Monday morning.[7]

Edgar Allan Poe and Edward Fitzgerald: Shadowy Sounds from Visionary Wings

Biographers Lyndall Gordon and Peter Ackroyd both argue that one of Eliot's earliest literary influences was Edgar Allan Poe (1809–1849), whose works he discovered in the waiting room of a dentist's office. It was a rhyme from a poem called "The Assignation" that captured his imagination: "Stay for me there, I will not fail / To meet thee in that hollow vale."[8] The narrator of "The Assignation," in preparing to recount a tale of supernatural horror, reinforces this dim perception of things unknown: "There are surely other worlds than this / other thoughts than the thoughts of the multitude / other speculations than the speculations of the sophist." With a sense of awe for the infinite variety of life, Poe ushers the aspiring artist into the world of imagination:

> Ours is a world of words: Quiet we call
> "Silence" — which is the merest word of all.
> All Nature speaks, and ev'n ideal things
> Flap shadowy sounds from visionary wings —
> But ah! Not so when, thus, in realms on high
> The eternal voice of God is passing by;
> And the red winds are withering in the sky!
> ["Al Aaraaf"][9]

Later in life, Eliot claimed that he could not be sure of the extent of Poe's influence on him, but he seems to be describing his own experience when he describes the average "cultivated" reader's receptivity to the poet:

Poe is the author of a few, a very few short poems which enchanted him for a time when he was a boy, and which do somehow stick in the memory. I do not think that he re-reads these poems, unless he turns to them in the pages of an anthology; his enjoyment of them is rather the memory of an enjoyment which he may for a moment recapture. They seem to him to belong to a particular period when his interest in poetry had just awakened.[10]

Poe undoubtedly appealed to the aspiring poet in moments of melancholy, capturing — with poems like "Tamerlane" — the fragility of youth:

> ... boyhood is a summer sun
> Whose waning is the dreariest one.
> For all we live to know is known,
> And all we seek to keep hath flown.[11]

Verses like this may have heightened the more fearful aspects of Eliot's coming of age, inspiring him to use poetry as an outlet for overwhelming emotions. It is difficult to explain the meaning of some of Poe's verses, but the emotional tone — achieved through regular rhythm and word choice rather than through a conventional narrative — is, for the adolescent, more affecting than logic. Though Eliot later dismissed Poe as an emotionally stunted man whose ideas are "*entertained* rather than believed,"[12] it seems clear that Poe appealed to him at a time when Eliot himself was most impressionable. Perhaps for that reason, much of Eliot's early poetry displays the same fearful, romantic tone.

At the age of fourteen, Eliot was equally fascinated by Edward Fitzgerald's (1809–1883) English translation of the *Rubaiyat* by Persian poet Omar Khayyam. He says, "It was like a sudden conversion; the world appeared anew, painted with bright, delicious and painful colours."[13] Khayyam, like Poe, saw the beauty of life in the shadow of death:

> Oh, come with old Khayyam, and leave the Wise
> To talk; one thing is certain, that Life flies;
> One thing is certain, and the Rest is Lies;
> The flower that once has blown forever dies.[14]

Fitzgerald's translation was certainly among the inspirations for T.S. Eliot's first poetic experiments. A pair of melancholy poems, "A Lyric" and "A Fable for Feasters," appeared in his high school newspaper in 1905. As would become his habit, Eliot continued to revise until he was satisfied that he had said what he meant to say. "A Lyric" blossomed two years later, and was published as "Song" in *The Harvard Advocate*:

> If space and time, as sages say,
> Are things which cannot be,
> The fly that lives a single day
> Has lived as long as we.
> But let us live while yet we may,
> While love and life are free,
> For time is time, and runs away,
> Though sages disagree.
>
> The flowers I sent thee when the dew
> Was trembling on the vine,
> Were withered ere the wild bee flew
> To suck the eglantine.
> But let us haste to pluck anew
> Nor mourn to see them pine,
> And though the flowers of love be few
> Yet let them be divine.[15]

Eliot says that, in the following years, he took the "usual adolescent course" of immersion in the popular English Romantic and Victorian poets — Byron, Shelley, Keats, Dante Gabriel Rossetti and Algernon Swinburne.[16] Until he was twenty-two, Eliot's favorite poetry was filled with images and rhymes that evoked a passionate response for very personal reasons. In later years, he maintained that this indiscriminate approach to poetry was an important part of his development. Perhaps for this reason, the mature poet strived to fill his own works with the kind of imagery and rhymes that evoke a passionate response from young readers. On this level, Eliot would always be a Romantic poet.

Fin de Siècle

At the end of the 19th century, popular American literature was largely defined by feelings of optimism, but T.S. Eliot says that Harvard undergraduates at this time were more interested in English literature than in American literature — especially English literature of the 1890s, which was characterized by feelings of "passionate boredom."[17] The apocalyptic air of the turn-of-the-century literature in the 1890s had been of languid contemplation — the sort of apocalypse that sounds a whimper instead of a bang. Ennui was the defining characteristic of this "tragic generation."

In London, William Butler Yeats had founded the Rhymers' Club, a venue that attracted poets of fashionable despair. The group, which included Arthur Symons, Ernest Dowson, John Davidson and Lionel Johnson, met regularly at a pub on Fleet Street to share poetry and criticisms. Symons and Dowson received their greatest inspiration not from Victorian-era peers, but from French Romantic poets like Charles Baudelaire, Paul Verlaine and Arthur Rimbaud. To Symons, the Rhymers' Club meetings were an attempt to approximate the intellectual climate of Paris. In 1900, he wrote:

> In Paris, it is the most natural thing in the world to meet and discuss literature, ideas, one's own and one another's work; and it can be done without pretentiousness or constraint, because, to the Latin mind, art, ideas, one's work and the work of one's friends, are definite and important things, which it would never occur to anyone to take anything but seriously. In England art has to be protected not only against the world, but against one's self and one's fellow artist, by a kind of affected modesty which is the Englishman's natural pose, half pride and half self-distrust.[18]

Perhaps it was this "affected modesty" that made several of these poets so tragic. For Dowson, Davidson and Johnson, success was short-lived: each of them died shortly after the turn of the century.

After Yeats, Ernest Dowson (1867–1900) was the most lyrical of the Rhymers, and the one whose poetry would have the most obvious influence on Eliot's poetry. Many of Dowson's poems reflect a feverish desperation to escape the too-busy world around him; he yearns for silence and rest, and envies the lives of religious figures, cloistered behind the walls of London churches, where they are saved from the chaos outside:

> Outside, the world is wild and passionate;
> Man's weary laughter and his sick despair
> Entreat at their impenetrable gate:
> They heed no voices in their dream of prayer.[19]
> ["Nuns of the Perpetual Adoration"]

Although he was shy and often antisocial, Dowson did not lead a monastic life. Beneath his timid exterior was a restless desire for new sensations. After his death in 1900, Arthur Symons wrote of his friend, "I have never known him when he could resist either the desire or the consequences of drink…. Under the influence of drink, he became almost literally insane, certainly quite irresponsible. He fell into furious and unreasoning passions; a vocabulary unknown to him at other times sprang up like a whirlwind; he seemed always about to commit some act of absurd violence."[20] In his restlessness, the poet transformed the deafening din outside the church walls into calls for Rapture:

> … without, the sounding street
> Heralds the world's swift passage to the fire:
> O Benediction, perfect and complete!
> When shall men cease to suffer and desire?[21]
> ["Benedictio Domini"]

Dowson believes that those who dwell with Christ will "prevail"—but he does not count himself among the victors.[22] For travelers like him, there are no fortune islands, only an escape to "the hollow lands, / Where the poor, dead people stray, / Ghostly, pitiful and gray."[23] Though this is hardly an alluring fate, he still yearns for the finality of death. Even death is preferable to the thought of growing old slowly. Dowson, like Edgar Allan Poe in "Tamerlane," is fearful that for the remainder of his life he will be plagued by autumnal memories of the "old, extinguished fire / Of our divine, lost youth."[24] Faced with this horror, he embraces death as an abrupt end to the trials of life:

> Let us go hence, somewhither strange and cold,
> To Hollow Lands, where just men and unjust
> Find end of labour, where's rest for the old,
> Freedom to all from love and fear and lust.
> Twine our torn hands! O pray the earth enfold
> Our life-sick hearts and turn them into dust.[25]
> ["A Last Word"]

Dowson spent the final year of his life in France, where he succumbed to tuberculosis on February 23, 1900. His existing poetry offers little hope in the future, but Symons does note in his eulogy that his friend was "full of projects" and had recently begun to read Charles Dickens "with a singular zest."[26]

William Butler Yeats and Arthur Symons: Dance on Deathless Feet

In the 1890s, William Butler Yeats (1865–1939) was known as an eccentric poet with a mostly regional appeal. He wrote about fairies, Druids and dreams rooted in the Celtic folklore of his homeland of Ireland. His quasi-mystical poetry was poorly received by the sullen members of the Rhymers' Club, but Yeats regarded himself as part of a larger literary movement, a descendant of Romantic writers like Johann Wolfgang von Goethe, William Blake and Robert Browning, whose work transcends time and place. In an 1896 essay he argues that, because of their work, poetry "gave up the right to consider all things in the world as a dictionary of types and symbols and began to call itself a critic of life and an interpreter of things as they are."[27] Yeats believed that when the arts realized their full potential, they might even replace religion as the guiding light of culture:

> The arts are, I believe, about to take upon their shoulders the burdens that have fallen from the shoulders of priests, and to lead us back upon our journey by filling our thoughts with the essences of things, and not with things. We are about to substitute once more the distillation of alchemy for the analyses of chemistry and for some other sciences; and certain of us are looking everywhere for the perfect alembic that no silver or golden drop may escape.[28]

Among his peers, Arthur Symons (1865–1945) was the most receptive to Yeats's ideas about the high purpose of poetry and the potential of symbolism to rescue man's soul from the material world. This was the impetus behind his influential book *The Symbolist Movement in Literature* (1899), which he warmly dedicated to Yeats.

T.S. Eliot picked up a copy of Symons's book in December 1908, halfway through his third year at Harvard, and it became a profound inspiration. Symons writes that symbolism is an attempt to spiritualize and humanize literature. The arts, he says, have the same power that passion and religion have, allowing us to escape our fears of death: "Each is a forgetfulness, each a symbol of creation; religion being the creation of a new heaven, passion the creation of a new earth, and art, in its mingling of heaven and earth, the creation of heaven out of earth."[29]

Symons used the writings of the French Romantics to illustrate his point, and in the process introduced many of them to the English-speaking world. It is possible that T.S. Eliot was already inclined toward an appreciation of French literature; his mentor, Irving Babbitt, had been a professor of French and comparative literature before he joined the Harvard faculty in 1894, and was convinced that "it is only under French influence that scholarship gets disengaged from pedantry and acquires urbanity and polish, that the standards of the humanist coalesce with those of the man of the world."[30]

Charles Baudelaire: Something New

Arthur Rimbaud, Paul Verlaine and Jules Laforgue, as well as many of their peers, were products of a literary tradition that began with *Les Fleurs du Mal* (*The Flowers of Evil*, 1857), a collection of sly ruminations on sex, death and urban blight by Charles Baudelaire (1821–1867). Many readers were outraged by the publication, and accused the self-indulgent poet of blasphemy. The book was subsequently banned, and Baudelaire was tried on obscenity charges by the French government. The poet may have intended to spark such controversy; his manner of self-expression was defiant by nature. From the very first poem in his collection, Baudelaire seems determined to offend his readers, accusing them of sharing the "evil" thoughts and inclinations that he writes about: "You know it, O reader, this monster effete, / — Hypocritical reader — my fellow — my twin!"[31]

Jules Laforgue writes with admiration that Baudelaire was the first major poet to *confess* rather than *pontificate*. Baudelaire, he said, spoke of Paris "from the point of view of one of her daily damned," showing readers "the boredom implicit in sensuality, together with its strange décor."[32] In a 1950 lecture, T.S. Eliot said, "From him, as from Laforgue, I learned that the sort of material that I had, the sort of experience that an adolescent had had, in an industrial city in America, could be the material for poetry; and that the source of new poetry might be found in what had been regarded hitherto as the impossible, the sterile, the intractably unpoetic."[33]

Baudelaire seems to have reminded Eliot of two poems that he had read years earlier. Around the same time that Eliot had discovered Poe and Fitzgerald, he also stumbled upon a pair of poems by two morose Scottish writers, John Davidson (1857–1909) and James Thomson (1834–1882), who conveyed their melancholy through landscape symbolism. Of John Davidson's "Thirty Bob a Week," Eliot later said, "I am sure that I found inspiration in the content of the poem, and in the complete fitness of content and idiom: for I also had a good many dingy urban images to reveal."[34] At the heart of the poem is a poor, angry clerk, unable to support his wife and children on his thirty-bob-a-week salary, but hopelessly resigned to his fate. "P'r'haps we are in hell for all that I can tell," Davidson muses, "And lost and damn'd and served up hot to God," but "I face the music, sir." It was the poet's description of the clerk's daily travels in London that seems to have exerted the most influence on the Eliot:

> For like a mole I journey in the dark,
> A-travelling along the underground
> From my Pillar'd Halls and broad Suburban Park,
> To come the daily dull official round ...[35]

James Thomson's "The City of Dreadful Night" is also filled with imagery of a blighted city "where Death-in-Life is the eternal king," and the inhabitants wander aimlessly like spirits in Hell. Twice the poet invokes the inscription above the gateway to Dante's Inferno: "Leave hope behind, all ye who enter here." His outlook is as bleak as Davidson's:

> The world rolls round for ever like a mill;
> It grounds out death and life and good and ill;
> It has no purpose, heart or mind or will.[36]

Though these poems may appear hopelessly pessimistic to the casual reader, Eliot instinctively understood that these poets were on a lifelong quest for something truly meaningful. In Baudelaire's words, he was "eager to plunge / Deep into the abyss — Hell or Heaven, what odds? / Deep into the Unknown, just to find something new!"[37]

Arthur Rimbaud and Paul Verlaine: Something Sacred

Arthur Rimbaud (1854–1891) is perhaps the most influential of Baudelaire's successors, which is quite an accomplishment when one considers that he *stopped* writing poetry at the age of nineteen. At age twenty, he ended his career as a writer with the prose piece *Une Saison en Enfer* (*A Season in Hell*), which summarizes his evolution as a poet and justifies his decision to abandon art. In the few short years that he was writing, he had accomplished more than most of his contemporaries ever would.

At age sixteen, Rimbaud was already ruminating on the lost innocence of his youth, regarding adulthood as a somber twilight of kings and idols:

> I long for the lost days of youth,
> For wanton satyrs and beastly fauns,
> Gods who, for love, bit the bark of branches
> And kissed blonde Nymphs in water-lily pools![38]
> ["Sun and Flesh"]

He praised the grandeur and romanticism of Greek mythology and eagerly discounted rational science and Christian charity — just as Friedrich Nietzsche would in *The Birth of Tragedy* two years later. He used grandiose language to prophesy a revival of Greek classicism:

> I believe in you! I believe in you! Divine mother,
> Aphrodite of the sea! Oh the way is bitter
> Now that another God has yoked us to his cross;
> Flesh, Marble, Flower, Venus: I believe in you![39]
> ["Sun and Flesh"]

In the following years, Rimbaud's poetry remained vivid and imaginative — from the anthropomorphism of "Le Bateau Ivre" ("The Drunken Boat") to his assigning of colors to all the vowels — and his pronouncements became increasingly self-important. "Socrates and Jesus, Holy and Righteous — foul!" he wrote, "Revere me: king of the Damned in the bloody dark!"[40]

In spite of his grand pronouncements, his boredom was "sweet as sugar on rotten teeth,"[41] and he was growing sick of his own precocious pomp. Dismissing rational science and Christian charity, he reached the defining crisis of his life, the struggle to make the turning world stand still.[42] In a fragmented poem called "Alchimie du Verbe" ("Alchemy of Words"), he shares his sacred vision of eternity:

> Rediscovered.
> What?— Eternity.
> Sea and sun
> As one.[43]

At age nineteen, he renounces this vision, convinced that he has been tricked by his own desire and pride. His "discomfort," he realizes, is the same discomfort felt by Baudelaire and his blasphemous disciples who politely shared their private hells with each other — it is simply a product of Western civilization. Rimbaud realizes that he cannot escape the suffering until he escapes the Western mindset. "The soul knows best," he says, explaining his resolution to bury philosophy, imagination and memories, and head into the wilderness, "I'll have to shut up if I want to end up as I'd hoped."[44] Rimbaud spent the rest of his life on a kind of spiritual safari, working as a commercial trader in Africa and the Far East.

In *The Symbolist Movement in Literature*, Arthur Symons says that Rimbaud's mind "was not the mind of the artist but of the man of action," adding that he "illustrates the danger of one's over-possession by one's own genius, just as aptly as the saint in the cloister does, or the mystic too full of God to speak intelligibly to the world, or the spilt wisdom of the drunkard."[45] Alternatively, perhaps Rimbaud had, in a very short time, gone as far as his poetry could take him. If, in his travels, he realized his goal of being able to "*possess truth in a single body and soul*,"[46] then he achieved what many of his peers could only write about. If not, at least he acknowledged the limitations of his own art, and fought to maintain hope in the possibility of something new.

Symons opines that Rimbaud's future in literature was Paul Verlaine (1844–1896). Verlaine was already an established poet, having written three books of melancholy love songs, when Rimbaud came to live with him and his wife in 1870. The two men began a tumultuous affair and, not long after the birth of his first child, Verlaine abandoned his family to travel with Rimbaud. During this period, Verlaine produced *Romances sans Paroles* (*Love Songs without Words*). Darker and more kinetic than his earlier work, it became his most celebrated book of poetry.

Before it was published, Verlaine impulsively shot Rimbaud. Soon after, he was sent to prison, where he converted to Catholicism and repented his debauchery. Thereafter, his life and poetry were characterized by a constant fluctuation between submission to animal desire and confessions of spiritual longing. Verlaine's conversion was the dominant subject of his next book, *Sagesse* ("Wisdom"), published in 1881. It was in this work, Symons argues, that his poetry became transcendent, expressing "the great secret of the Christian mystics: that it is possible to love God with an extravagance of the whole being, to which the love of the creature cannot attain. All love is an attempt to break through the loneliness of individuality, to fuse oneself with something not oneself, to give and to receive, in all the warmth of natural desire, that inmost element which remains, so cold and so invincible, in the midst of the soul."[47]

Jules Laforgue: An Art of the Nerves

Although Eliot was inspired by Rimbaud and Verlaine, the poet at age twenty saw more of himself in their contemporary Jules Laforgue (1860–1887). Like Eliot, Laforgue was shy and solitary; reading and writing were his most trusted methods of interaction with the world.

Laforgue was thus over-intellectualized (as opposed to over-socialized, like the clowns and charming ladies of his poems); he lacked faith in his ability to interact socially. He felt like an onlooker — a ghost — rather than a participant in life. Arguably, poetry was both the cause and the product of his isolation, as well as the touch of madness that came with it.

Laforgue's own inspiration for poetry-writing was a vague mystical notion of the Oneness of the universe, partly derived from Eduard von Hartmann's *Philosophie des Unbewussten* (*The Philosophy of the Unconscious*). In his earliest poetry, Laforgue uses von Hartmann's term "the Unconscious" to signify a God-like force that unites and pervades everything in the universe. As he got older, the poet's writing shifted from lofty pontifications on the Unconscious to witticisms on the minutiae that comprises the Unconscious. In 1882, he writes: "Now I am a dilettante in everything, with little attacks of universal nausea from time to time. I watch the Carnival of life go by with its police sergeants, artists, sovereigns, ministers, lovers, etc. I smoke cigarettes, I write verse and prose, do an occasional etching, and wait for death."[48]

Under this new persona, Laforgue resolves to create an impression of the Unconscious by focusing on the details in much the way that American poet Walt Whitman had done in his 1855 poem "Song of Myself." Whitman's poem presents readers with a collage of people, places and things that, in his mind, helped to define the eclectic culture of his United States of America. Similarly, in Laforgue's poetry, police sergeants, artists, sovereigns, ministers and lovers become "the great melodic voice resulting from the symphony of the consciousness of races and individuals."[49] His 1885 book of poetry *Les Complaintes* (*The Complaints*) is mostly a collage of interior monologues ascribed to men and women, rich and poor, living and dead. The playful ramblings of these characters emphasize the poet's boredom with the trivialities of every day life — the posturing of "clowns" (including himself) and "charming women" who make up his world — and a desire to look beyond an Epicurean lifestyle. Ironically, he rarely does. Most of the time, he is satisfied to mock his characters with their own thoughts, words and deeds. The resulting poetry is little more than a distraction for the bored poet; it offers no real insight or revelation.

Laforgue's landscapes offer more revealing impressions of the Unconscious. Like Baudelaire before him, he was obsessed with the darker recesses of industrialized Paris; he reveled in sordid details of "black, choked-up subterranean" canals, flowing alongside abandoned buildings with "dish-rag gray windows."[50] In his final poems, collected after his death in 1887, Laforgue finally achieves a balanced syncopation of voices, images and ideas, creating an intense cumulative effect.

Based on these final poems, some literary critics have credited him with the invention of *vers libre*, literally "free verse"— free of stylistic rules, and often free of discernible logic. The opening lines of "L'Hiver qui vient" ("The Coming of Winter") demonstrate the confidence with which he invents his own unlikely rhythm:

> Sentimental blockade! Cargoes due from the East! ...
> Oh, rainfall! Oh, nightfall!
> Oh, wind!
> Halloween, Christmas, and New Year's,
> Oh, my smokestacks lost in the drizzle, all
> My factory smokestacks!
> Where can one sit? The park benches are dripping and wet;
> The season is over, I can tell you it's true
> The woods are so rusty, the benches so dripping and wet,
> And the horns so insistent with their constant halloo! ...[51]

He continues to vary the rhyme scheme and, in a manner that is almost cinematic, to change voice and setting (as well as time frame), as if in constant search of a suitable poetic form. When he stops searching, the whole is immeasurably greater than the sum of its parts — the search itself is the revelation of the Unconscious.

One of Laforgue's most revealing works is a prose piece called "Hamlet, or the Consequences of Filial Piety." Laforgue's interpretation of the indecisive Danish prince falls between popular interpretations by Johann Wolfgang von Goethe and Sigmund Freud. According to Goethe's interpretation, Hamlet's madness is over-intellectualization; he is unable to act because he is too busy thinking about *how* he should act. According to Freud's interpretation, Hamlet's dilemma is specific to the nature of the task he wants to perform: he can't avenge his father's death because he is troubled by the Oedipal desire to kill his father and take his place. Freud's diagnosis explains why Hamlet is able to kill others, both directly (as in the case of Polonius) and indirectly (as in the case of Rosencrantz and Guildenstern), but is unable to kill his father's murderer.

The latter interpretation does not apply to Laforgue's version of the story, which establishes that Hamlet is not the true son of the queen but a product of the king's affair with a dead gypsy fortune-teller. Nevertheless, Laforgue's Hamlet *still* fails to murder his uncle. As in Shakespeare's play, he arranges for players to act out a scenario resembling the murder of his father, and his uncle's response reveals his guilt. At the moment of confirmation, however, Laforgue's Hamlet shrugs it off ("Well, this has been punishment enough for them in my opinion," he says[52]) and prepares to flee the kingdom with a promiscuous actress named Kate.

Far less noble than Shakespeare's and Goethe's character and more reprehensible than Freud's, Laforgue's Hamlet is a sophisticated sociopath. Initially, he is unable to act because he does not want to accept the responsibility of being a "hero," a man of action with the will power to control people's lives. He would rather be a clerk or a librarian than a prince. "If one could only take things always with the broad sweep of the waves," Hamlet muses, "and let the rest take care of itself!"[53] After another internal debate, he begins training for murder. He gives himself pep talks and, like a good paranoiac, decides that nobody understands him, that "they are all against me,"[54] that he must be a predator if he is to avoid being a victim. Then, he embarks on a comic, small-scale killing spree — tearing the wings from butterflies, decapitating snails, slicing the legs off of toads, stomping anthills and slashing flowers. Afterwards, Hamlet visits the cemetery and seriously begins to contemplate death, suddenly overwhelmed by the impermanence of life:

> They also existed, the little people of History, learning to read, doing their nails, lighting their dirty lamps every evening, amorous, greedy, vain, delighting in compliments, handshakes and kisses, eating up the gossip of the bells in the belfry, saying: "What will the weather be tomorrow? Now winter is coming.... We have had no plums this year." Ah, all this is well that has no end. Forgive the Earth, O Silence! The little fool isn't too sure what she's doing; and on the day Conscience pays its staggering bill to the Ideal, it will be set down with sad ditto marks in the column of miniature evolutions of the Unique Evolution, in the column of negligible quantities. But these are words, words, words! That will be my motto until someone has proved to me that our speech has some connection with a transcendent reality.[55]

Hardened by contemplation, he coldly dismisses memories of the drowned Ophelia ("Dirty little thing, fished up by the dam! After she'd soaked herself so aimlessly in my library, how else could she end?"[56]), then wonders at his own detachment ("How could someone as good-hearted, as golden-hearted as I, have done such a thing!"[57]). Finally, he turns the blame toward Fate. He is resolved to become a murderer when he gets distracted by Kate, and his own idealized vision of her. Hamlet convinces himself that she will understand him as Ophelia, that "dear gluey little tart,"[58] never could. Laforgue offers hints that Hamlet's idealization of Kate is doomed; already he recognizes her as "one of those women in a drawing room at whom you gaze indifferently and distantly rather than ardently, madly, and tenderly." Still, he clings to her desperately as they make plans to flee to Paris.

On the way out of Elsinore, they encounter Ophelia's brother Laertes, who accuses Hamlet of "an absence of moral sense," adding that "whenever one ends up as a madman, it's because he began by acting the part."[59] With this psychoanalytical indictment, Laforgue brings the all-too-human hero into the modern age. Eliot's Prufrock, like Laforgue's Hamlet, feels too insignificant to be capable of making life-altering decisions. Prufrock says: "No! I am not Prince Hamlet, nor was meant to be."

Inventions

By 1919, Eliot understood that the French Romantic poets had influenced his own poetic development by providing him with a point of departure. In an essay entitled "Reflections on Contemporary Poetry," he says that when a young writer finds an established writer with whom he shares a certain kinship (as Eliot did with Laforgue), "he may be changed, metamorphosed almost, within a few weeks even, from a bundle of second-hand sentiments into a person. The imperative intimacy arouses for the first time a real, an unshakeable confidence."[60] He goes on to say that this is not mere admiration but a quickening; it does not lead to imitation, but to metamorphosis. It is the initiation of the poet into the world of poetry, the first stage in the development of his own individual voice.

Eliot's first cycle of poems employs the techniques of the French Symbolists, and progresses from beauty to horror. His earliest Harvard poems are fragmentary pieces featuring faded, withered flowers — imagery reminiscent of Baudelaire. In November 1908, after he had discovered Symons and Laforgue, the flowers become "fanged and red," springing "from the limbs of the dead."[61] In a poem called "Song (The moonflower opens to the moth)," the speaker begs defeatedly: "Have you no brighter tropic flowers / With scarlet life, for me?"[62] In "Nocturne," composed the following year, the young "Romeo," tired of dull conversations with his Juliet, makes arrangements for her to be stabbed while on a midnight stroll. He then marvels at the way her blood shines in the moonlight, "the perfect climax all true lovers seek!"[63] Like Laforgue, Eliot seems bored with the thoughts and words of nubile women, to the point of homicidal aggression. He justifies his impulses with lofty contemplation of the Absolute. Still following the lead of Baudelaire and Laforgue, Eliot turned his attention to landscapes, producing a putrid "yellow evening" and "a heap of broken barrows."[64] He also responds to music and theater. An operatic performance of Richard Wagner's *Tristan and Isolde* fills him with intense passion, but the intensity slowly wanes, and leaves him feeling like "the ghost of youth."[65]

Much of the poetry Eliot wrote in 1910 is nearly derivative of Laforgue.[66] While Laforgue always remained standoffishly amused by his subjects, however, Eliot dares to express his most personal, and horrifying, emotions. Laforgue is simply a mask that Eliot wears; as he writes more and more, the mask slips. In "Suite Clownesque," Eliot's jellyfish-comedian interrupts Laforguean posturing with a moment of fearful insecurity: "Do you think that I'm all right?"[67]

Just as noteworthy among the year's compositions are "Easter: Sensations of April" and "Silence." In the former, the poet focuses on a young girl as she returns home from church with a bright red geranium. In time, the geranium withers and fades, like Eliot's memory of *Tristan and Isolde*; this seems to be the first time that he associates the loss of passion with metaphysics and religion. "Silence" might be compared to Rimbaud's "Eternity," for it is a record of a near-religious experience of "the ultimate hour." Rimbaud suffered deep disappointment and doubt in the aftermath of such an experience. For Eliot, the silence is nothing short of terrifying.

In September 1910, after completing his undergraduate studies and spending the summer with his family in Gloucester — a summer full of sun-baked afternoons, cakes and tea, and "guesses at eternal truths"[68] — Eliot planned a trip abroad. In October, he left for Paris — the home of his literary idols.

Suggested Reading (1905–1910)

Poems Written in Early Youth

"A Fable for Feasters" (1905)
"A Lyric: If time and space, as Sages say" (1905)
"Song: If time and space, as Sages say" (1906)
"At Graduation 1905" (1905)
"Song: When we came home across the hill" (1906)
"Before Morning" (1908)
"Circe's Palace" (1908)
"On a Portrait" (1909)
"Song: The moonflower opens to the moth" (1909)
"Nocturne" (1909)
"Humouresque (After J. Laforgue)" (1909)
"Spleen" (1910)
"Ode" (1910)

Inventions of the March Hare

"Convictions (Curtain Raiser)" (1910)
"First Caprice in North Cambridge" (1909)
"Second Caprice in North Cambridge" (1909)
"Suite Clownesque" (1910)
"Easter: Sensations of April" (1910)
"Silence" (1910)
"Mandarins" (1910)
"Goldfish (Essence of Summer Magazines)" (1910)
"Fourth Caprice in Montparnasse" (1910)

Prufrock and Other Observations

"Conversation Galante" (1909)

◆ PART II ◆

A Passion for Wholeness (1910–1911)

It does not matter at what point you first break into the system of European poetry. Only keep your ears open and your mouth shut and everything will lead you to everything else in the end.

— C.S. Lewis

The Teachings of Irving Babbitt

In the fall of 1906, T.S. Eliot became a student at Harvard University. At that time, the school was under the leadership of his cousin, Charles Eliot, who had been president of Harvard since 1869. Over the course of three and a half decades, Charles Eliot had practically invented the American university as we know it today — instituting a system that separated students into professional schools rather than instructing all undergraduates in the humanities. Charles Eliot believed in the prevailing notion that *the business of America was business*, and he encouraged graduate-level study in the humanities for those called to an academic life.[1] T.S. Eliot took advantage of the opportunity for a liberal program of study by concentrating almost exclusively on the humanities; in his freshman year, he enrolled in courses in Greek, English, German and French literature, as well as ancient and modern philosophy.[2] He was guided by three influential professors: Irving Babbitt (1865–1933), George Herbert Palmer (1842–1933) and George Santayana (1863–1952).

Irving Babbitt was a classicist who disagreed with Charles Eliot's policies. In his book *Literature and the American College* (1908), Babbitt writes that President Eliot freed college students from a rigid curriculum in the hope that they would pursue the course of study that best helps them to fulfill their unique potential. But Babbitt believed that this was not how the typical student responded; in his experience, students chose whatever course of study required the least amount of effort. He further argued that the growth of the individual genius was stunted by the modern tendency of students to limit their academic pursuits to one specialized field of study and neglect the humanist's "passion for wholeness." T.S. Eliot obviously agreed; his readings were heavily influenced by Babbitt's conservative views on literature and on religion.

As a classical studies professor, Babbitt considered it his goal to bridge the gap between the Greco-Roman world and the modern world that his students knew. In his book, he there-

20

fore emphasizes the secular humanism of those ancient civilizations over the religion of those that succeeded them. In Babbitt's opinion, ancient Greece — the foundation of Western civilization — was the most humane of all cultures, and its literature represents the ideal combination of sympathy and discipline within the individual. By contrast, he argues that the culture of medieval Christianity, which repressed the prevailing thought of Greek and Roman civilization for nearly a thousand years, was detrimental to individual growth. Historical Christianity, he writes, reserved sympathy only for those who followed the same discipline and persecuted those who did not. Secular humanism — which Babbitt opines is more sympathetic than historical Christianity and more disciplined than vague humanitarianism — was dormant until the Renaissance, when it finally prevailed over divinity in the works of William Shakespeare and prompted Western literature to acknowledge that we can learn much from the religions and philosophies of different cultures.

What was important to Babbitt was not so much a particular belief or set of beliefs, but *open-mindedness* to many beliefs taken in context of the histories and cultures that could be studied by the American scholar. In his book, he encourages his students to read as much as possible and look for shared, universal ideas among literary, philosophical and religious works:

> In the case of an author like Virgil, for instance, he should be familiar not only with the classical Virgil, but also with the Virgil of after-centuries, — with Virgil the magician and enchanter who haunted the imagination of the Middle Ages, with Virgil the guide of Dante, and so on, down to the splendid ode of Tennyson. If he is dealing with Aristotle, he should be able to show the immense influence exercised by Aristotle over the medieval and modern European mind, both directly through the Latin tradition and indirectly through Averrhoes and the Arabs.... He should neglect far less than has been done heretofore the great patristic literature in Greek and Latin, as giving evidence of the process by which ancient thought passed over into thought of the medieval and modern types.[3]

Babbitt admits that the humanist's broad course of study is intimidating (and surely it is even more intimidating at the beginning of the 21st century than it was in Babbitt's time), but he insists that this is how we become well-rounded thinkers. He summarizes his thoughts on literature and the American college by saying that there are three types of scholars: receptive, originative and assimilative. He considered the assimilative to be the best type, and that is what the young Eliot aspired to be, hoping to embody "that subtle alchemy by which mere learning is transmuted into culture."[4]

Just as Poe and Fitzgerald had awakened the romantic poet within Eliot, so Babbitt awakened the classicist. In his 1919 essay "Tradition and the Individual Talent," Eliot echoes Babbitt in his statement that it is important for all students, and especially writers, to read as widely as possible — not only to develop their personal taste but to develop a sense of the whole of literature, which will serve as a frame of reference for their writing. Eliot argues that wide reading allows students of literature to organize and assess the thoughts and ideas they encounter; it also allows the writer to avoid imitating any one voice or group of voices. A poet evolves as "a receptacle for seizing and storing up numberless feelings, phrases, images, which remain there until all the particles which can unite to form a new compound are present together."[5] Then the poet fuses the personal and the historical — his original voice emerging in relation to voices of the past.[6]

As Eliot formulated his early poetry, he was also developing his own metaphysical beliefs, synthesizing what he had learned from those who came before him. For a time, he followed the lead of his teacher, who said that the genuine humanist "believes that the man of to-day, if he does not, like the man of the past, take on the yoke of a definite doctrine and discipline, must at least do inner obeisance to something higher than his ordinary self, whether he calls this something God, or, like the man of the Far East, calls it his higher Self, or simply the Law."[7] Through his studies, Eliot traced this idea back to the beginnings of Western literature.

The Soul of Homer

At Harvard, Eliot read Homer, whose epics *The Iliad* and *The Odyssey* are generally believed to have been written sometime between 1000 and 800 B.C.E., offering the earliest glimpses of the Western worldview. They demonstrate that the ancient Greeks imagined the universe ruled by a collection of gods — personifications of sky, sea, love, war and so on — who were often at odds with each other, and who made life volatile for humans. The focus of Homer's epics, however, is on those humans who are able to curry favor with the gods by realizing their individual potential.

The main hero of *The Iliad* is the warrior Achilles. The epic poem champions his strength and courage, hailing him as the strongest of Greek soldiers. At the same time, it reveals his all-too-human character flaws and the limitations of his strength. When Agamemnon insults his comrade's honor, Achilles refuses to fight, and his pride causes the death of a close friend and nearly leads to the defeat of his people. Though he overcomes his pride and returns to battle, *The Iliad* ends with the hero's death — reminding us that Achilles is not a god. Achilles himself is only too aware of this and, although he has no reassuring thoughts of the afterlife (the Greek warriors believe that darkness is the only thing awaiting them), he chooses to face death because such courage is the fulfillment of his individual potential. No man, Homer illustrates, is greater than his destiny.

In contrast with the physical strength of Achilles, Odysseus — the hero of Homer's second epic — boasts intellectual strength which allows him to look beyond the curtain of death into the darkness that awaits the soul. *The Odyssey* begins ten years after the end of the Trojan War. For all that time, Odysseus has been waylaid on his journey home. Eventually, he comes to the island of a beguiling witch named Circe, who tells him to consult the blind prophet Tiresias about his destiny. There is only one problem: Tiresias is dead. Nevertheless, Odysseus is supremely confident of his abilities and sails to the edge of the ocean to find a gateway to Hades, the subterranean land of the dead. Here, the hero performs an animal sacrifice, drawing a legion of ghosts to him — including the disembodied souls of several soldiers who fought alongside him in the Trojan War. Agamemnon, the general who sacrificed his daughter to the gods before leading the Greeks in battle, tells Odysseus that his wife murdered him when he returned home. Mighty Achilles solemnly claims that he would rather be a slave among the living than a hero among the dead. Tiresias predicts a peaceful death for Odysseus, many years in the future ... though what lies beyond death remains a somber eventuality. The hero resumes his journey.

Homer's heroes must find meaning in life, not death. Perhaps for this reason, Eliot populated his own literary works with some of the minor figures from these ancient epics — Agamemnon resurfaces in "Sweeney among the Nightingales" (published in 1918) and Tiresias is the central figure in *The Waste Land* (published in 1922) — using them to work out the meaning of his own life. In a 1926 lecture, T.S. Eliot expresses his dissatisfaction with this limited view of the world, in essence saying that the poet's works accurately perceive and record the mortal world at a given moment but fail to extend "the frontiers of this world."[8] For Eliot, Homer was simply a starting point.

The Birth of Tragedy

Whereas Homer's epics focus on the destinies of heroes who recognize their place in the universe, the major Greek tragedies — written several hundred years later — reveal the existential suffering of heroes at odds with universal dictates. It seems that the birth of tragedy resulted from a tendency among Greek poets living in the 5th century B.C.E. to feel estranged from the mythic gods of antiquity. As tragedians focused more and more on the human characters, as opposed to the gods, they created new myths reflecting a troubled view of the cosmos.

The tragedy can be traced to the Festival of Dionysus, founded by Athenian leader Pisistratus around 535–533 B.C.E., to honor the Greek god of wine and ecstasy who dies and is reborn each year.[9] The annual festival was held in early spring, as a celebration of the god's revival. For Athenians, it was also a celebration of freedom — freedom from inhibitions, social constructs and even death. Classicist Edith Hamilton writes that all day-to-day business stopped so that everyone could participate in the festivities; even prisoners were released so that they could take part.[10] For one week, people indulged the irrational human impulses that their increasingly rational culture viewed as dangerous; the festival itself functioned as a cathartic purging of these dangerous tendencies, and ultimately inspired reverence of social order.

According to Hamilton, the main event was a symbolic rendering of this communal catharsis. Community theaters hosted a competition among playwrights to capture the spirit of the Dionysian myth — transcendence through excess and pain. In many of the famous Greek tragedies, such as Aeschylus's trilogy *The Oresteia* (first produced in 458 B.C.E.) and Sophocles's *Oedipus* trilogy (probably written between 429 and 425 B.C.E.), unconscionable behavior leads the hero to a haunting awareness of human potential at its most destructive. The heroes speak to the audience in calm, rational Apollonian verse but their actions are rash and violent, threatening social order and the integrity of universal law. In the end, these tragic heroes receive just punishment, according to the laws of nature, for their lack of humility. The tragedians imply that the Dionysian quest may lead to self-awareness, but it will also lead to self-destruction. We are only human, after all.

In Homer's epics, the rule of cause-and-effect applies to the hero's relationship with the gods. When a hero is humble and respectful, the gods grant him good fortune. When he is arrogant or foolish, the gods punish him. Odysseus ultimately returns home and lives a long life because he is respectful of the gods. By contrast, in Aeschylus's trilogy *The Orestia*, messages from the gods are often unclear. Having failed in their attempts to be godlike, the tragic heroes (Clytemnestra and Orestes) cannot even hope for salvation when appealing directly to the gods, because the gods apparently are neither omniscient nor omnipotent.

In the first play, *Agamemnon*, the title character returns home from the Trojan War only to be slain by his wife Clytemnestra. The murder, she says, is an act of justice — an answer to the murder of her daughter Iphigenia, whom Agamemnon offered as a sacrifice to the gods at the beginning of the Trojan War. Aeschylus, speaking through a chorus of Greek citizens, raises the possibility that Agamemnon sacrificed his daughter in response to the evil counsel of his comrades in arms rather than at the request of the gods. Another chorus of citizens wonders aloud how such a fate could justly befall the great hero Agamemnon: How could the gods have allowed him — a great hero, honored by the gods in the Trojan War — to be killed by a woman? Their only explanation is an ambiguous one: Perhaps he is suffering from an ancient curse on his family — one that began when an ancestor killed a fellow family member. To the chorus, however, this does not seem like divine justice but rather a self-perpetuating cycle of violence and suffering.

> Here is anger for anger. Between them
> who shall judge lightly?
> The spoiler is robbed; he killed, he has paid.
> The truth stands ever beside God's throne
> eternal: he who has wrought shall pay; that is law.
> Then who shall tear the curse from their blood?
> The seed is stiffened to ruin.[11]

In the trilogy's second play, *Choephori* or *Libation-Bearers*, Agamemnon's son, Orestes, further perpetuates the family curse. He returns home, in disguise, to avenge his father's murder. After much internal debate over whether or not he will offend the gods if he murders his mother, the oracle of Apollo endorses his plan of action. Orestes hesitates, wondering if the oracle can be trusted (apparently, a message from an oracle is not as definitive as getting the okay from Apollo himself). A bloodthirsty chorus of Trojan women, enslaved by the Greeks, urges Orestes to action. First, Orestes kills Aegisthus, his mother's lover and co-conspirator. Then, after his friend Pylades advises him that it is better to offend the law of man than to offend the law of the gods, he murders his mother. This action summons the Furies — enforcers of an "old law" that predates the Olympian gods. Their mission: to punish him by driving him mad with fear.

In the third part of the trilogy, *The Eumenides*, Apollo — the god of intellectual and spiritual enlightenment — personally directs Orestes to Athens, where the goddess Athena presides over a trial for the murder of his mother. The trial becomes the arena for a struggle between the Olympian gods, who seem to govern according to inconsistent whims, and the Furies, who are determined to restore a simple order to the universe. The Furies contend that, by inspiring fear, they can achieve this goal:

> There are times when fear is good.
> It must keep its watchful place
> at the heart's controls. There is
> advantage
> in the wisdom won from pain.
> Should the city, should the man
> rear a heart that nowhere goes
> in fear, how shall such a one
> any more respect the right?[12]

Apollo responds, referring to the origin of Athena (the less-than-impartial judge), who was born from the head of Zeus and never had a mother. The father, Apollo concludes, is indispensable in the creation of life; the mother is not. Following this logic, Apollo concludes that Clytemnestra's crime of patricide is more reprehensible than Orestes' crime of matricide.

When the jury finds for the defendant, the Furies are enraged. Perhaps they understand that they have been tricked, but they are unable to match wits with the Olympians. Instead, they threaten to curse the city of Athens. At this point, Athena employs her own wit and intelligence to make peace with the Furies. She promises that the people of Athens will henceforth regard the Furies with reverence instead of fear, and offers them a sacred place in the new order of the Olympians. The Furies accept, becoming the Eumenides or "kindly ones." Thus, chaos is averted through reason and reverence, rather than fear and violence. The verdict reflects the entire culture's understanding that only through reason and reverence can people expect a life without undue suffering. This seems to be the beginning of democratic law and of the use of philosophy and religion as enforcers of social custom.

By the time that Euripides (480–406 B.C.E.) succeeded Aeschylus and Sophocles as the chief carrier of the mythological tradition, early philosophers had called the effectiveness of the ancient religious myths into question. Plato's *The Republic* (c. 360 B.C.E.) suggests that even Socrates's protégé did not believe that reverence for the Olympians and the Furies could help to insure order. Perhaps for that reason, he banned Homeric myths from his fictional republic, saying that they "are harmful to those who hear them, for every man will be ready to excuse his own evil conduct if he believes these things are done, and have been done in the past by [gods]." Plato advises:

> We must seek out such artists as have the talent to pursue the beautiful and the graceful in their work, in order that our young men shall be benefited from all sides like those who live in a healthy place, whence something from these beautiful works will strike their eyes and ears like a breeze that brings health from salubrious places, and lead them unawares from childhood to love of, resemblance to, and harmony with, the beauty of reason.[13]

In later years, Eliot would take up the mythology of the Furies in his play *The Family Reunion* (1939) — a later attempt to reconcile the questions of his youth with the answers he'd found in religion. In that work, the creatures seem to represent a man's metaphysical dread in the absence of clearly defined religious beliefs. During his time at Harvard, Eliot was subject to vague metaphysical dread, but he would for years attempt to follow the Greek philosophers — and his Harvard professors — to a life based purely on reason. As a young academic, Eliot sought to replace the religious training of his youth with studies of Plato and Aristotle, which left him with a fragmented view of the metaphysical world.

The Epistemology of Plato

In addition to Irving Babbitt's course on French literary criticism, which required students to read the classics so that they would have a stronger foundation for critical judgment, Eliot was greatly influenced by George Herbert Palmer's course on the history of philosophy and George Santayana's course on the philosophy of history, both of which he took during his undergraduate years. These courses introduced Eliot to the Greek philosopher Heraclitus, who argued that all of the materials which make up the universe exist in flux. The mere juxtaposition of these two courses — studying philosophy from the perspective of history, and history from the perspective of philosophy — proves as much; it's all relative to our point of view. Life itself, according to Heraclitus, is like a river, constantly moving and changing, even while we continue to call it by the same name.

George Santayana embraced this complex worldview, which made him — like Babbitt — something of an outsider among the Harvard faculty and a bit of a hero to Eliot. Like W.B. Yeats and Arthur Symons, Santayana put his faith in the Ideal represented by poetry. In his first book, *The Sense of Beauty* (1896), he writes:

To feel beauty is a better thing than to understand how we come to feel it. To have imagination and taste, to love the best, to be carried by the contemplation of nature to a vivid faith in the ideal, all this is more, a great deal more, than any science can hope to be. The poets and philosophers who express this aesthetic experience and stimulate the same function in us by their example, do a greater service to mankind and deserve higher honour than the discoverers of historical truth.[14]

Santayana argued that the best expression of the experience of Beauty is in the parables of Plato (427–347 B.C.E.).

The character Socrates dominates Plato's written dialogues, and he is usually portrayed dismantling the theories of arrogant sophists with careful rhetoric. That said, Socrates (at least, as he is presented in Plato's dialogues) does not use rhetoric simply to disprove the theories of others; he also uses it as a means of advancing his own beliefs about human nature. If life is flux, he says, then there must be something changeless — a frame of reference — in order for humans to know that they are experiencing flux, and thus to know anything about the world.

In one of Plato's dialogues, the character Meno poses an epistemological question that raises this issue: *How can we recognize truth unless we already know what truth is, and therefore already know what we are looking for?* Socrates responds that "the human soul is immortal; at times it comes to an end, which they call dying, at times it is reborn, but it is never destroyed.... As the soul is immortal, has been born often and has seen all things here and in the underworld, there is nothing which it has not learned; so it is in no way surprising that it can recollect the things it knew before."[15] In other words, the soul already knows what it seeks to know; this knowledge Socrates calls the Good. Facing his own death in the *Phaedo*, Socrates says that the goal of human life is not fulfillment of individual potential but realization of "the good which must necessarily bind and hold all things together."[16] Thereby one purifies his own soul, escapes future reincarnation, and — at the time of death — enters into the family of gods.[17]

In *The Republic* Socrates explains that his knowledge of the afterlife is based on the personal experience of a great warrior named Er. After Er was killed in battle, Socrates says, his soul traveled to a mysterious place where he saw two openings — one to the right, leading upward into heaven, and one to the left, leading downward into Hades. Er took the lower path, so that he could return to earth and tell people what he had seen there. He saw that the souls below continued to exist according to the habits of their previous lives — still committing acts of violence, hate and jealousy even after their deaths. Eventually, the souls that he was watching journeyed to the Plain of Oblivion and drank from the River of Forgetfulness, then fell asleep. The story continues: "After they had fallen asleep and it was the middle of the night, there was a sound of thunder and a quaking of the earth, and they were suddenly wafted thence, one this way, one that, upward to their birth like shooting stars."[18] The souls, Er realized, were being reborn into a new mortal life, where they would continue to live by their habits. Reincarnation, Socrates concludes, is necessary because the souls have not yet attained the highest knowledge that is available to them. Only through a love of learning can the soul regain its natural state of oneness with the Good, and break the earthly habits that trap it in the cycle of reincarnation.

Other passages in Plato's *The Republic* define the Good as that which allows a man to understand the difference between objects perceived through the senses and ideas recollected by the immortal soul. Plato refers to the immortal ideas as Forms, and famously uses allegory to explain his theory of Forms: A group of prisoners have been trapped inside a cave since childhood, their hands bound, facing a wall. Sunlight streams through the entrance of the cave, but the prisoners are able to see only the wall — never the sun. Everything that passes by the entrance of the cave casts a shadow onto the wall in front of the prisoners. Knowing nothing but the shadows, they believe that the shadows are real. Only when they are released can they see that the shadows are distorted imitations of the real.

In this allegory, the shadows represent the world we apprehend through our physical senses. The "real" things that pass by the entrance of the cave represent the Forms, which are knowable only through reason. The sun is the Good, which allows us to see the difference. Socrates concludes: "Education then is the art of doing this very thing, this turning around, the knowledge of how the soul can most easily and most effectively be turned around; it is not the art of putting the capacity of sight into the soul; the soul possesses that already but it is not turned the right way or looking where it should. This is what education has to deal with."[19]

A student of literature may take to heart the ancient Greek aphorism "Know thyself," since Plato proposes that we already have the answers. Such a student learns to trust those teachings that reinforce whatever beliefs he already has. Eliot had been brought up to respect tradition, which explains why he gravitated toward Babbitt. Eliot scholar Howard Howarth suggests that he was probably also influenced by his mother's "sensitivity to the beauty of the antique church." Howarth points out that Charlotte Eliot composed a series of poems dramatizing the stories of the New Testament in which, despite her Unitarian beliefs, she expresses the beauty of Catholic rituals and sacred objects.[20] Howarth also theorizes that, in a comparable way, George Santayana's "religion of beauty" grew out of his upbringing in the Spanish Catholic Church.[21] This connection provides us with a partial explanation for the young Eliot's affinity with Santayana's sentiments, and an interest in Plato's Forms.

Socrates says that a man who "believes that there is such a thing as Beauty itself, who can both see it and the things which share in it, and does not confuse the two" lives in reality, instead of a dream.[22] According to Santayana, that type of man will have a better understanding of the world and a greater sense of purpose in life. Ten years after he praised the parables of Plato in *The Sense of Beauty*, Santayana wrote a more carefully reasoned explanation of his personal philosophy, based largely on the writings of Plato's student Aristotle. At the time the book was published, T.S. Eliot was an undergraduate.

The Metaphysics of Aristotle

In his essay "Physics," Aristotle (384–322 B.C.E.) writes that everything that exists is a composite — not of natural elements in flux, as suggested by Heraclitus and Plato, but of three principles: the *underlying nature* of a thing ("as bronze stands to a statue, or wood to a bed, or the formless before it acquires a form to anything else"), *the lack* which is the opposite of that underlying nature, and *something else* which makes it clear "what sort of opposites are involved, how the principles stand to one another, and what the underlying thing is."[23] Whereas Plato argues that all objects have in themselves a "source of their movements and changes"[24] (Forms), Aristotle suggests that the *something else* which determines the nature of a thing may be human interpretation of the object.

This theory of the three principles helps to illuminate Aristotle's concept of the human soul. He believes that the soul, "the cause and the first principle of the living body,"[25] is not a physical body and that it exists only in conjunction with physical senses of the body. We are nevertheless dependent on the soul, rather than the senses, for knowledge because "actual perception is of particulars, while knowledge is of universals; and these are somehow in the soul itself."[26] In short: Forms exist only in the soul, which itself exists only in conjunction with a living body. Aristotle does not mean for us to infer, however, that the soul has the same limitations as the body; he suggests a pervasive connection between the individual soul and the whole of Nature: "the soul is in a way all existing things."[27] In this statement we find Aristotle's justification for a philosophy of metaphysics — a study of nature as a composite of the particular and the universal — which he calls the primary discipline.

Taking a scientific approach to the theories of his teacher Plato, Aristotle argues that what we perceive as the essence of a thing, whether it exists in our mind or in the object itself, is whatever is "in virtue of" the thing itself. He adds, "The good, then, must be one with the essence of good, and the beautiful with the essence of beauty, and so with all things which do not depend on something else but are self-subsistent and primary. For it is enough if they are this, even if there are no Forms; and perhaps all the more if there are Forms."[28] He further theorizes that "the bad" does not exist in essence, but as the absence of essence — a concept that would become the basis for neo–Platonism.

Unlike Plato, Aristotle believes that art teaches us about life in a way that experience cannot: "experience is knowledge of individuals, art of universals."[29] Furthermore, he believes that it is only through knowledge of universals that the soul can exist in virtue of itself. In other words, it is only through education in the arts that man can achieve his potential. With this in mind, it is not difficult to understand why Aristotle became a guardian of the less rational traditions in Greek antiquity — specifically, the worship of the Olympian gods — as well as other religious traditions. An early anthropologist, Aristotle believed that religious mythology and philosophy have a similarity of purpose:

> Our forefathers in the most remote ages have handed down to us through posterity a tradition, in the form of a myth, that these substances are gods and that the divine encloses the whole of nature. The rest of the tradition has been added later in mythical form with a view to the persuasion of the multitude and to its legal and utilitarian expediency; they say these gods are in the form of men or like some of the other animals, and they say other things consequent on and similar to these which we have mentioned. But if we were to separate the first point from these additions and take it alone — that they thought the first substances to be gods — we must regard this as an inspired utterance, and reflect that, while probably each art and science has been developed as far as possible and has again perished, these opinions have been preserved like relics until the present. Only thus far, then, is the opinion of our ancestors and our earliest predecessors clear to us.[30]

In his essay "The Poetics," Aristotle explicitly defends epic and tragic poetry by explaining how they reflect the human condition while revealing the universal truths that enable the soul to transcend mortal life.

This view had a profound effect on T.S. Eliot, who studied Aristotle under the tutelage of Harold Joachim at Oxford in his postgraduate years. Five years after completing his studies with Joachim, T.S. Eliot cited Aristotle as an example of the transcendent intelligence of the classical literary mind:

> He was primarily a man of not only remarkable but universal intelligence; and universal intelligence means that he could apply his intelligence to anything. The ordinary intelligence is good only for certain classes of objects; a brilliant man of science, if he is interested in poetry at all, may conceive grotesque judgments: like one poet because he reminds him of himself, or another

because he expresses emotions which he admires; he may use art, in fact, as the outlet for the egotism which is suppressed in his own specialty. But Aristotle had none of these impure desires to satisfy; in whatever sphere of interest, he looked solely and steadfastly at the object; in his short and broken treatise he provides an eternal example — not of laws, or even of method, for there is no method except to be very intelligent, but of intelligence itself swiftly operating the analysis of sensation to the point of principle and definition.[31]

The Life of Reason

In his book *The Life of Reason* (1905–1906), Santayana writes that Aristotle uses reason to prove that "everything ideal has a natural basis and everything natural an ideal development,"[32] and therefore his philosophy is the classic formulation of the ideal life. Santayana dismisses modern philosophers, accusing them of "imaginative apathy" while accusing Western civilization of overemphasizing the physical sciences. Historians and scientists "may furnish a theatre and properties for our drama," Santayana says, "but they offer no hint of its plot and meaning."[33] This statement justifies Eliot's decision to study the humanities in college, but even Santayana seems to realize that such a study is not an end in itself. One craves a personally meaningful *conclusion*.

For meaning, one might be inclined to turn to religion, but on this topic Santayana expresses grave reservations. Too often, he says, religion discards reason in favor of fanaticism and mysticism. He argues that fanaticism doubles the efforts of the will to compensate for the absence of common sense, causing the fanatic to forget his true aim. Likewise, the mystic often mistakes vanity for unity and asserts his own will in defiance of reason. Religion may have the noblest of goals — it is "a more conscious and direct pursuit of the Life of Reason than is society, science, or art"[34] — but it also has the tendency to deaden the individual's awareness of his ties to the universal. In practice, religion may limit one's sense of community and estrange him from popular morality, with potentially dangerous results.

Santayana places much of the blame for these tendencies on the "Hebrew tradition," which he says has popularized an unhealthy understanding of monotheism. He argues that the Greeks had a more enlightened perspective — not because they were polytheistic but because they were more open-minded. Their culture was not exclusively monotheistic or polytheistic; rather, monotheism and polytheism were compatible. In ancient Greece, it was the universal religious impulse that was important:

> To say God or the gods was only to use different expressions for the same influence.... When religion appears to us in this light its contradictions and controversies lose all their bitterness. Each doctrine will simply represent the moral plane on which they live who have devised or adopted it.[35]

Santayana argues that most people's religions are chosen *for* them, part of their ancestry and upbringing. When religious beliefs are ingrained at an early age, the religion of one's childhood often seems more "real" and more inspiring, but Santayana says that it is important to recognize and embrace the universal impulse behind the religion rather than the worldly dogmas. The impulse, he points out, is what unites us, while dogmas divide us. In place of dogma, we should augment the religious impulse with reason. In the final analysis, Santayana believes that the ideal life requires a balance of the two: reasonable religion is his goal.

Finding few reasonable religions in the world, Santayana goes beyond philosophy, into the realm of poetry, to satisfy his own personal religious impulse. Philosophical poetry, he writes, aims to "satisfy the cravings of a forgotten part of the soul and to make a home for those elements in human nature which have been denied overt existence."[36] While he acknowledges that poetry has the potential to be just as irrational as dogma, poetry is nevertheless a more accurate representation of those fleeting moments of beauty in which a human being knows truth beyond intellectual comprehension. The experiences introduce to us "something deeper than Nature and something higher than God, depriving these words of the best sense in which a philosopher might care to use them."[37] Poets use myths and symbols to convey intuitions of something beautiful beyond reason. This is perhaps why poets like W.B. Yeats became convinced that art would, or *should*, replace religion. It also reinforced T.S. Eliot's love for Symbolist poetry — which he felt much more deeply than the religious doctrines of his youth. In the years to come, Eliot would argue that the French poets had revealed his own unconscious awareness of the metaphysical world.

In 1910, George Santayana published a book about three philosophical poets whose works seemed to him to sum up the whole of European thought: Lucretius represents natural philosophy, Dante Alighieri represents supernatural philosophy and Goethe represents Romantic philosophy. Years later, his student T.S. Eliot named the three bodies of work that he considered the most vital for modern philosophical poets: the Greek epics of Homer, the Christian mythology of Dante and the humanist drama of William Shakespeare.[38] To understand Eliot and his philosophical search, one must (as his own literary criticism indicates) be familiar with these three poets and understand how each builds on the previous one: how Greek philosophy evolved and helped to shape Christianity during the age of the Roman Empire, how Dante struggled to reconcile the two during the Middle Ages and how and why Shakespeare resurrected the humanism of the Greeks and opened the doors to the Modern Age.

The Metamorphoses of the Roman Empire

In a 1951 lecture, T.S. Eliot explained that when he read *The Aeneid* of Virgil (70–19 B.C.E.) for the first time, he felt more comfortable with the Roman heroic epic than he had with Homer's Greek epics. "The explanation I should now give," he said, with the advantage of hindsight, "is simply that I instinctively preferred the *world* of Virgil to the *world* of Homer — because it was a more civilized world of dignity, reason and order."[39] In an earlier essay, Eliot had referred to Virgil as a mature reflection of Western civilization and "the classic of all Europe," because he simultaneously remembered Homer's world without metaphysical frontiers and anticipated the more satisfying (for Eliot) Christian system of belief:

> In Homer, the conflict between the Greeks and the Trojans is hardly larger in scope than a feud between one Greek city-state and a coalition of other city-states: behind the story of Aeneas is the consciousness of a more radical distinction, a distinction, which is at the same time a statement of *relatedness*, between two great cultures, and, finally, of their reconciliation under an all-embracing destiny.[40]

Just as Odysseus was a "man of many moves," so the Roman Empire was a culture of constant movement — an ever-turning world that only gradually (and, some might argue, belatedly) adopted Christianity as its pivotal center. Because the Romans' emphasis on politics somewhat mitigated the influence of religion, their culture tolerated a variety of religious ideas from every corner of its vast empire — which, in the first century B.C.E., encompassed all land on the Mediterranean Sea (most of Europe, Palestine, Asia Minor and the northern coast of Africa). The Romans greatly admired the culture of the Greeks, and incorporated much Greek mythology and philosophy into their own tradition. Toward the end of the first century B.C.E., Virgil wrote a companion piece to Homer's *The Odyssey*, telling it from the perspective of a Trojan warrior named Aeneas, legendary founder of Rome.

The Aeneid is set in the aftermath of the Trojan War. Its hero — like Odysseus — faces a number of diversions on the path home. In Aeneas's case, "home" is a promised land that the gods call Hesperia. By the time he arrives there, the warrior is overwhelmed by doubts about the purpose of his journey and his life. He wonders why he alone escaped the siege of Troy, and seeks the counsel of a seer, the Sybil. In a cave on the side of a cliff near Cumae, the Sybil tells Aeneas how he can safely enter Hades and consult his deceased father for advice. First, he must obtain the Golden Bough, a sprig that will allow him safe passage into Hades. Aeneas travels to a shadowy valley where the sprig is said to grow and returns with it to the Sybil, who leads him into the underworld.

Virgil's description of Hades echoes those given by both Homer and Plato (the latter recounted Odysseus's descent in *The Republic*). Aeneas sees legions of souls clinging to their mortal lives in the grimmest parts of the underworld. Beyond that, however, lies a more comforting sight — the blessed fields of Elysium where purified souls await reincarnation. It is here that Aeneas encounters his father, Anchises, who explains to his son the metaphysics of the human soul. His explanation seems to be based on a combination of ideas from ancient Greek mythology and newer, more mature philosophical ideas. Virgil writes of a great spirit — "a Mind interfused / Through every fiber of the universe," from which all earthly life forms emerge — and of the corruption that haunts us in our mortal life and beyond, until we are purified again:

> Their life-force is drawn from fire, their creative seeds
> Are of heavenly source, except as they are clogged
> By the corrupting flesh, and dulled by their earthly
> Habiliments, and limbs imbued with death.
> From these derive our fears and our desires,
> Our grief and our joy, nor can we compass the whole
> Aura of heaven shut as we are in the prison
> Of the unseeing flesh. And furthermore,
> When on the last day we are lost to the light,
> We do not shed away all evil or all the ills
> The body has bequeathed to us poor wretches,
> For many flaws cannot but be ingrained
> And must have grown hard through all our length of days.
> Therefore we souls are trained with punishment
> And pay with suffering for old felonies —
> Some are hung up helpless to the winds;
> The stain of sin is cleansed for others of us
> In the trough of a huge whirlpool; or with fire
> Burned out of us — each one of us we suffer
> The afterworld we deserve: and from thence are sent
> Through wide Elysium, and some few maintain
> Ourselves in the Fields of Bliss, until length of days

> When time has come full circle, cleanses us
> To corruption's very core and leaves a pure
> Element of perception, a spark of the primal fire.
> After the cycle of a thousand years
> God summons all these in a great procession
> To the waters of Lethe, so that when they visit
> The sky-encircled earth, being bereft
> Of memory, they may begin to want
> The body on again.[41]

It is difficult to delineate the historical ideas and influences expressed in this passage. Specific names (like Elysium and Lethe) belong to Greek mythology, but some of the broader ideas (pantheism; reincarnation) might just as easily come from Egypt, the Middle East or the Far East. The passage might be said to illustrate the idea that the Roman Empire's policy of religious tolerance allowed many traditions to flourish and that, gradually, those traditions — presented in poetry as a seamless set of fixed ideas — began to meld in the minds of the people and in their art.

On the other hand, Ovid's epic poem *Metamorphoses*, written approximately twenty years later, emphasizes the variety of myths and ideas rather than melding them. The effect is schizophrenic, perhaps reflecting restlessness in Roman culture itself. Ovid begins by remembering Hesiod's *Theogony*, the oldest Greek account of the origin of the universe. From a chaotic mass of disconnected elements, "some god (or kinder nature)"[42] separates sky from earth, earth from sea. During the process of evolution that follows, two generations of gods come into being. In time, mankind is also created from the divine substance of the original god or nature, possibly by the second-generation god Prometheus. Ovid explains that four degenerative Ages of Man — Gold, Silver, Bronze and Iron — followed the creation. During the Age of Silver, the younger generation of Gods (the Olympians) usurped the older generation. Throughout the Age of Iron, the Olympians interacted with humans, until the death of humanity's last epic hero. Before the dawn of the current age, the gods withdrew from the world of men — to return only in dreams, visions and prophecies. Ovid's tales end here, in an age of confusion.

The *Metamorphoses* is a series of confused morality plays, which eagerly indulge in the details of human acts of pride and rashness, while glamorizing the haughty and impulsive nature of the immortal gods. Ovid's overall message seems to be that *change* is the only truth in the world, and he is compelled to show us that mortals and immortals alike are eternally guided by passion. (One imagines that Plato would have protested the work with particular zeal.) The gods undergo physical metamorphoses in order to pursue their passions on earth, while humans are physically transformed as a reward or punishment for acting on their own passions or for inciting the passions of the gods. Star-crossed lovers Pyramus and Thisbe prematurely take their lives, and become mulberry trees; the prophet Tiresias is turned into a hermaphrodite after he strikes coupling serpents with a walking stick; princess Philomela becomes a songbird after she is raped and her tongue cut out by her barbarous brother-in-law. Toward the end of the work, Ovid turns from mythology to mystical philosophy, perhaps trying to reassure himself that life is not insignificant. He remembers that he was once — in a past lifetime — a soldier fighting in the Trojan War, and therefore insists that "souls cannot perish" and "the spirit is always the same even though it migrates the different bodies." He continues:

> And since I am already embarked upon this great sea,
> Have given full sails to the wind, hear me out: nothing
> Endures in this world! The whole of it flows, and all is
> Formed with a changing appearance; even time passes,
> Constant in motion, no different from a great river,
> For neither a river nor a transitory hour
> Is able to stand still; but just as each wave is driven
> Ahead by another, urged on from behind, and urging
> The next wave before it in an unbroken sequence,
> So the times flee and at the same time they follow,
> And always are new; for what has just been is no longer,
> And what has not been will presently come into being,
> And every moment's occasion is a renewal.[43]

At first glance, Ovid's cosmology has more in common with the thoughts of Heraclitus than with the thoughts of Socrates, Plato or even Virgil. Pyramus and Thisbe, Tiresias and Philomela would reappear, alongside the thoughts of the great philosophers, in Eliot's early poetry, enhancing the 20th-century poet's sense that this variety and flux offered the only true characterization of the universe. Upon closer inspection, we recognize that Ovid was writing at a pivotal time in the history of Western civilization, when Christianity was competing violently with the mythologies of the past. Similarly, Eliot was writing at a pivotal time when Christianity was competing violently (at least in Harvard's academic circle) with both the mythologies of the past and the science of the future.

The Birth of Christianity

As an undergraduate, Eliot was acutely aware that classical culture would eventually convert to Christianity, but his own conversion would be just as gradual and hard-won. He could not accept Christianity without attempting to understand it fully, and that meant understanding its origins, its development, and eventually its many modern incarnations.

Among the many subcultures in the vast Roman Empire of the early first century C.E. was the Hebrew culture in Palestine. According to stories passed down for thousands of years, the one true God had made a covenant with the Hebrews, and called them His chosen people. In the later part of the 4th century B.C.E., the Hebrews were ruled by Romans who allowed them to continue to worship according to their own beliefs, so long as their practices did not interfere with Roman law. For hundreds of years, their religion evolved within a mixed culture and adapted traditions of both Greek and Hebrew heritage.

According to the Christian Gospels, the long line of Hebrew prophets ended with John the Baptist, who witnessed the fulfillment of the prophecies that God would send a savior. John was baptizing a man from Nazareth when he "saw the heavens opened, and the Spirit like a dove descending upon him: And there came a voice from heaven, saying, Thou art my beloved son, in whom I am well pleased" (Mark 1: 9–11). Jesus of Nazareth, the proclaimed Son of God, taught the Jewish people in Palestine about a new covenant with the one true God — a covenant that dispensed with traditional Jewish rites and practices and elevated two commandments above all other traditions. The first commandment: "Thou shalt love the Lord thy God with all thy heart, and with all thy soul, and with all thy mind, and with all thy strength." The second: "Thou shalt love thy neighbor as thyself" (Mark 12: 29–31). Jesus preached a message of consolation to the impoverished people of Israel. Blessed be the poor, he said, for "your reward is great in heaven" (Luke 6: 23). His teachings made mortal suffering sound like a prologue to eternal bliss — a prospect that was well received by the lower classes, who embraced the prophet.

Some Jews were not as easily converted to the new religion. Fearing that Jesus sought to overturn the old commandments handed down by Moses, they vigorously questioned his claim to be the son of the Hebrew God. "We know that God spake unto Moses," they said. "As for this fellow, we know not from whence he is" (John 9: 28–29). Jesus replied, "Think not that I come to destroy the law, or the prophets: I am not come to destroy, but to fulfill" (Matthew 5: 17). He explained that Moses, and other prophets, had foretold his coming — referring to a prophecy that appears in the book of Deuteronomy, chapter 18, verse 15: "The Lord thy God will raise up unto thee a Prophet from the midst of thee, of thy brethren, like unto me; unto him ye shall hearken."

After Jesus's death, some of his followers also pointed to Isaiah's prophecy of a virgin-born son who shall "know to refuse the evil, and choose the good" (Isaiah 7: 14–15), Jeremiah's prophecy of a king of the house of David who "shall execute judgment and justice in the earth" (Jeremiah 23: 5), and a reference in the book of Daniel to a vision of the Son of Man, descending from heaven to take dominion over all things (Daniel 7: 13). Some even cited a poem by Virgil, the fourth of his *Eclogues*, which refers to a child that will come to redeem Rome. (Eliot himself said that Virgil "makes a liaison between the old world and the new, and of his peculiar position we may take the fourth *Eclogue* as a symbol."[44]) Many Jewish traditionalists remained unconvinced, and Jesus and his disciples had many enemies. Eventually, it was the leaders of the old Jewish community who demanded his crucifixion, transforming him into a martyr, and (in the eyes of his followers) a symbol of God's supreme love for humanity.

Roman critics, by contrast, were quietly baffled by the seemingly irrational beliefs of the early Christians. In the first hundred years after the crucifixion of Jesus, many Romans viewed Christianity as a minor cult or superstition, or a sect within Judaism. Among educated Roman writers, references to Christianity were largely dismissive. However, as the religion grew and spread into the west, mainly due to the influence of the apostle Paul, Roman philosophers began to study and question the new religion. In 178 C.E., a Platonist named Celsus wrote a lengthy criticism of Christianity, entitled *A True Discourse*. He based much of his criticism on the observation that while Christianity stemmed from the prophecies of Judaism, the followers of Jesus did not uphold any of the Jewish traditions. To his way of thinking, this meant that Christianity had no tradition to claim as its own. Furthermore, Celsus believed that the very basis of the Jewish and Christian religions — the single-minded worship of one true God — was undermined by the excessive adoration of Jesus. (There was, as yet, no fixed Christian doctrine of the Holy Trinity.) For the Jews, he concluded, Christianity was nothing short of simple-minded heresy. For Greeks and Romans, Jesus was unexceptional. The essential humanity of Jesus' teachings, Celsus said, had been better expressed in the dialogues of Plato, whose appeal to men's rationality was, in its humility, easier to accept than Jesus' claim that he was speaking for God.

Despite such criticisms, Christianity quickly spread throughout the Roman Empire, uniting people of all traditions under the God of Abraham, making them "one body in Christ" (Romans 12: 5). The simplicity of the "new covenant" was no doubt very appealing to the disenfranchised classes, who had neither the time nor the education to make a fruitful study of Greek philosophy. Christianity was a religion for the masses — one that provided comfort, despite the struggles of daily life, through its promise of salvation. The apostle Paul traveled widely and preached that eternal salvation was possible through faith, which he refers to as a kind of hope-without-object:

> We are saved by hope: but hope that is seen is not hope: for what a man seeth, why doth he yet hope for? But if we hope for that we see not, then do we with patience wait for it. Likewise the Spirit also helpeth our infirmities: for we know what we should pray for as we ought: but the Spirit itself maketh intercession for us with groanings which cannot be uttered. And he that searcheth the hearts knoweth what is the mind of the Spirit, because he maketh intercession for the saint according to the will of God. And we know that all things work together for good to them that love God, to them who are called according to his purpose [Romans 8: 24–28].

Jesus said it more simply: "All things are possible to him that believeth" (Mark 9: 23).

The message that "all things are possible with God" became a common response to the rational criticisms that were leveled against Christianity by Roman scholars. Over time, however, followers of Christianity did make attempts to reconcile some basic principles of Greek philosophy with Christian thought. The Gospel of John, believed to have been written toward the end of the first century A.D., begins with a recapitulation of the Jewish creation story: "In the beginning was the Word, and the Word was with God, and the Word was God." (John 1: 1). The phrase "the Word" is the English translation of the Greek *logos*, a key concept in the philosophy of Heraclitus. Considered in the context in which Heraclitus used it, John's "logos" might be interpreted as the divine Reason that simultaneously penetrates and orders everything in existence, and connects the human mind to the Mind of God. The Gospel of John goes on to say that, in Jesus, "the Word was made flesh" (John 1: 14). In Platonic terms, Jesus is the Form of the divine Reason.

In centuries to come, some of the most important figures involved in shaping the Christian doctrine as we know it today continued this effort to reconcile the Greek and Jewish traditions with Christianity. The apostle Paul had faith that Christianity would ultimately overwhelm the two older traditions: "For the Jews require a sign, and the Greeks seek after wisdom: But we preach Christ crucified, unto the Jews a stumbling block, and unto the Greeks foolishness: But unto them which are called, both Jews and Greeks, Christ the power of God, and the wisdom of God. Because the foolishness of God is wiser than men; and the weakness of God is stronger than men" (I Corinthians 1: 22–25).

It is clear from Eliot's college-era writing that he was studying Christianity. Later, his adult poetry makes frequent allusion to stories and passages in the Bible — beginning with a reference to John the Baptist ("Though I have seen my head [grown slightly bald] brought in upon a platter, / I am no prophet") in "The Love Song of J. Alfred Prufrock" and continuing through the *Four Quartets*, where he paraphrases Paul's teachings about hope. For the time being, however, the young Eliot remained skeptical. He still had not found a mediator who could make Christianity seem vital in the way that his Harvard professors had made Greco-Roman ideals seem vital to him. All he could do was study the lives and writings of other philosophers and poets who, like him, sought meaning in a world that had moved beyond Greco-Roman values. One such journeyman who impressed him was St. Augustine, whose voice eventually found its way into *The Waste Land*.

The Confessions of St. Augustine

By the early fourth century C.E., the stability of the Roman Empire was in dire jeopardy, owing to political corruption, urban decay, public health problems and military dissolution. Augustine of Hippo (354–430) saw the world he knew crumbling around him, and he longed to find a rock of the ages that would outlast this "end time." During his years of searching, he read the letters of the apostle Paul. Paul preached about a God that transcends time; Augustine directly addresses this God in his spiritual autobiography, *Confessions*: "The countless days of our lives and of our forefathers' lives have passed by within your 'today.' From it they have received their due measure of duration and their very existence. And so it will be with all the other days which are still to come. But you yourself are eternally the same."[45]

This realization is, for Augustine, humbling and reassuring, but he writes that his piety was hard-won. He remembers being obliged to memorize *The Aeneid* as a child, and having spent many hours lamenting the cruel fate of Dido, who sacrificed herself for the unrequited love of Aeneas. He writes that he was drawn to tales of tragedy because they fanned the flames of his youthful melancholy; he thrived on the writings of Homer because they made the gods equally melodramatic. Illustrating Plato's greatest fears, he recalls thinking that criminals should not be punished since "all who did as they did could be shown to follow the example of the heavenly gods, not that of sinful mortals."[46]

Believing himself to be justified in the pursuit of his desires, the young Augustine moved to Carthage and indulged his most carnal impulses — experiences worthy of the tawdry tales of Ovid's *Metamorphoses*. Later, he confesses to God, "I wandered away, too far from your sustaining hand, and created of myself a barren waste."[47] He acknowledges that his prayers for lasting happiness were overwhelmed by his desires for immediate gratification. "Give me chastity and continence," he begged, "but not yet."[48] Over the years, his moral suffering became more intense. After a nine-year sojourn among dualist pseudo–Christians known as Manicheans, he turned to philosophy for solace. Augustine says that the greatest hindrance to finding peace was his reluctance to surrender his will to the religious impulse without the consent of his reason. His studies in philosophy had ignited in him a passion for "the wisdom of eternal truth," and he became too proud of his education to embrace doctrine that seemed simple-minded by comparison. Nevertheless, he was dissatisfied with philosophy. Aristotle's *Categories* left him cold, and the teachings of the Manicheans failed to resolve one overwhelming question:

> Where then is evil? What is its origin? How did it steal into the world? What is the root or seed from which it grew? Can it be that there simply is no evil? If so, why do we fear and guard against something which is not there? If our fear is unfounded, it is itself an evil, because it stabs and wrings our hearts for nothing. In fact the evil is all the greater if we are afraid when there is nothing to fear. Therefore, either there is evil and we fear it, or the fear itself is evil.[49]

It was philosophy that finally led him to Catholic Christianity. Not long after he renounced Manicheanism, Augustine discovered Plato. Scholars concur that the so-called "neo-platonic" distillation of the Greek philosopher's teachings convinced Augustine that everything is One, and that "whatever is, is good; and evil, the origin of which I was trying to find, is not a substance, because if it were a substance, it would be good."[50] Evil, Augustine concludes, is "nothing but the removal of good until finally no good remains."[51] By extension, wickedness is merely a perversion or corruption of the human will when it turns away from God, who created all things and made them good. This realization reinforced Augustine's growing humility, and he concludes that his previous suffering was due to the fact that he had loved only temporal things, rather than loving the world around him as a temporal manifestation of the eternal God.

For Augustine, there was one more step in the conversion to Christianity, and it stemmed directly from the teachings of Paul the Apostle. Augustine writes: "I understand ... *that the impulses of nature and the impulses of the spirit are at war with one another.* In this warfare I was on both sides."[52] He needed a mediator that could help to fortify him against the impulses of nature — a mediator between God and man. He found that mediator in Jesus Christ, "the Word made flesh," who is, for Christians, "*a man, like them,* and also *rules as God over all things, blessed for ever.*"[53]

During this time period, more and more of Augustine's contemporaries also turned to Christianity as a respite from the moral chaos of the Roman Empire. For Augustine, as for millions of people, Christianity provided meaning and hope in a changing world: "One thing passes away so that another may take its place and the whole be preserved in all its parts."[54] Hadn't Jesus himself spoken of a baptism by fire?

The Inferno of Dante

Toward the early 14th century, the work of Italian poet Dante Alighieri (1265–1321) illustrates the revitalizing influence of the Greco-Roman tradition on the fully formed orthodoxy of the Catholic Church. Dante, like the scholars of the Church who inspired him, was deeply moved by the writings of the classical period and struggled to assimilate the beauty of that world into his own Christian belief system.

For centuries, the Catholic Church had taught that an individual who accepts Jesus Christ as his Lord and Savior will be forgiven his sins and welcomed into a blessed afterlife. Those who had not been baptized into the church were condemned to eternal suffering apart from God. For Dante, this meant that the souls of all of the heroes and poets of the classical age, who existed before the coming of Christ, were eternally suffering. In his masterpiece *Divina commedia* (*The Divine Comedy*), Dante takes an allegorical journey through the three realms of the afterlife that were recognized by the Catholic Church: Hell, Purgatory and Paradise. Each of these realms is populated with historical and literary figures.

Lost in a dark wasteland, Dante (as "the Pilgrim") entreats Virgil, his literary idol, to guide him on a journey through the afterlife, so that the traveler can share his discoveries with people on earth. Like Odysseus and Aeneas before him, the Pilgrim descends into "the starless air of Hell."[55] There, he finds the spirits of his literary predecessors (Homer, Ovid, etc.), along with a host of influential Greek philosophers (including Heraclitus, Socrates and Plato), all confined to a kind of permanent limbo because they were born before mankind was redeemed by the birth of Christ.

Dante defines the shades he sees in the underworld as "the form of our desire,"[56] a definition which is illuminated by the teachings of St. Thomas Aquinas (1225–1274), arguably Dante's most profound philosophical influence. In his *Summa Theologica*, Aquinas writes that "the soul will remain perpetually in whatever last end it is found to have set for itself at the time of death, desiring that state as the most suitable, whether it is good or evil.... After this life, therefore, those who are found good at the instant of death will have their wills forever fixed in good. But those who are found evil at that moment will be forever obstinate in evil."[57] Among the "evil" shades in Dante's Inferno are those pre–Christian thinkers who have been "neither faithful nor unfaithful to their God."[58] The two travelers descend through seven circles of increasing horror, but the Pilgrim seems most disheartened by the sight of this initial group — generations upon generations of well-meaning souls who never had a chance at redemption. He laments: "I wondered how death could have undone so great a number."[59]

By the time he and his guide emerge from the Inferno and begin climbing the mountain of Purgatory, the Pilgrim is developing a better understanding of the simple message of Jesus Christ about love. Turning his back on the natural philosophy of the Greeks, he asks for divine inspiration to help him relate his soul's journey home. The journey, he says, begins with love — even the most base, physical love for another human being — and strives for a union that is beyond comprehension:

> Just as a fire's flames always rise up,
>   Inspired by its own nature to ascend,
>   Seeking to be in its own element,
> Just so, the captive soul begins its quest,
>   The spiritual movement of its love,
>   Not resting till the thing loved is enjoyed.[60]

When he gets to Paradise, the Pilgrim is guided by Beatrice, who is for him the ideal embodiment of Love, and greeted by the great saints of the medieval Catholic Church. Here he asks the question that has been nagging him since the beginning of his journey: *Why must all those who were born before Christ reside with the sinners? Did they not love?* He is told simply that God's will, His Eternal Judgment, is too high for mankind to comprehend.

T.S. Eliot was familiar with Dante in 1909 when he read George Santayana's *Three Philosophical Poets*. Howard Howarth writes that Eliot had, by then, discovered the Italian poet in "the Harvard way" — his professors encouraged him to read Dante "without preliminaries on grammar, to splash through him, half understanding, and wait till later to clear up problems."[61] At the time, Eliot was still under the influence of the French Symbolists, and he recognized similarities between Baudelaire's morbid ruminations and the first section of Dante's *Divine Comedy*, which was filled with vivid depictions of squalor and suffering. It was not until much later in life that Eliot began to understand the role of these haunting images within the grand scheme of the *Divine Comedy*.

In 1950, he explained that he had worked his way back, chronologically, to Dante: the French Symbolists helped him to understand the Elizabethan and Jacobean poets; the Elizabethan and Jacobean poets eventually led him back to Dante. In the years between college and religious conversion (1914–1927), Eliot was focused on Elizabethan and Jacobean verse, which he came to regard as the height of achievement in English literature.

The Legend of Shakespeare

It is difficult to pinpoint the beginnings of a distinctly English literature, and almost as difficult to pinpoint the beginnings of English drama. It has been suggested that the English tragedy, which came into its fullest expression during the reign of Queen Elizabeth I (1558–1603), began developing as an art form as early as the 12th century, and that several of the earliest examples were dramatizations of the murder of Thomas Becket, the Archbishop of Canterbury who was assassinated in his own church by representatives of the monarchs of England and France.[62] For centuries, the shrine of St. Thomas Becket in Canterbury was a popular site of pilgrimage for Christians in England and a common subject for storytellers. In *The Canterbury Tales*, Geoffrey Chaucer (1343–1400) recounts the personal histories of thirty pilgrims on their way to receive the saint's blessings. The first to speak is a knight, who regales the others with a noble tale of honor and love — the stuff of Arthurian legend.

Tales of Christian piety and knightly virtue continued to dominate English literature until the early 16th century. One of the most-cited examples of the time period is *Everyman*, a morality play believed to have been written soon after 1485. *Everyman* is a Christian allegory in which the nondescript eponymous character must come to terms with his own mortality. He seeks comfort from family and friends, but learns that only his good deeds can comfort him in the afterlife. In 1927, T.S. Eliot wrote that he regarded this play as the best example of more "refined" early period of English drama,[63] which ended in the 16th century, as the works of Thomas Kyd (1558–1594) and Christopher Marlowe (1564–1593) paved the way for William Shakespeare.

Shakespeare was born in 1564, during the early years of the reign of Protestant monarch Elizabeth I, and it is possible that Protestantism was a significant childhood influence. The Renaissance movement and the Protestant Reformation had ended the dominance of the Roman Catholic Church and repopularized the humanist ideals of Greek and Roman antiquity, emphasizing naturalism, individualism and secular reason over religious faith and the supernatural. This shift in values had a significant influence on English theater; medieval morality plays like *Everyman* gave way to more realistic, character-based dramas.

Shakespeare's plays were pivotal to this change. W.B. Yeats argues that "Shakespeare wrote at a time when solitary great men were gathering to themselves the fire that had once flowed hither and thither among all men, when individualism in work and thought and emotion was breaking up the old rhythms of life, when the common people, sustained no longer by the myths of Christianity and of still older faiths, were sinking into the earth."[64] The implication of this statement is that the Renaissance produced existential feeling and, for the first time (at least in England), made it possible for art to exert a greater influence than religious instruction. Walter Kaufmann, in his book *From Shakespeare to Existentialism*, presents Shakespeare as the father of Romantic literature: "He celebrated the world in a most un–Christian manner: its beauties and its grossness; love between the sexes, even in its not particularly subtle forms; and the glory of all that is transitory, including intense emotion. Suffering and despair were to his mind not revelations of the worthlessness of *this* world but experiences that, if intense enough, were preferable to a more mediocre state."[65] Shakespeare's unrivaled talent for complex characterization, he concludes, paved a road for the philosophy of existentialism, and eventually the modern novel.

Of course, this is a narrow appraisal of Shakespeare's significance. With a historical figure as omnipresent as Shakespeare, there are many different perspectives. F.E. Halliday, a 20th-century biographer, writes that Shakespeare's body of work is governed by "a philosophy derived from the Middle Ages and a commonplace to the Elizabethans: that of an ordered universe at the heart of which was God, while on the terrestrial plane was the King, another fixed centre about which all subjects should revolve in orbits as orderly as those of the sun, planets, and stars about the earth."[66] Though Halliday certainly does not identify Shakespeare as a Christian, this perspective suggests an artist with a far more concrete belief system than Kaufmann suggests.

Very early in life, T.S. Eliot felt a need to come to terms with the legacy of Shakespeare. In a 1905 letter, Eliot's mother writes to the headmaster of Milton Academy that her teenage son has read and memorized most of Shakespeare's works. Almost thirty years later, Eliot confessed that, as a student, "the only pleasure that I got from Shakespeare was the pleasure of being commended for reading him; had I been a child of more independent mind I should have refused to read him at all."[67] He says that he was intimidated by Shakespeare's legacy — as the center of the Western canon, the nearest thing to an undeniable "classic" author in the English language — to the point that he could not respond to the playwright's work in an unbiased way. Perhaps as a result, in his early years as a literary critic, Eliot tended to be overly critical of Shakespeare's works.

To his credit, Eliot strove to present to his readers a portrait of Shakespeare within the context of the Elizabethan age: Shakespeare as man and writer, rather than as literary god. Shakespeare, Eliot said, did not fully develop his own genius: he was "fortunate" to live in a time and place that was ripe for the rebirth of literature, and he inherited the "already highly developed ... verse instrument"[68] of Thomas Kyd, author of *The Spanish Tragedy*. Eliot also lavished considerable praise on Shakespeare's peer Christopher Marlowe, whose own style (Eliot said in 1918) was in some ways more accomplished than Shakespeare's: "Shakespeare's is more exactly a vice of style, a tortured perverse ingenuity of images which dissipates instead of concentrating the imagination." He wrote, "Marlowe's vice is one which he was gradually attenuating, and even, what is more miraculous, turning into a virtue."[69] What Eliot admires in Marlowe are his powers of concentration and self-evaluation. What he fails to acknowledge, at least initially, is that Shakespeare only appears to lack these powers because he is constantly evolving as a thinker. At the beginning of Shakespeare's career, the Bard almost certainly existed in Marlowe's shadow. *Titus Andronicus*, Shakespeare's fifth play, is an homage of sorts to Marlowe's *Tamburlaine the Great*. It was only with his more poetical works, notably *Romeo and Juliet* and *A Midsummer Night's Dream*, that Shakespeare came into his own. By the time the first quarto edition of *Romeo and Juliet* was published in 1597, both Kyd and Marlowe were dead. Shakespeare had no peers of equal standing, though many Elizabethan dramatists closely followed his lead.

Eliot and Shakespeare, "Hamlet and His Problems"

As a pioneer, Shakespeare may have had only a hazy conception of what he was trying to accomplish: a reconciliation of the traditional belief system of Roman Catholicism with the humanist leanings of Renaissance thought. It is much easier for us to analyze *Hamlet* with several centuries of literature and philosophy between us and that ambitious play. *Hamlet*, like Thomas Kyd's *The Spanish Tragedy*, begins with a ghost — one hungry for revenge. In Shakespeare's play, the ghost is the title character's father, the former king of Denmark. One night, several members of the castle guard and a skeptical nobleman named Horatio see the tortured spirit of the king, and become convinced that this sighting is a harbinger of impending doom. Eager to hear the ghost's full message, they resolve to share their secret with Hamlet, believing that the ghost will speak to his son. Hamlet has been unremittingly melancholy since his father's death, and his passions are inflamed when the ghost explains that he was murdered by his brother Claudius, who subsequently took his throne and married his queen.

When next we see him, Hamlet appears quite mad — he is still contemplating death, but his thoughts and words are unfocused. When he encounters Polonius, Hamlet tells him, "Yourself, sir, shall grow old as I am, if, like a crab, you could go backward" [II.ii.197–205]. Moments later, Hamlet meets with his old friends Rosencrantz and Guildenstern and reveals to them the cause of his apparent madness. What torments him is not the simple realization that Denmark is filled with cruelty and injustice, but questions stemming from the realization that this was true *even before he realized it*. His window on the world has been darkened, and Hamlet does not so much want to avenge his father's murder as he wants to regain his simple, innocent perspective on life. Since his awakening, life itself—the way that he experiences life—seems so complex as to be meaningless. Hamlet now fears that everything is relative—that there are no eternal truths, only human perceptions subject to time and death.

Tormented by this possibility, Hamlet contemplates suicide. He is not, however, a resolute stoic—he has too many questions, and death is too great a mystery for him to face it casually. "Thus," he says, "conscience does make cowards of us all" [III.i.84]. Hamlet turns his thoughts to revenge, setting into motion a chain of events reminiscent of Kyd's play. In *The Spanish Tragedy*, the mad king Hieronimo avenges his son's murder by performing in a stage play alongside the murderers. The play ends with the fatal stabbing of his son's killers. In *Hamlet*, the mad prince is merely an onlooker. Ultimately, Hamlet lacks the courage of the ancient Greek and Roman heroes, men of action for whom "the readiness is all." He has no problem, however, murdering Polonius or sealing the fates of his friends Rosencrantz and Guildenstern. At times, we see, he is completely guided by passion. Thus he may be described as genuinely mad—a schizophrenic who is at one moment unable to focus his thoughts and, the next, unable to control his actions.

These self-contradictions seem to be the basis of Eliot's criticism of the play. According to Eliot, it is full of "superfluous and inconsistent scenes," full of "stuff that the writer could not drag to light, contemplate, or manipulate into art."[70] Eliot suggests that Shakespeare's play, like Hamlet's madness, conveys only frustration and confusion:

> For Shakespeare it is less than madness and more than feigned. The levity of Hamlet, his repetition of phrase, his puns, are not part of a deliberate plan of dissimulation, but a form of emotional relief. In the character Hamlet it is the buffoonery of an emotion which can find no outlet in action; in the dramatist it is the buffoonery of an emotion which he cannot express in art. The intense feeling, ecstatic or terrible, without an object or exceeding its object, is something which every person of sensibility has known; it is doubtless a subject of study for pathologists. It often occurs in adolescence: the ordinary person puts these feelings to sleep, or trims down his feelings to fit the business world; the artist keeps them alive by his ability to intensify the world to his emotions. The Hamlet of Laforgue is an adolescent; the Hamlet of Shakespeare is not, he has not that explanation and excuse. We must simply admit that here Shakespeare tackled a problem which proved too much for him.[71]

Years later, Eliot admitted that his early criticisms of Shakespeare may have been "jaundiced."[72] He realized that his criticisms of *Hamlet* were criticisms of his own work written between 1910 and 1918—his own early attempts to assimilate conflicting beliefs, disparate emotions and a heap of broken images into a coherent whole.

Interlude in Paris

In 1910, in his final semester as an undergraduate, Eliot began work on "Portrait of a Lady," one of his first major poems. The earliest-written section of the poem borrows symbolism from

Eliot's earlier works — flowers (lilacs and hyacinths) and piano notes "recalling things that other people have desired."[73] In this particular poem, Eliot uses the symbols to build a character rather than an abstract impression. The "lady" of the title is an older woman — probably a remnant of the Boston society that Eliot is eager to leave behind and reminiscent of Laforgue's marionettes. The lady, however, is not the true focus of Eliot's poem. Much as novelist Henry James uses his narrators' observations about other characters to reveal the nature of the narrator himself, Eliot's poem reveals more about the speaker than his subject.

The lady is peacefully resigned to the unambitious nature of her life. She sits, serving tea to friends, and places the heavy burden of responsibility for passionate living on the speaker: "You will go on, and when you have prevailed / You can say: at this point many a one has failed."[74] At this, the speaker feels anything but youthful; he knows that he is not a man of action, and his fear of failure is overwhelming. The symbols of Eliot's early poems — those sights and sounds and smells that once evoked fleeting feelings of transcendence — now begin to seem like tired representations, "the withered leaves / Of our sensations."[75] The lady speaks of April sunsets and Paris in the spring, and the poet compares her voice to a broken violin on an August afternoon. His fear: Life has ended before it began.

In October 1910, Eliot drafted another segment of the poem, set "among the smoke and fog of a December afternoon,"[76] amid an atmosphere of death. The speaker is more direct this time, expressing gratitude for the other's sympathetic ear. There is a certain desperation in it, and eventually the speaker's composure begins to crack. He feels a distressing impulse building beneath the staid conversation and elegant parlor music — a primal rhythm that is fighting its way to the surface:

> Among the windings of the violins
> And the ariettes
> Of cracked cornets
> Inside my brain a dull tom-tom begins
> Absurdly hammering a prelude of its own,
> Capricious monotone
> That is at least one definite "false note."[77]

In the same month, T.S. Eliot arrived in Paris and composed the first of what have become known as the "Bolo Verses." The main character, King Bolo, is a crass man of action who, in "The Triumph of Bullshit," directly addresses the staid marionettes of Eliot's more academic poetry: "For Christ's sake stick it up your ass!"[78] Critics have suggested that the fictional King Bolo persona was an important emotional outlet for the repressed and frustrated poet, and it is clear that Eliot never intended for them to be analyzed alongside his academic poetry. He confined the bawdy experiments to private correspondence, never imagining that they would be published.

The Bolo Verses are helpful for what they tell us about Eliot during this time in his life. In Paris, Eliot granted himself a bit more freedom of expression, and may have begun to experience some relief from the anxiety that he associated with Boston society. It is no coincidence that, around the same time, he struck up one of the most intimate relationships of his life, with a medical student named Jean Verdenal. The two carried on a lasting correspondence for several years, and it was Verdenal who heard Eliot's most revealing confessions during that time. While in Paris, Eliot also encountered a significant new intellectual influence in the weekly lectures of Henri Bergson at the Collège de France in the fall of 1910.

Henri Bergson: Creative Evolution

The philosophy of Henri Bergson (1859–1941), expounded in his popular 1907 book *Creative Evolution*, harks back to the early days of Western thought — specifically, to Heraclitus, who said that all things are in constant flux. Bergson's philosophy is based on this idea as it pertains to human consciousness. Like George Santayana, Bergson says that philosophical reflection is the ongoing enhancement of human purpose, and what is more, that human consciousness is part of the ongoing evolution of life itself.

Bergson uses the paradoxical proofs of Zeno of Elea (c. 490–430 B.C.E.) to prove his theory. Zeno, in Socratic fashion, asks the student to accept the notion that time can be infinitely divided: an hour into minutes, a minute into seconds, a second into milliseconds, a millisecond into microseconds, a microsecond into nanoseconds, and so on indefinitely. He then asks the student to accept that, before a nanosecond can pass, one million picoseconds must pass; before a picosecond can pass, one million femtoseconds must pass; before a femtosecond can pass, one quintillion attoseconds must pass, and so on indefinitely. He concludes that it is impossible for any unit of time to ever "pass," because an infinite number of smaller units would have to pass first. Therefore, time is simply a construction of the human imagination.

To the practical mind, this is worthless theory. We know that time is real, because we experience change: day passes into night, we grow old and die. Zeno's paradox has not made time seem unreal to us, but it does force us to analyze our everyday definition of time. We usually perceive time as continuous. Bergson compares this perception of time to the "cinematographical method"[79] — when we see a filmstrip projected onto a screen, we interpret it as a moving image, even though our intellect knows that it is in fact a series of still frames. The cinematographical method is not an intellectual comprehension of time, but a practical interpretation. Bergson says that the same thing is true of our perception of life — we interpret it as a series of fragments, though in fact everything is inextricably connected.

Bergson says that the *intellect* is not made for everyday survival; it is *instinct* that transforms intellectual ideas into practical, livable "reality." The goal of instinct is physical survival. The goal of the intellect is to create meaning in life by organizing, harmonizing and unifying — by making time stand still. The intellect, according to Bergson, is attracted to the "stable and unchangeable."[80] What then is the "stable and unchangeable" that the intellect apprehends? We might turn to Plato's theory of Forms, but Bergson refutes this answer. He says it is natural for the intellect to try to organize new experiences according to preexisting ideas or Forms, and that it is this natural function of the intellect which preexists, not the ideas or Forms themselves. Because this "natural function" cannot be turned off, we cannot trust our intellect to give us an objective view of unchangeable reality.

It follows then, that Bergson hopes to rely on instinct to find the meaning of life. He knows, however, that only a very highly developed instinct — "instinct that has become disinterested, self-conscious, capable of reflecting upon its object and of enlarging it indefinitely"[81] — would bother to seek meaning. This highly developed instinct he calls *intuition*. Intuition acts as a mediator between instinct and intellect, recognizing that "life does not quite go into the category of the many nor yet into that of the one; that neither mechanical causality nor finality can give a sufficient interpretation of the vital process."[82] Intuition, however, is fleeting — usually overwhelmed by the more vital forces of instinct and intellect. Instinct has no need for intuition because it demands no higher meaning than physical survival, and intellect dismisses intuition because intellect cannot understand intuition. Bergson says that the goal of philosophy is to help us to seize moments of intuition and bring them together. Only then, he says, will we realize the natural function of the human mind and understand that life is a *process*:

> To act and to know that we are acting, to come into touch with reality and even to live it, but only in the measure in which it concerns the work that is being accomplished and the furrow that is being plowed, such is the function of human intelligence. Yet a beneficent fluid bathes us, whence we draw the very force to labor and to live. From this ocean of life, in which we are immersed, we are continually drawing something, and we feel that our being, or at least the intellect that guides it, has been formed therein by a kind of local concentration. Philosophy can only be an effort to dissolve again into the Whole. Intelligence, reabsorbed into its principle, may thus live back again its own genesis. But the enterprise cannot be achieved in one stroke; it is necessarily collective and progressive.[83]

Two years before Bergson's *Creative Evolution* was published, Albert Einstein published his famous paper on the theory of relativity, which proposed that space is not three-dimensional and time is not separate from space. Time, Einstein showed, is relative to the observer; there is no universal flow of time. This reevaluation of the popular concepts of space and time necessitated a reevaluation of the scientific terms used to describe the natural world. It also led Einstein to the belief that mass is nothing but energy, and laid the groundwork for quantum mechanics.

In 1907, Bergson foresaw a major paradigm shift: "The more physics advances, the more it effaces the individuality of bodies and even of the particles into which the scientific imagination began by decomposing them: bodies and corpuscles tend to dissolve into a universal interaction."[84] In the following decades, quantum physicists demonstrated that we are all physically part of the world around us: our bodies are made up of atoms; atoms are made up of subatomic particles; subatomic particles are made up of packets of energy called quanta— *not* smaller, solid particles. At this level, *we exist as the connective tissue that makes up everything in the natural world*. Bergson's teachings reinforced the apparent truth that there can be no finality, no unification, in this new science.

Accordingly, Bergson proposes that a new kind of philosophy should develop alongside modern physics, teaching us how to go beyond intellect: "We should no longer be asking where a moving body will be, what shape a system will take, through what state a change will pass at a given moment: the moments of time, which are only arrests of our attention, would no longer exist; it is the flow of time, it is the very flux of the real that we should be trying to follow."[85]

In pursuit of such a progressive philosophy, Bergson turned to poetry. Although poetry is divided into lines and words and poems, he says, it still aspires to convey the inspiring possibility of wholeness or oneness: "All these words run now one after another, seeking in vain, by themselves, to give back the simplicity of the generative idea." Though it seeks an impossible goal — because ideas, like our physical selves, exist only as *the connective tissue that makes up everything in the natural world*—poetry offers intuitive glimpses of eternal life.

Walt Whitman: Mosaic

More than any other poet of the 19th century, Walt Whitman (1819–1892) anticipated the idea of creative evolution. T.S. Eliot never claimed much enthusiasm for Whitman's work, but he inadvertently may have absorbed some of the poet's philosophy and style through the early work of Jules Laforgue, who had translated Whitman's poems into French and apparently shared his fascination with cityscapes. Whitman's poetry, like the early poetry of Laforgue, does not ask us to see the world through the poet's eyes but prompts us to reflect on the life that surrounds and penetrates us. Whitman's subject is America, because he believes that such a progressive view of the natural world is best illustrated by the unity and variety in every-day American life.

Whitman wove his masterpiece, "Song of Myself," from a plethora of casual observations of life in New York. The poem itself is a haphazard catalogue of people, places and things that the poet witnessed and reflected upon while preparing to write. He seems to have made every effort not to disregard anything that caught his attention or to discriminate among his stimuli in any way. He absorbs everything, unfiltered, because in everything he sees God:

> I see something of God each hour of the twenty-four, and each moment then,
> In the faces of men and women I see God, and in my own face in the glass,
> I find letters from God dropt in the street, and every one is sign'd by God's name,
> and I leave them where they are, for I know that wheresoe'er I go,
> Others will punctually come for ever and ever.

Whitman records his observations in simple, unrhymed verse to prove to the common reader that poetry can find the Divine in the everyday and that transcendence is not reserved for academics in foreign lands. By showing us a mosaic of men and women doing casual, mundane things — finding the beauty in even the most ungraceful and uncouth acts — he demonstrates that we need not look hard to find the Divine; it is all around us, even *through* us. By tying all of these observations together in a moment of reflection on the particular and the universal, he shows us how every man may, through poetry, "be his own priest"[86]:

> Stop this day and night with you and you shall possess the origin of all poems
> You shall possess the good of the earth and sun, (there are millions of suns left,)
> You shall no longer take things at second or third hand, nor look through the eyes
>   of the dead, nor feed on the specters in books,
> You shall not look through my eyes either, nor take things from me,
> You shall listen to all sides and filter them from your self.[87]

In these moments of reflection, simplicity and silence, the poet steps outside of time, no longer searching for beginning and end, but reveling in the fleeting dual experience of individuality and universality. Afterwards, the poet casually dismisses the problem of perceiving the particular and the universal at the same time: "Do I contradict myself? / Very well then I contradict myself, / (I am large, I contain multitudes.)"[88] The moment, even after it has passed, makes him ecstatic beyond words, because he knows that, if he remains observant, it will not be his last moment of intuition.

Portrait of the Artist As a Young Man

Unlike Whitman, whose studies of Eastern philosophy had helped him to come to terms with ideas that Western thinkers tended to regard as self-contradictory, Eliot was overwhelmed by thoughts of an ultimate reality that consisted of countless subjective realities. He yearned for a simpler, more ordered universe, and his desperation soon began to manifest itself in fearful imaginings of violence. In his February 1911 poem "Interlude: In a Bar," the speaker finds himself in a room filled with shifting smoke — a recurring image that seems to represent cloudy thought, confusion over the "form" of life. It is also perhaps a suggestion of impurity. Life, Eliot writes, seems "broken and scarred."[89] He repeats the word *broken*, and remembers the fearful drumming from "Portrait of a Lady," in "Bacchus and Ariadne: 2nd Debate between the Body and Soul," which he composed during the same month.

The title of this poem is a reference to a tale in Ovid's *Metamorphoses*. Ariadne, the daughter of King Minos, was abducted from her home by the warrior Theseus and later abandoned on the island of Dia. The god Bacchus heard her wailing there and tried to comfort the young princess by transforming her into a constellation. It is possible that this story of apotheosis was somehow comforting to Eliot. In the poem, he reassures himself that a "triumph" — by which he seems to mean divine intervention — is imminent.

In March, Eliot wrote a few lines ("He said: this universe is very clever") that suggest he was struggling to reconcile popular science and traditional religion. What, he seems to wonder, is the role of the Western religious tradition in a Bergsonian universe? A letter written to Jean Verdenal a few months later indicates that he has no respect for any of the intellectuals or Christians with whom he has been interacting, and his philosophical studies seem only to frustrate him.[90] Eventually, Eliot began to regard his quest for metaphysical answers as a threat to his personal sanity. In "He said: this universe is very clever," he compares the Absolute to a syphilitic spider weaving her web of intrigue. These lines say much about the poet's sexually charged angst: the supreme knowledge that he seeks is characterized as a monstrous female, diseased and possibly mad, with the clear intention of devouring him.

In April, Eliot embarked on a tour of Europe. He began in London, then traveled to Munich and northern Italy in July. It was during this time period that he wrote "The Love Song of J. Alfred Prufrock." In a sense, Prufrock had existed in Eliot's mind since 1910, when he wrote "Spleen." In that poem, he describes Life as a little old man, well-dressed but bland, waiting "on the doorstep of the Absolute."[91] In "Prufrock," Eliot's little man is still waiting, but his façade of patience is cracking. At the beginning of the poem, Prufrock is on his way to a party, but consumed by dread. He envisions himself as a patient on a surgeon's table, and later as an insect about to be dissected. Paradoxically, he also views himself as the surgeon. He is not sure whether he will be able to put himself back together when the evening is over. It occurs to Prufrock that perhaps he is a lost cause — a man searching for companionship and objective meaning in a world that can provide neither.

It was probably Bergson's influence that prompted Eliot to use the physical metaphors of surgery and dissection to represent his state of anxiety. He is torn apart by an inner conflict between evolved intellect and primitive sexual instinct. Early in the poem, Prufrock dwells on "one-night cheap hotels" and oysters (famed for their aphrodisiac properties), yellow fog that rubbed and "licked its tongue into the corner of the evening," the sight of bare arms and the smell of perfume — all vaguely erotic symbols. The speaker assures himself that "there will be time," but he is also hyper-sensitive to the passage of time. An overactive intellect keeps him from saying anything revealing, and from making any kind of human connection with the women around him. "Do I dare?" he asks, but always the moment passes, leaving him more frustrated and growing older by the minute. Finally, he surrenders, ashamed, and imagines a reverse evolution: "I should have been a pair of ragged claws / Scuttling across the floors of silent seas."

Turning from the false comforts of religion ("I am no prophet") and philosophy ("I am not Prince Hamlet"), Prufrock eventually withdraws into his own imagination. He trades his formal suit for white flannel trousers and goes for a walk on the beach, where he has a vision of singing mermaids. While composing this section, Eliot may have been thinking of Homer's mermaids, the Sirens, who (like syphilitic spiders) ensnared Odysseus's entire crew with the beauty of their song. Or he could have been thinking of Oberon's beatific vision in Shakespeare's *A Midsummer Night's Dream*:

> ...Once I sat upon a promontory,
> And heard a mermaid, on a dolphin's back
> Uttering such dulcet and harmonious breath,
> That the rude sea grew civil at her song,
> And certain stars shot madly from their spheres,
> To hear the sea-maid's music [II.i.148–153].

Whether the mermaids are meant to be beguiling or comforting is perhaps irrelevant. "I do not think that they will sing to me," Prufrock sulks, before retiring to a chamber of the sea — evoking Edgar Allan Poe's horrifying dream of necrophilia in "Annabel Lee":

> And so, all the night tide, I lie down by the side
> Of my darling — my darling — my life and my bride,
>   In her sepulchre there by the sea —
>   In her tomb by the sounding sea.[92]

It is significant that "Prufrock" has a stronger cadence than anything Eliot had written before it. Though the poem does not have a consistent rhyme scheme, it demonstrates that Eliot is becoming more focused, developing what he would later call the auditory imagination. "Prufrock" is sometimes melodic, like a fantasy mermaid's song, and sometimes primal, like the tom-tom drum; it is ragtime music playing beneath a classical façade. The rhythm draws us in, and then the poet startles us with an uncomfortable observation or a discomforting question, making us wonder, *What does he mean?* For Eliot, there were no easy answers — only contradictory fragments of answers. Something less than madness but more than feigned madness was driving him on. By the fall of 1911, he was back at Harvard, pursuing a postgraduate degree in philosophy.

Suggested Reading (1910–1911)

Prufrock and Other Observations

"Portrait of a Lady" (1910–1911)
"Preludes" (1910–1911)
"The Love Song of J. Alfred Prufrock" (1911)
"Rhapsody on a Windy Night" (1911)

Inventions of the March Hare

"First Debate between the Body and Soul" (1910)
"The Triumph of Bullshit" (1910)
"Entretien Dans un Parc" (1911)
"Interlude: In a Bar" (1911)
"Bacchus and Ariadne: 2nd Debate between the Body and Soul" (1911)
"The Smoke that Gathers Blue and Sinks" (1911)
"He said: this universe is very clever" (1911)

"Inside the Gloom" (1911)
"Interlude in London" (1911)
"Ballade Pour La Grosse Lulu" (1911)
"Do I know how I feel? Do I know how I think?" (1911 or 1912)
"Hidden under the heron's wing" (19??)
"The Engine" (19??)
"Fragments: There was a jolly tinker…" (19??)
[Columbo and Bolo Verses] (19??)

◆ Part III ◆

Appearance and Reality
(1911–1915)

On the way toward our goal we must be content, for a time, with fragmentary views.
They will, erelong, come into a certain unity with one another; but for that unity
we must wait, until each idea has had its own partial and preliminary presentation.
— Josiah Royce

Prelude

Back in Boston in the fall of 1911, Eliot completed a number of poems. He wrote the final section of "Portrait of a Lady"—a melancholy surrender to the dying fall. He composed the fourth (and final) of his "Preludes," which reads like a nostalgic reflection on the poetry of his early youth. He also wrote a love poem called "La Figlia Che Piange" ("The Weeping Girl"), which lingers on an image of an idealized young woman, the object of a solitary hero's affections:

> She turned away, but with the autumn weather
> Compelled my imagination many days,
> Many days and many hours:
> Her hair over her arms and her arms full of flowers.[1]

This is a voice full of peaceful, loving resignation — not at all like the crass, unimaginative King Bolo or the passive-aggressive Prufrock. For the first time, Eliot appears capable of love. "La Figlia Che Piange" foreshadows what many biographers have referred to as the poet's tragic would-be love affair—a platonic relationship with a young Bostonian named Emily Hale, whom he would meet in the fall of 1912.

During the years 1912 and 1913, Eliot wrote very little poetry; he feared that the creative well had run dry. At the time, however, he was subconsciously absorbing new ideas for future work. As a graduate student, Eliot immersed himself in a study of Eastern philosophy and religion. He enrolled in Charles Rockwell Lanman's course on Indic philology in the fall of 1911, and learned to read Sanskrit. In 1912, he took a course on Indian philosophy with James Haughton Woods, and studied the *Upanishads* and the *Bhagavad Gita* (which Eliot would refer to, in 1929, as a philosophical poem second only to Dante's *Divine Comedy*). He also attended a year-long seminar on Buddhism given by Masaharu Anesaki.[2] During this time, his unflagging desire to *know more* was enhanced by a growing desire to *love more*.

The Brihadaranyaka Upanishad

In the late 1800s, Hinduism was a particularly troubling subject for American academics. Poets like Walt Whitman and Henry David Thoreau had been inspired by English translations of ancient Eastern texts; in fact, Thoreau longed for the day when the great Eastern philosophical texts would be placed side-by-side with "Bibles, with Homers and Dantes and Shakespeares."[3] Most Western philosophers, however, were confounded by Eastern ideas. In his 1875 book *Indian Wisdom*, Oxford professor Monier Williams observes that "most educated persons are beginning to be conscious of the duty of studying fairly and without prejudice the other religions of the world." He bases his comparative study on the notion that "traces of the original truth imparted to mankind" may be found in any religious system.[4] Despite his supposed open-mindedness to Eastern influences, Williams was unable to synthesize the apparent contradictions within the Hindu system of belief and facetiously concluded that the ancient religion was "vaguely pantheistic, severely monotheistic, grossly polytheistic, and coldly atheistic."[5] In a sense, of course, he is correct. Hinduism embraces all of the world's religions, explaining their apparent contradictions as misapprehensions of the human mind.

Classical Hinduism is based upon the Vedas, scriptures written by a succession of poets between 1500 and 1000 B.C.E.[6] Throughout the Vedas, and particularly in the *Rig Veda*, there are indirect references to the immortality of the soul and the afterlife, but these subjects remain vague (as they did in the early Greek epics) until the writing of the *Upanishads*, a later part of the Vedas which are sometimes referred to as the Hindu mystical doctrines. Sankara, an early teacher of the Vedanta school of Hinduism, based his teachings on eleven "fundamental" Upanishads, of which the *Brihadaranyaka Upanishad* is the longest and most comprehensive.[7]

According to this particular Upanishad, all gods — from local demigods to the deities of all major world religions — are one being, which is referred to as the Self. Indologist Max Muller explains, "As a lump of salt, when thrown into water, becomes dissolved into water, and could not be taken out again," so "does this great Being, endless, unlimited, consisting of nothing but knowledge, rise from out these elements, and vanish again in them."[8] Multiplicity, the Upanishad explains, is a product of human perception only. A famous parable, related in a poem by John Godfrey Saxe and sometimes attributed to the Muslim mystic Jelaluddin Rumi, illustrates this point. The parable is set in a city that is entirely inhabited by the blind. One day, word arrives that an elephant is passing by the walls of the city. Since none of the citizens has ever seen an elephant, they send their three wisest men to study it. Upon their return, each of the men offers a different description. One of them compares the elephant to a snake. Another compares it to a pillar. The third describes it as a wide, flat, leathery creature. Afterwards, the three wise men, each convinced that he alone has experienced the truth first hand, refuse to speak to each other. The explanation: the blind men studied the elephant through limited means. The first touched the elephant's tail, the second its leg and the third its ear. None of them perceived the elephant in its entirety. In one modern-day telling, the parable concludes: "So it is with us. We see Allah one way, the Hindus have a different conception, and the Christians a third. To us, all our different visions seem incompatible and irreconcilable. But what we forget is that before God we are like blind men stumbling around in total blackness."[9]

The goal of mankind, according to the *Brihadaranyaka Upanishad*, is to attain a higher consciousness, to realize the unity of all things — all gods and all modes of consciousness and to comprehend the divinity of life itself. Realization of the Self is the moment in which the individual dissolves into the sea of absolute consciousness:

> In that unitive state one sees without seeing, for there is nothing separate from him; smells without smelling, for there is nothing separate from him; tastes without tasting, for there is nothing separate from him; speaks without speaking, for there is nothing separate from him; hears without hearing, for there is nothing separate from him; touches without touching, for there is nothing separate from him; thinks without thinking, for there is nothing separate from him; knows without knowing, for there is nothing separate from him.[10]

The *Brihadaranyaka Upanishad* teaches that we cannot know the Self through waking consciousness alone; we must consider our states of consciousness during sleep. Only through meditation can we achieve a state of consciousness that unites the waking state, the deep sleep state and the dream state. In this unitive state, we can achieve self-realization, and understand that all things — even apparent contradictions — are one. Such a realization allows us to overcome all of our worldly fears and attain peace according to our true nature. If we do not attain this higher level of consciousness, we are doomed to reincarnation, as in the stories of the ancient Greek poets and philosophers, until we get it right.

There are other obvious parallels to later philosophies and religions of the West. In 1 Corinthians 13: 13, the Christian apostle Paul writes that we should always live by the virtues of faith, hope and charity — especially charity. Another parable, at the end of the *Brihadaranyaka Upanishad*, also emphasizes three virtues that should govern all beings: humility, charity and mercy. Of these three virtues, charity is the one intended for mankind. The parable reads as follows:

> The threefold descendants of Pragapati, gods, men, and Asuras (evil spirits), dwelt as Brahmakarins (students) with their father Pragapati. Having finished their studentship the gods said: "Tell us (something), Sir." He told them the syllable Da. Then he said: "Did you understand?" They said: "We did understand. You told us 'Damyata,' Be subdued." "Yes," he said, "you have understood."
>
> Then the men said to him: "Tell us something, Sir." He told them the same syllable Da. Then he said: "Did you understand?" They said: "We did understand. You told us, 'Datta,' 'Give.'" "Yes," he said, "you have understood."
>
> Then the Asuras said to him: "Tell us something, Sir." He told them the same syllable Da. Then he said: "Did you understand?" They said: "We did understand. You told us, 'Dayadham,' 'Be merciful.'" "Yes," he said, "you have understood."
>
> The divine voice of thunder repeats the same, Da Da Da, that is, Be subdued, Give, Be merciful. Therefore let that triad be taught, Subduing, Giving, and Mercy.[11]

The Bhagavad Gita

The *Bhagavad Gita* was composed between the first and third centuries C.E. to reconcile differences between many strains of Hindu thought. It has been called "the halfway point between the spontaneous insights of the *Upanishads* and the later, highly formalized philosophical systems" such as Vedanta.[12] The *Gita* essentially proposes that different paths work for different people at different times in their lives, but maintains that all paths lead to the same goal. It may be subdivided into three parts: karma yoga, the path of action; jnana yoga, the path of knowledge; and bhakti yoga, the path of devotion.

The *Gita* begins with the dilemma of the warrior Prince Arjuna, a man of action like the

Greek Achilles, who is called to duty in a just war that pits him against friends and family. Conflicted, he asks the god Krishna — a representation of the eternal Self — to advise him. Krishna tells him that he must eventually take the path of action — not out of desire for success or reward, but out of a sense of duty. By doing so, he will remain true to his nature as a warrior and serve a higher power. Krishna reassures the Prince that, later, wisdom will help to obliterate his anxieties about the outcome of his decision, including his fear of death.

According to the *Gita*, the afterlife is determined by one's state of mind at the time of death. Krishna explains that death is not fearful to one who knows the Self, because he recognizes that he is part of the eternal divinity:

> Those who worship other gods with faith and devotion also worship me, Arjuna, even if they do not observe the usual forms. I am the object of all worship, its enjoyer and Lord. But those who fail to realize my true nature must be reborn. Those who worship the devas [Hindu demigods] will go to the realm of the devas; those who worship their ancestors will be united with them after death. Those who worship phantoms will become phantoms; but my devotees will come to me.[13]

Finally, Krishna advises that, throughout life, and especially at the moment of death, one must tread the path of devotion. Through the power of devoted meditation, one surrenders to the will of the universe and achieves peace. A meditative prayer appears at the end of many of the Hindu sacred texts: "Om shantih shantih shantih." A. Parsatharathy, a modern-day Hindu teacher, explains that this phrase is intended to bring peace on three different fronts:

> Santih means peace. The three santihs are symbolically meant to appease the three sources of disturbance that may interfere with their learning. They are:
>   Adhidaivikam: Refers to the cosmic disturbance caused by the phenomenal powers like rain, thunder, lightning, etc. Hence the first santih is chanted aloud to appease those disturbances coming from a distance.
>   Adhibhautikam: Relates to the environmental intrusion like noise around, animal prowling, insect crawling etc. The second chant is, therefore, softer than the first to indicate that it is directed to offset the adjacent, external distraction.
>   Adhyatmikam: Pertains to disorders emanating from one's own body and mind. Like sickness, worry and anxiety etc. The last chant, therefore, is in whispers. Directed to quieten [sic] such internal perturbation.[14]

This prayer obviously made an impression on T.S. Eliot — it would eventually appear as the finale of *The Waste Land* — but he longed for a more rigid, formalized system of beliefs. For a time, he found what he was looking for in Buddhism.

The Light of Asia

It is easier to discern the origins of Buddhism than the origins of Hinduism, since they stem from the teachings of one historical figure: an Indian prince named Siddhartha Gautama (563–483 B.C.E.). It is written that Siddhartha lived a sheltered life until he was twenty-nine years old, at which time he discovered the sufferings of the world, renounced his earthly possessions and became a wandering ascetic. For six years he spent all of his time and energy on meditation, sleeping as little as possible and eating only the food that was given to him. His lifestyle, however, did not produce the results he expected, so he eventually rejected self-denial and self-mortification as a means to enlightenment. Exhausted, he sat beneath a pippala tree in the northeastern Indian city of Gaya, and resolved not to move until he had received enlightenment. He later gave his first sermon to a group of monks in Gaya, where he became known as the "Buddha," or Enlightened One.

The historical Buddha taught that a human being is a compound of transitory aggregates (body, feelings, perceptions, mental formations and consciousness), and that all of these aggregates are reconfigured at the time of death. According to his belief system, all existing things are subject to change at any time, leaving no constant such as the soul. The Buddha therefore spoke exclusively about life, rather than death. In his first sermon — shared orally for some five hundred years before it was recorded in the *Sutta Pitaka* of the Pali Canon — he laid out the basic tenets of his philosophy for living, in Four Noble Truths. They can be summed up as follows:

1. Mundane existence is suffering.
2. Suffering is caused by selfish desire. (This may be clarified by the Hindu concept of karma. Karma is sometimes defined as a theory of moral cause and effect: "What goes around comes around" or "We get what we deserve, not what we desire." *Bad* karma perpetuates a cycle of rebirth — not, as the Greeks believed, of the soul, but of a different consciousness in another lifetime.)
3. Renouncement of selfish desire can end suffering and lead to a state of enlightenment, which Buddhists call Nirvana.
4. There is a formula for renouncing selfish desire, known as the Eightfold Path. It consists of right views, right aspiration, right speech, right action, right livelihood, right endeavor, right watchfulness and right meditation. (The Eightfold Path may be more simply interpreted as a balance between self-indulgence and self-mortification.)[15]

Buddhism has no notion of God that is comparable to the Hindu concept of the Self or the Platonic concept of the One, because Buddhism does not ask metaphysical questions. The need for a concept of God is essentially nullified by the concept of "Buddha," a mentor who teaches how to transcend life by embracing the eternal truth about ongoing change. The Buddha is not meant to be a Godhead or a Christ figure, but an illustration of the full potential of human beings. The historical Buddha lived to be roughly 80 years old and preached many sermons. On his deathbed, he delivered the following message to his followers: "All things are impermanent. Work out your own salvation with diligence."[16]

In the centuries following the Buddha's death, followers of his teachings split into sects, which ultimately became the Theravada (sometimes called Hinayana) and Mahayana schools. It is often said that Theravadists, who emphasize a path of individual study (particularly of the Pali Canon), adhere more closely to the recorded teachings of the historical Buddha. The Theravada school was embraced by several prominent Western philosophers, including German Idealists Arthur Schopenhauer and Friedrich Nietzsche, and the early 20th-century American philosopher F.H. Bradley, who argued that neither the knower nor the thing known can exist independent of the other. Furthermore, he said that no act of knowing can be independent of the object known; all of these things are interdependent, and the entire universe is nothing but consciousness. Mahayana Buddhism, by contrast, emphasizes a path of action and, perhaps for that reason, it has had a more pervasive influence on the Western world.

Eliot's first brush with Buddhism came from *The Light of Asia*, a lengthy poem by Sir Edwin Arnold (1832–1904), which he read while still in prep school.[17] "I must have had a latent sympathy for the subject-matter," Eliot later wrote, "for I read through it with gusto, and more than once."[18] Arnold's epic account of the life of the historical Buddha begins with the immaculate conception of a "king of kings," which casts the tale in a familiar Christian mold. When he reaches adulthood, Arnold's Buddha asks the same question that many Western philosophers and theologians have asked: Why would a God that is both benevolent and omnipotent allow suffering in the world? The Buddha then undertakes a solitary quest into the wilderness, resolving to "cast away my world to save my world."[19] This is arguably an overly Westernized introduction to Buddhism.

Under the tutelage of his professor Masaharu Anesaki, Eliot pursued a more authentic understanding of the religion during his postgraduate years. Anesaki's understanding, in contrast with Arnold's, shows a closer affinity to Hinduism than to Western religion. His 1928 book *A History of Japanese Religion*, which originated in the author's lectures at Harvard, indicates what Eliot most likely would have been taught. Anesaki writes:

> The central idea in Buddhist teaching is the gospel of universal salvation based on the idea of the fundamental oneness of all beings. There are in the world, Buddhism teaches, manifold existences and innumerable beings, and each of these individuals deems himself to be a separate being and behaves accordingly. But in reality they make up one family, there is one continuity throughout, and this oneness is to be realized in the attainment of Buddhahood on the part of each and all, in the full realization of the universal communion.[20]

Despite the fact that his formal study of Hinduism and Buddhism emphasized the fundamental differences of perspective between Eastern and Western religion, Eliot was privately inclined toward a synthesis of all the belief systems he had studied. Judging by his later poetry, he focused his attention on the images and ideas where they seemed to overlap.

Buddhism, Christianity and the Fire Sermon

Academics the world over have compared Buddhism and Christianity, attempting to reconcile two of the world's most popular religions. Irving Babbitt wrote that both religions strive for "the peace that passeth understanding."[21] In his book *Introducing Buddhism*, Kodo Matsunami points out that, in both religions, "there is an ultimate truth, often interpreted as the saving power which transcends the individual."[22] Siddhartha Gautama and Jesus of Nazareth both carried messages of that "saving power," and both resisted temptation: Siddhartha was visited by Mara (the lord of misfortune, sin, destruction and death) during his final night under the tree of enlightenment; Christ was visited by Satan during his forty days and nights in the wilderness.

The differences, however, between these two religions are equally striking. Matsunami compares the setting of the two temptation stories — a tree of enlightenment and a desert waste land. The setting of Buddha's enlightenment is reminiscent of the Edenic setting of the first book of the Hebrew Bible — a setting which emphasizes a state of abundance. The setting of the later books of the Hebrew Bible, and of Christ's temptation, emphasize a state of scarcity, implying the need for redemption. These settings, Matsunami suggests, are indicative of the circumstances in which the two religions were founded:

> Some scholars presuppose that Christianity was originated in the vast expanse of cattle-breeding waste land, whereas Buddhism was originated in a fertile farm land.... Accordingly, the characteristic of Christianity is more likely brutal as symbolized in the crucifixion of Jesus Christ on the cross, and that of Buddhism is tranquil as symbolized in the passing-away of recumbent Buddha.[23]

That said, certain Buddhist texts nevertheless include some rather brutal-sounding symbolism. For example, the historical Buddha's "fire sermon" from the *Sutta Pitaka*, says that everything — the senses and their objects alike — is burning:

> The ear is on fire; sounds are on fire; ... the nose is on fire; odors are on fire; ... the tongue is on fire; tastes are on fire; ... the body is on fire; things tangible are on fire; ... the mind is on fire; ideas are on fire; ... mind-consciousness is on fire; impressions received by the mind are on fire; and whatever sensation, pleasant, unpleasant, or indifferent, originates in dependence on impressions received by the mind, that also is on fire.[24]

The Buddha, of course, is speaking figuratively. He goes on to explain that this all-consuming fire is the fire of passion, hatred, infatuation, birth, old age, death, sorrow, lamentation, misery, grief, despair — all the manifestations of worldly life. It is only through rejection of these things, he says, that we can find peace.

To the Western mind, the Buddha's fire sermon may be reminiscent of the Old Testament prophecies of Isaiah or Jonathan Edwards's 17th-century sermon "Sinners in the Hands of an Angry God," both of which use fire to symbolize earthly suffering and inspire fear of God. These teachings, however, are very different. In Isaiah and Edwards, fear is not interpreted as an outcome of ignorance but as proof of man's moral unworthiness. Furthermore, these teachings emphasize that salvation is possible only through divine intervention, rather than through simple rejection of earthly passion.

The Old Testament prophet Isaiah, who began to preach in Jerusalem around 740 B.C.E., spoke of a violent redeemer. As a young man, Isaiah answered God's call to become a messenger to the Israelites, who were not keeping their side of the covenant with God during the time of Assyrian conquest. The prophet asked how long he should minister to the people and the voice of God responded, "Until the cities be wasted without inhabitant, and the houses without man, and the land be utterly desolate" (Isaiah 6: 11). For the next forty years, Isaiah preached his fire sermon: "Behold, the day of the Lord cometh, cruel both the wrath and fierce anger, to lay the land desolate: and he shall destroy the sinners thereof out of it" (Isaiah 13: 9). He preached salvation for those who remained faithful, urging them to seek shelter in the mountain of Zion: "Enter into the rock, and hide thee in the dust, for fear of the Lord, and for the glory of his majesty" (Isaiah 2: 10). God assures Isaiah that "when thou walkest through the fire, thou shalt not be burned; neither shall the flame kindle upon thee" (Isaiah 43: 2). The wicked people who disobey God will be consumed and, afterward, the righteous survivors will begin to rebuild on the ruins of the old.

Jonathan Edwards's sermon to the New England Puritans is comparable. In it, a wrathful deity dangles humanity over the fiery pit of damnation, and rescues them not because of their own worthiness but because of His infinite grace:

> That world of misery, that lake of burning brimstone is extended abroad under you. There is the dreadful pit of the glowing flames of the wrath of God; there is hell's wide gaping mouth open; and you have nothing to stand upon, nor anything to take hold of; there is nothing between you and hell but the air; it is only the power and mere pleasure of God that holds you up.[25]

Considering T.S. Eliot's family background and New England education, and the degree to which the Puritan strain of thought pervaded American life in the early 20th century, it seems likely that he was at least somewhat familiar with Edwards's most famous sermon. In his early graduate years, Eliot was eager to slough off his own Puritan instincts. He was still somewhat drawn to the secular humanism of his teacher Irving Babbitt, whose own study of

Buddhism had led to an understanding of Christ as an enlightened, fully actualized human being. Eliot was also largely under the influence of Henri Bergson's philosophy, which had forced him to question the existence of objective reality. Idealist philosopher Josiah Royce (1855–1916) may have been another significant influence. In the fall of 1913, Royce taught Eliot in a course entitled "A Comparative Study of Various Types of Scientific Method." That same year, Royce published one of his key works, *The Problem of Christianity*.

Josiah Royce: The Problem of Christianity

Royce's book seeks to answer one vital question: "In what sense, if any, can the modern man consistently be, in creed, a Christian?"[26] The author argues neither that Christianity should be preserved in its present form nor that the religion has outlived its usefulness. Instead, he makes the case that Christian doctrine should be reevaluated by modern man, in accordance with the intentions of Jesus Christ, and following the example of the apostle Paul. Royce explains: "The true moral code of Christianity has always been and will remain fluent as well as decisive. Only so could it express the Master's true spirit.... The early apostolic Churches fulfilled the Master's teachings by surpassing it, and were filled with the spirit of their Master just because they did so."[27]

Royce distinguishes the teachings of Christ from the teachings of the Church after the apostle Paul. He points out that Jesus taught a message of love but did not deliver doctrine: "Apart from insisting upon the loving spirit, apart from the one rule to extend the Kingdom of Heaven and to propagate this spirit of love among men, the Master leaves the practical dimensions of the lover to be guided by loving instinct rather than by conscious doctrine."[28] Royce believes Jesus deliberately avoided a rigid system of moral rules, and that he intended for his followers to develop his teachings further. Paul, the self-proclaimed thirteenth apostle, did so by uniting Christ's followers within what Royce calls "a corporate entity,"[29] transforming the vague notion of Christian love into Loyalty, defined by the author as "the willing and thorough-going devotion of a self to a cause, when the cause is something which unites many selves in one."[30] Paul organized the Church as a spiritual community made up of individuals who consciously devoted themselves to that community, and he believed that such steadfast devotion could have only been accomplished through the divine grace of Christ's sacrifice on earth — through his atonement for our sins. Such devotion, Paul preached, is the path to salvation at the time of Christ's second coming.

Herein, Royce argues, lies the problem of Christianity for the modern world: Centuries passed without fulfillment of the prophecy of Christ's return, and "those little apostolic churches, where the spirit daily manifested itself, gave place to the historical church of the later centuries, whose possession of the spirit has often been a matter of dogma rather than of life, and whose unity has been so often lost to human view."[31]

Much of the dogma of the historical church of later centuries stems from the Pauline idea of the Moral Burden of humanity, which Royce considers an essential feature of Christianity. He argues that the idea of the Moral Burden — Royce's term for original sin, the idea that humans are sinful by nature and cannot achieve salvation without divine help — fosters humility, and a gives us a "reasonable regard for the larger connections of our obligations and our powers."[32] It connects us not only to God, but to the entire spiritual community. When the idea of the Moral Burden is used to justify specific cultural taboos (for instance, the essentially Puritan aversion to recreational sex), it becomes a matter of dogma rather than of life.

Royce prefers a more flexible definition of sin: "Whatever willful deed does not spring from love of God and man, and especially whatever deed breaks with the instinctive dictates of whole-hearted love, is sin."[33] Only through willful repentance can the guilty sinner become part of the community of believers; only through the community can he then be saved: "Man the individual is essentially insufficient to win the goal of his own existence. Man the community is the source of salvation."[34] Specifically, Royce continues, salvation is granted through a "steadfastly loyal servant" who acts on behalf of the community of believers — like Christ or Buddha. He writes:

> So far as I can venture to judge, no other religions that have attempted to appeal to the deepest and most universal interests of mankind have been so free as both Buddhism and Christianity are from bondage to national, to racial, and to worldly antagonisms and prejudices. No others have made so central, as they both have done, the conception of a personal saviour of mankind, whose dignity depends both upon the moral merits of his teaching and his life, and upon the religious significance of the spiritual level to which he led the way, thus moulding both the thoughts and the lives of his followers.[35]

Because of this vital link between the individual believer and the community of believers, Royce writes, the Christian doctrine of life is a distinctly social doctrine. For that reason, Royce rejects mysticism, which tends to remove the individual from the community.

In his final years at Harvard, however, T.S. Eliot was drawn to mysticism, perhaps because it seemed to him to present a more compelling view of Christ's expression of the deepest and most universal interests of mankind than did the traditional teachings of the Church. He undertook an intense study of the lives of Benedictine monk Saint Bernard of Clairvaux (1090–1153), English mystics Walter Hilton (?–1396) and Dame Julian of Norwich (1342–after 1413), Spanish mystics St. Teresa of Avila (1515–1582) and St. John of the Cross (1542–1591), alchemist Jacob Boehme (1575–1624) and French quietist Madame Guyon (1648–1717). He also took exhaustive notes on Evelyn Underhill's 1911 book, *Mysticism: A Study in the Nature and Development of Man's Spiritual Consciousness*, using it as a main point of reference in his studies.

Mysticism

Underhill writes that a mystic is a "person with a genius for God,"[36] one who has effectively transcended the world of the senses and attained union with the Absolute. Each of us, she explains, has a "hunger for the Absolute" and a natural ability to discover it for ourselves, but most people disregard this hunger because it does not play a clear role in our physical survival. Lovers, artists and religious converts alike have some intuitive sense of the Absolute, rooted in the idea of their beloved — the object of their passion. Herein, Underhill continues, lies a clue to realizing the mystic way: We begin with the desire to *love more*, rather than simply a desire to *know more*. One of the earliest English mystics, the nameless author of *The Cloud of Unknowing*, writes, "All rational beings, angels and men, possess two faculties, the power of knowing and the power of loving. To the first, to the intellect, God who made them is forever unknowable, but to the second, to love, he is completely knowable, and that by every separate individual."[37] Underhill concludes, "Those who 'feel to think' are likely to possess a richer, more real, if less orderly, experience than those 'think to feel.'"[38]

She goes on to outline the steps of the mystic way, beginning with an Awakening, "a long period of restlessness, uncertainty and mental stress," coupled with an "intuition of either a transcendent or an immanent God often accompanied by feelings of joy." This prompts a Purgation / Purification, a willful rebuilding of one's consciousness, "altering the self's attitude toward the world through detachment and mortification." This in turn leads to Illumination, a "steady and voluntary surrender of the awakened consciousness, its feeling, thought, and will, to the play of those transcendental influences."[39] According to Underhill, many seekers, visionaries and poets who reach this point believe that they have attained the Absolute. True mystics, however, go on to face a Dark Night of the Soul, wherein they realize that they have not yet been unified with God — they have only seen fleeting glimpses of the Absolute. Unsatisfied with an illusion, they suffer a stagnation of intellect, a void of emotions, and complete inhibition of the will. To overcome this, they must completely surrender their individuality, giving up all hopes and fears. When this is done, the mystic becomes one with the Absolute, like a drop of rain dissolving in the ocean.

Underhill traces the origins of mysticism to the dawn of Christianity, suggesting that it derived from three primary cultures: Greek, Oriental and Christian. During the time of the Roman Empire, the teachings of Jesus Christ melded with a number of Middle Eastern religions and philosophical traditions — including Manicheanism and neo-Platonism. For the Manicheans, as for many Gnostic sects, the Living God is one with the world in which we exist and can be experienced by us during our time on earth. For them, the goal of life was union with this divine essence.[40] The Roman philosopher Plotinus (204–270) was an outspoken critic of the Gnostic sects, but such beliefs were nevertheless a major influence on his interpretations of Plato.

Plotinus writes that the beauties of physical reality are mere shadows of Beauty, which is derived from the One, the source of all things. The One, Plotinus explains, is knowable to each of us if we block out all of the unnecessary sights and sounds of the world around us, and "invoke a new manner of seeing, a wakefulness that is the birthright of us all, though few put it to use."[41] It is present only to those who are willing to suspend discursive reasoning and surrender their individuality, "only to those who are prepared for it and are able to receive it, to enter into harmony with it, to grasp and to touch it by virtue of their likeness to it."[42] By using our soul's *intuitive* power to perceive the unity of all things, we become godlike. Plotinus describes his own personal experience of this mystical state as follows:

> Roused into myself from my body — outside everything else and inside myself — my gaze has met a beauty wondrous and great. At such moments I have been certain that mine was the better part, mine the best of lives lived to the fullest, mine identity with the divine. Fixed there firmly, poised above everything in the intellectual that is less than the highest, utter actuality was mine.[43]

This moment of unity, Plotinus adds, is the individual soul's attainment of its earthly goal. It becomes the Soul, having recovered *its true nature* and returned at last to its starting point: "When we look at it, we then attain the end of our desires and find rest. Then it is that, all discord past, we dance an inspired dance around it."[44]

Evelyn Underhill says that mysticism — which differs from neo-Platonism in that it is "an experience of Reality, not a philosophic account of Reality" — has found its "best map" in Christianity.[45] The doctrine of the Trinity and the Incarnation of Jesus Christ, she argues, "has best been able to describe the nature of the inward and personal mystic experience."[46] Underhill has a particular affinity with Dame Julian of Norwich, whose writings express a very elaborate understanding of the Trinity. On May 13, 1373, Julian — believing that she was fatally ill — prayed that she might be purged and purified by God's mercy. She was rewarded with sixteen divine visions, which revealed to her the true nature of Christ:

> We are double by God's creating, that is to say substantial and sensual. Our substance is the higher part, which we have in our Father, God almighty; and the second person of the Trinity is our Mother in nature in our substantial creation, in whom we are founded and rooted, and he is our Mother of mercy in taking our sensuality ... by the power of his Passion, his death and his Resurrection he unites us to our substance.[47]

In essence, Jesus is the means through which we can know God while we are in our earthly (sensual) existence: an intermediary, the Word made flesh.

The Burnt Dancer

Walter Hilton, a contemporary of Julian of Norwich, presents a more austere vision of mystical union with God: "As fire wasteth all bodily thing that may be wasted, right so the love of God burneth and wasteth all sin out of the soul and maketh it clean, as fire maketh clean all manner metal."[48] Later mystics like John of the Cross (1542–1592) adopted the same imagery of trial by fire. John was raised by Jesuits in Medina, Spain, where he helped Teresa of Avila to establish a monastery of the Carmelite Order. Later, he was imprisoned as a result of internal politics and, for nine months, he lived in a small, dark cell. It was here that he conceived his masterpiece, *The Dark Night of the Soul*.

This work begins with an eight-stanza poem, in which the author cryptically outlines his inner journey. John writes of a pivotal state of hopelessness in the life of the aspiring mystic:

> God thus leaves them in darkness so great that they know not whither to betake themselves with their imaginations and reflections of sense. They cannot advance a single step in meditation, as before, the inward sense now being overwhelmed in this night, and abandoned to dryness so great that they have no more any joy or sweetness in their spiritual exercises, as they had before; and in their place they find nothing but insipidity and bitterness."[49]

This, he explains, is the turning point: God is trying to transmit himself to the individual in "pure spirit," rather than through thought or sense. To continue, one must overcome the seven deadly sins — spiritual pride, avarice, luxury, anger, spiritual gluttony, envy and spiritual sloth — and surrender completely to God. "This darkness," John writes, "must continue so long as is necessary to destroy the habit, long ago contracted, of understanding things in a natural way, and until the divine enlightening shall have taken place."[50] When the time comes, the soul in the darkness is set on fire. This is the final stage of spiritual purification:

> The first action of material fire on fuel is to dry it, to expel from it all water and all moisture. It blackens it at once and soils it, producing a disagreeable smell, and drying it by little and little, makes it light and consumes all its foulness and blackness which are contrary to itself. Finally, having heated and set on fire its outward surface, it transforms the whole into itself, and makes it beautiful as itself. The fuel under these conditions retains neither active nor passive qualities of its own, except bulk and weight, and assumes all the properties and acts of fire. It becomes dry, being dry it glows, and glowing, burns; luminous, it gives light, and burns more quickly than before.... It is in this way we have to reason about the divine fire of contemplative love.[51]

The mystic does not simply *acknowledge* the fire, does not *understand* the fire; he *becomes* the fire that consumes the darkness.

In June 1914, T.S. Eliot began writing poetry again, though he later told Conrad Aiken that he was unsatisfied with the results. Over the summer he composed "The Burnt Dancer," "Oh Little Voices of the Throats of Men," and "The Love Song of St. Sebastian." In these works, Eliot's voice begins to appear almost schizophrenic: self-immolating and sadomasochistic in "Sebastian" (clearly inspired by Robert Browning's dramatic monologue "Porphyria's Lover"), escorted to the brink of nihilism by spectral "appearances" in "Little Voices" (which was almost certainly influenced by Eliot's study of philosopher F.H. Bradley), and lured like a helpless moth to the all-consuming flame in "The Burnt Dancer." Eliot regarded each of these scenarios as forced.[52]

The poet himself was fascinated with the poetic imagination of the mystics but unable to embrace the mystic way as his own path. Eliot may have been dissuaded by another influential mentor, English mathematician Bertrand Russell (1872–1970), who had entered his life in the spring of 1914. When Russell came to Harvard to teach a course in symbolic logic, he had just published his famous essay "Mysticism and Logic."

Bertrand Russell: Mysticism and Logic

Russell contends that the world's greatest philosophers have always felt the need to balance insight and reason. It is this balance, he says, that elevates metaphysical philosophy above both science and religion, which compete with each other. Russell traces this competition back to Plato, who he argues was unfavorably biased toward spontaneous insight. Pointing to Plato's allegory of the cave, Russell writes: "In this passage, as throughout most of Plato's teaching, there is an identification of the good with the truly real, which became embodied in the philosophical tradition, and is still largely operative in our own day. In thus allowing a legislative function to the good, Plato produced a divorce between philosophy and science, from which, in my opinion, both have suffered ever since and are still suffering."[53] Russell regards Heraclitus, Plato's forerunner, more favorably. Though his physics seems primitive to modern readers, Russell argues that the philosophy of Heraclitus balances scientific observation and poetic imagination. He finds the ancient philosopher to be a reasonable mystic who applies "a certain intensity and depth of feeling" to his deductions about the nature of universe.[54]

Russell's main objective is to understand how philosophers in the twentieth century can, in the tradition of Heraclitus, reconcile science and spirit. He begins his inquiry by identifying the principal modern-day mystical beliefs: (1) Intuition is a more important source of knowledge than Reason, and the intuition of the great mystics reveals that (2) Plurality and division are illusory, therefore (3) Time must be an illusion and (4) Evil cannot exist. In criticism of the first belief, Russell mounts an attack on Henri Bergson:

> Bergson, under the name of "intuition," has raised instinct to the position of sole arbiter of metaphysical truth. But in fact the opposition of instinct and reason is mainly illusory. Instinct, intuition or insight is what first leads to the beliefs which subsequent reason confirms or confutes; but the confirmation, where it is possible, consists, in the last analysis, of agreement with other beliefs no less instinctive.[55]

Russell seeks not to undermine "the spirit which inspires those beliefs"[56] but to combine that spirit with true reason.

In fact, Russell has great admiration for mysticism as an attitude towards life. He even argues that mysticism offers a greater truth than evolutionism. The latter, he writes, "fails to be a truly scientific philosophy because of its slavery to time, its ethical preoccupations, and its predominant interest in our mundane concerns and destiny."[57] Russell goes on to say that mysticism combined with reason may be a more worthwhile attitude toward life than moral instruction from popular religious institutions. If Evil is an illusion, he argues that "those who forget good and evil and seek only to know the facts are more likely to achieve good than those who view the world through the distorting medium of their own desires."[58] In Russell's view, however, mysticism *without* reason is, at best, problematic. Like T.S. Eliot, he himself was unable to embrace the mystic way.

First Debate Between Body and Soul

Eliot's biographer Lyndall Gordon argues that "the turning-point in Eliot's life came ... in 1914 when he was circling, in moments of agitation, on the edge of conversion." She alludes to his poem "The Burnt Dancer," as well as to three fragments that would eventually find their way into *The Waste Land* ("After the turning," "I am the Resurrection," and "So through the evening"), as proof that he was beginning to be swayed more by "strange images" than by logic.[59] Eliot writes of a constant emotional and intellectual "turning," concluding in stillness without peace. The poet catches a glimpse of the beauty of Christian salvation in "I am the Resurrection," but he cannot sustain the vision. Disheartened, he ends "So through the evening" with a drowning that is reminiscent of the conclusion of "Prufrock."

Gordon points out that, among Eliot's student notes, "there is a warning from Evelyn Underhill that vision through the senses is imperfect, capricious, often a delusion. One must await a purely spiritual communication."[60] For the time being, Eliot's longing for a spiritual awakening did not lead him to surrender to God. In his own mind, perhaps, it was the beginning of a dark night of the soul. In July, Eliot wrote to his friend Conrad Aiken, "Some people say that pain is necessary ('they learn in suffering,' *etc*), perhaps others that happiness is. Both beside the point, I think: what is necessary is a *certain kind* (could one but catch it!) of *tranquility*, and *sometimes* pain does bring it."[61]

Soon after, Eliot traveled to Marburg University in Germany to study philosophy on a Harvard scholarship. For a few weeks, he seems to have been content, but his studies were abruptly cancelled when the Germans declared war on Russia on August 1. England declared war on Germany three days later and, after two weeks in seclusion at the university, Eliot left Marburg for the relative safety of London. On September 8, he wrote to his brother from his new flat at 28 Bedford Place, just off of Russell Square, saying that he was feeling intellectually stimulated by the atmosphere of wartime London. During his time there, Eliot wrote three short verses to capture momentary impressions of that particular time and place. "Morning at the Window" was probably composed in his Bedford Place flat, soon after arrival. "Paysage Triste" recounts an outing in which the poet exchanged momentary glances with a sexually "experienced" stranger. He recalls the exchange of glances, as the lights go down at the opera house, where he is surrounded by less tantalizing society women. "Afternoon" is a Laforgue-esque juxtaposition of the worldviews of these society women ("amateur comedians") and a larger worldview (presumably that of Eliot himself) represented by the art housed in the nearby British Museum.

In "Paysage Triste" and in a fourth verse often attributed to this time period, entitled "Suppressed Complex," Eliot's sexual longing manifests itself with increasing desperation and even hostility toward women. His lack of sexual experience, combined with extreme insecurity, led him to perceive "experienced" women as a threat to his dignity; he abhors the thought that a woman with no concept of "the unconscious, the ineffable, the absolute,"[62] might regard him as inferior, simply due to his lack of sexual experience. Perhaps, given his slightly Puritanical upbringing, he felt guilty for wanting that experience so badly.

Racked by what he regarded as distinctly American anxieties, Eliot longed for some kind of mental and emotional rest. Already, he was planning a life in exile from America — an escape from the attitudes that had defined his personality. On September 22, he met Ezra Pound, who was more than willing to assist Eliot in his escape. After reading "The Love Song of J. Alfred Prufrock," Pound became an advocate for the young poet and tried to convince him to remain in London indefinitely. Pound emphasized that it was the only sensible decision for Eliot to make if he intended to be a serious poet. Eliot, as usual, was filled with doubt. He confessed to Aiken that he felt he had written nothing satisfactory since "Prufrock."[63] Later, reflecting on "The Love Song of St. Sebastian," he writes that he does not honestly expect to do anything satisfactory for years to come.[64] Unsatisfied with his poetry and his studies of mysticism, he turned back again to philosophy.

F.H. Bradley: Notes Towards the Absolute

In October, Eliot went to the University of Oxford to study Aristotle under the tutelage of professor Harold Joachim, a disciple of British philosopher F.H. Bradley. The previous year, Eliot had read Bradley's book *Appearance and Reality*, and it had already begun to influence his way of thinking. For the next two years, Eliot worked to complete his doctoral dissertation, eventually published as *Knowledge and Experience in the Philosophy of F.H. Bradley*. It was the longest piece of writing he would compose in his life.

Eliot begins, as Bradley does, by examining the nature of human experience, which both philosophers accept as the basis of knowledge. Out of personal experience comes our perception of *subjects* and *objects*. The subject is the experiencer, the perceiver, the knower; the object is the experienced, the perceived, the known. Eliot explains using the example of a person looking at a flower. The person is the subject; the flower the object. Some philosophers adopt an *idealist* view of the world, arguing that the flower exists only because it is perceived. Others take a *realist* view of the world, arguing that the flower has its own independent existence, and would exist even if it were not perceived.

Eliot argues that, between the idealist point of view and the realist point of view, "there is no absolute point of view from which a decision may be pronounced."[65] He follows Bradley to the conclusion that knowable reality is a fusion of the two — that the sum of *interactions* between subjects and objects produces the world we know:

> My existence is dependant upon my experience of the red in the flower, and the existence of the flower is dependant upon its unity in feeling (as red) with me. Whatever relations the flower may afterwards be discovered to have, its nature must be such that its being under these conditions experienced as red will be essential to the whole account of it. The red flower, we can say, will be the sum of its effects — its actual effects upon other entities — and this sum must form a system, must somehow hang together.[66]

Eliot continues to explain Bradley's philosophy of subject-object coalescence, but he does not agree with Bradley that this line of thought leads to the all-inclusive Aristotelian

Absolute.[67] Eliot has no preconception of reality as a whole; for him, the Absolute is an enigma. Thus, Eliot's own personal system of metaphysics is a heap of irreconcilable fragments: "The world as we are acquainted with it from this limited point of view is an artificial construction, and, our point of view not being large enough to grasp the whole, we consider the rest simply as the debris of our own slight structure."[68] It seems he longed to be comforted by the teachings of Aristotle, who assures us of the existence of a soul that "is in a way all existing things."[69] Certainly, he believed that Bradley's belief in the Absolute was genuine and heart-felt. Perhaps he even envied Bradley, but he still could not accept the same conclusion for himself. In a 1915 letter to Norbert Wiener, he writes: "It does not exist for me, but I cannot say that it does not exist for Mr. Bradley. And Mr. Bradley may say that the Absolute is implied *for* me *in* my thought — and who is to be the referee?"[70]

Eliot uses Bradley's philosophy to determine what we can know for certain about the world we live in, and how we are to understand Reality. Bradley's conclusion is that "Reality is spiritual,"[71] and thus cannot be fully comprehended by the scientific mind. For Eliot, this is an unsatisfactory solution, and yet it is the only conclusion he can come to. Eliot must have felt as if Bradley had led him through the desert to an oasis, only to find that he himself could not drink the water. This might well have turned him into a cynic, but instead it increased Eliot's resolve to find his own answers.

In *Appearance and Reality*, Bradley writes that "metaphysics is the finding of bad reasons for what we believe upon instinct, but to find these reasons is no less an instinct."[72] The philosopher was not trying to be cynical. Though his prose can be dry and even off-putting, he nevertheless demonstrates an affinity with the most passionate of human seekers: "When poetry, art, and religion have ceased wholly to interest, or when they show no longer any tendency to struggle with ultimate problems and to come to an understanding with them; when the sense of mystery and enchantment no longer draws the mind to wander aimlessly and to love it knows not what; when, in short, twilight has no charm — then metaphysics will be worthless."[73] Bradley also waxes pragmatic, finding ample reason for a man to pursue philosophy, if that is his true instinct: "There is, so far as I can see, no other certain way of protecting ourselves against dogmatic superstition. Our orthodox theology on the one side and our common-place materialism on the other side ... vanish like ghosts before the daylight of free skeptical enquiry."[74] Like Baudelaire, Rimbaud, Nietzsche, Yeats and so many before him, Bradley cries out — admittedly, with the soft-spoken demeanor of a humble philosopher who warns of the dangers of "spiritual pride"— for constant reappraisal of humanity's purpose: "Existing philosophies cannot answer the purpose. For whether there is progress or not, at all events there is change; and the changed minds of each generation will require a difference in what has to satisfy their intellect."[75]

Bradley, like a modern-day Buddha, advised his readers to work out their own salvation with diligence. He prefaces his book *Appearance and Reality* by apologizing for it — suggesting that it is useful only to "stimulate enquiry and doubt." The author insists that he is nothing more than a "learner among learners."[76] Likewise, in his career as a literary critic and a man of letters, Eliot would also profess his limitations before offering opinions on any topic. As a scholar, he would remain always in the shadow of F.H. Bradley. Using Bradley's philosophy as a tool to stimulate enquiry and doubt, Eliot pursued his own answers through poetry and religion.

Eliot, Bradley and Symbolism

Bradley provided a bridge between Eliot's confessional poetry and the schizophrenic master-piece *The Waste Land*, in which Eliot illustrates that Bradleyan relativism has left him with a worldview held together by spit and chicken wire. It was through his writing on Bradley that Eliot came to understand that his true vocation was philosophical poetry — a battleground of concepts and ideas, words and symbols. In his dissertation, he defines a concept as "that which a word denotes" and an idea as "that to which a word refers in reality, this reference being contingent."[77] Greenness is a concept; a green book is an idea. As for the words we use to distinguish the two, Eliot agrees with Bradley that language is not merely a development of our ideas, but also a development of our reality.[78] Take, for example, the word *ghosts*. Depending on the beliefs of the individual using or encountering the word, "ghosts" may or may not refer to something that is assumed to be real. Yet by using the word, an assumption is made that it must be one or the other, and this assumption changes our experience of the world:

> The ghost conceived as real is a special kind of content with characteristics continuous with those of the fragment of reality in which he is set; the idea, from one point of view apart from the world and attached to it, yet contains already the character of the world, a world, as I said before, which shows by the very fact that the idea can be attached to it that it is somehow prepared for the reception of that idea....[79]

Eliot is finding his own way to observations made by Sigmund Freud (1856–1939): "Words, since they are the nodal points of numerous ideas, may be regarded as predestined to ambiguity; and the neuroses (e.g. in framing obsessions and phobias), no less than dreams, make unashamed use of the advantages thus offered by words for purposes of condensation and disguise."[80]

No doubt thinking of his own early poetry, Eliot examines Bradley's statement that a flower may become the sign or symbol of an emotion. The poet goes one step further: a withered flower may become the sign or symbol of a particular moment in our history. A flower may be the sign of an idea, he concedes, but he wonders how an idea could possibly be the sign of a reality.[81] A sign, according to Eliot, may refer to different realities which exist in memory, anticipation and / or imagination. This leads him to contemplate the effect of time on consciousness: "The past lived over is not memory, and the past remembered was never lived.... You either live the past, and then it is present, or you remember it, and then it is not the same past as you once lived: the difference is not between two objects, but between two points of view."[82] The implication is that there is a plethora of points of view which may be conjured by a particular sign or symbol. If so, how are they to be reconciled?

Eliot explains, "When the poet says *I lived with shadows for my company* she is announcing at once the defect and the superiority of the world she lived in. The defect, in that it was vaguer, less of an idea, than the world of others; the superiority, in that the shadows pointed toward a reality, which, if it had been realized, would have been in some respects, higher type of reality than the ordinary world — compared to which the ordinary world would be less real, and which the ordinary world might be said to 'mean.'"[83] For metaphysical purposes, Eliot concludes, the notion of idea as symbol is useless because there is no knowable consensus. For poetry, the notion warrants further discussion. If one is to say that any example of symbolic language is more real (true to experience) than any other, one must acknowledge that there is some common ground providing a basis for comparison. The critic and the literary artist alike must have criteria.

Eliot asserts that the ideas of great poets are not, in any sense, arbitrary. A madman, he writes, may produce ideas that are more imaginative, but in great poetry such ideas are more than "simply personal."[84] In his book *The Interpretation of Dreams* (first edition 1900), Sigmund Freud plunders his own dreams for ideational material that represents not only his own emotional state but the human condition at large. Eliot the poet plunders the whole of literature and philosophy for much the same reason, and understands full well that he is not the first — and will not be the last — to do so. Ideally, critical appraisals of symbolic language must be made by analysis of an individual's point of view. Eliot puts this in metaphysical terms: "In order to know what a particular event is, you must know the soul to which it occurs."[85]

Of course, neither the event nor the soul exists independently. In the same way, Eliot says, "there is properly speaking, no relation between the symbol and that which it symbolizes because they are continuous."[86] The symbol could not exist without that which it symbolizes, and the former could not be known as such without the symbol which partially defines it. No Forms without substance, no existence without essence, and vice versa. In Bradley's philosophy, we are left with an incomplete knowledge of the Absolute, a "conception of an all-inclusive experience outside of which nothing shall fall." Eliot, feeling restrained by the limitations of his own personal experience, cannot make the final leap to all-inclusive experience: "From a psychological point of view, things perceived are connected so far as they are perceived to be connected. If we contemplate several objects, and recognize them as disconnected, they *are* disconnected except for metaphysics, and that is the complete statement of the case."[87]

Confronted with the latest developments in physics, Eliot also opines that physical theories are as confounding as metaphysical theories: "If the ultimate is some kind of energy or motion[,] it is not an object but at most a half-object, since it possesses some internality. At this point the theory would become metaphysical, passing from one type of object to another; and two types can only be held together by an act of faith."[88] Perhaps reluctantly, he concludes that even the most scientific philosophy can be based on "nothing but faith."[89] Like Bradley, Eliot asserts the importance of Bradleyan relativism to stimulate enquiry and doubt, through which we ultimately acknowledge that "the world of practical verification has no definite frontiers."[90] Eliot, however, was not looking for a world without frontiers. He had an instinctive need for rational order and, for the time being, he was unwilling or unable to surrender his intellectual search for personal faith.

T.E. Hulme: Castles in the Air

Eliot's most striking poem from this period of crisis is "The Death of Saint Narcissus," which takes metamorphosis for its theme. Eliot's major inspiration was "Conversion," a short poem by T.E. Hulme (1883–1917), a member of Ezra Pound's small circle of avant-garde poets. Hulme had developed his own poetical sensibilities much the way that Eliot had. He championed the French *vers libre*, while calling for a revival of classical poetry in favor of outdated romanticism (which he called "spilt religion"). Hulme's diagnosis of the state of poetry in the first decade of the 20th century was unflinchingly critical:

> The latter stages in the decay of an art form are very interesting and worth study because they are peculiarly applicable to the state of poetry at the present day. They resemble the latter stages

in the decay of religion when the spirit has gone and there is a meaningless reverence for formalities and ritual. The carcass is dead and all the flies are upon it. Imaginative poetry springs up like weeds, and women whimper and whine of you and I alas, and roses, roses all the way. It becomes the expression of sentimentality rather than of virile thought.[91]

Like Eliot, Hulme believed that the modern age was characterized largely by fragmentation. "The world is a plurality," he asserts, comparing it to an ash-pit of cinders; "it is impossible to include it all under one large counter such as 'God' or 'Truth' and the other verbalisms, or the disease of the symbolic language."[92] Hulme believed that poetry has the power to bring the world to unity — but not by using terms like the Ideal or the Absolute. He was more emphatic in his rejection of existing philosophies and religions than Eliot had dared to be. "Truths don't exist before we invent them," he said. "They respond to man's need of economy, just as beliefs to his need of faith."[93] Accordingly, Hulme resolved to produce impressionistic poetry in free verse, considering it a more "sincere" art for an age in which the greatest thinkers denied the possibility of Absolute truth: "We shall no longer strive to attain the absolutely perfect form in poetry. Instead of these minute perfections of phrase and words, the tendency will be rather towards the production of a general effect.... [The modern] no longer deals with heroic action, it has become definitely and finally introspective and deals with expression and communication of momentary phrases in the poet's mind."[94]

The goal of the poet, Hulme says, is to achieve a "sense of wonder," "an other-world, through-the-glass effect."[95] Rule #1: "Never, never, never make a simple statement."[96] In his poem "Conversion," Hulme conveys a moment of transcendence through a peculiar combination of sensory details, rather than through abstract language about ideas and emotion. He avoids abstract words like "transcendence" because it "suggests easy comprehension when there is no easy comprehension."[97] In effect, he hopes to produce a unique impression. Through such achievement, literature becomes an ever-growing lexicon for an infinite diversity of impressions. As a classical scholar, Eliot agreed with Hulme's prescriptions for modern poetry and his conception of literature as a "building up of this *state of reference*."[98] As a poet, Eliot had already begun to achieve his effect through allusion.

The Death of Saint Narcissus

Eliot's powers of allusion are on display in "The Death of Saint Narcissus," a 1915 poem that juxtaposes Catholic theology with Greek mythology. On the one hand, the historical Saint Narcissus was a bishop in Jerusalem during the second century c.e. Late in his life, he was accused of a crime he did not commit. He responded by leaving his church to become a hermit in the desert. Eventually, his name was cleared and he returned to Jerusalem, where he lived to a very old age. On the other hand, in Ovid's *Metamorphoses*, Narcissus is a beautiful boy who is cursed by a spurned lover and falls desperately in love with his own reflection in a lake. Realizing the impossibility of consummating a union with his other self, Narcissus violently beats himself to a bloody pulp. Exhausted and fatally wounded, he then melts into the water like wax into a fire, leaving behind a white flower instead of a corpse.

Eliot's Saint Narcissus is a combination of the two: a wandering ascetic who imagines himself undergoing a series of metamorphoses. Much of the imagery is perversely erotic, ranging from images of self-molestation to a startling final image of ecstatic self-immolation. As in Ovid's tale, the driving force in Eliot's poem is desire — but this desire, overtly carnal and destructive, is simultaneously an urge for spiritual transcendence. Saint Narcissus, like J. Alfred Prufrock, is afraid of what he may become. He longs for religious purification but imagines the metamorphosis tainted by his carnal, destructive desire. In the end, Saint Narcissus welcomes death's "burning arrows," as Eliot's Saint Sebastian did, simply because they provide a deliverance from self. In an early draft of the poem, Eliot described the arrows as "penitrant" — a combination of penitent and penetrating.[99]

Eliot obviously realized the perversity of his poem because he taunts readers the same way Baudelaire did, like a carnival barker: "Come in" (hypocritical reader — my fellow — my twin!) "under the shadow of this gray rock, / And I will show you" what you secretly long to see: soul and body laid bare, purity defaced.[100] In the shadow of Hulme (a stark contrast to the reserved, prosaic F.H. Bradley) we see Eliot at his most volatile. He indulges his "sick moments" — what Hulme might call "the fundamental ennui and chaos out of which the world has been built, and which is as necessary to it as the listeners are to the intellectuals"[101] — in a dance for God.

The ending evokes pre–Christian rituals as well as Christian martyrdom — further proof that Eliot was still struggling with religious belief. The poem may stem, in part, from Hulme's thoughts on the usefulness of ritual:

> A man cannot deliberately make up his mind to think of the goodness of God for an hour, but he can perform some ritual act of admiration whether it be the offering of a sacrifice or merely saying amen to a set prayer. Ritual tends to be constant, even that seeming exception the impromptu prayers of a Non-conformist minister are merely the stringing together in accidental order of set and well-known phrases and tags. The burning of candles to the Virgin if only one can escape from some danger. The giving of a dinner, or getting drunk in company as a celebration — a relief from concentrated thinking.[102]

This is exactly what T.S. Eliot needed — *relief from concentrated thinking.*

For the time being, only Eliot's poetry provided him any relief, and the relief was fleeting. In the following years, Eliot's personal metamorphosis — into a British citizen, a married man, teacher, bank clerk, staid literary critic — was part of an ongoing search for sustained relief. For years, he was unable (or unwilling) to act on the conclusion that his study of F.H. Bradley had led him to. He continued to suppress the religious impulse behind his concentrated search until it began to burn him from the inside out.

Suggested Reading (1911–1915)

Prufrock and Other Observations

"Portrait of a Lady" (1910–1911)
"Preludes" (1910–1911)
"La Figlia Che Piange" (1911)
"Morning at the Window" (1914)

Inventions of the March Hare

"Prufrock's Perviglium" (1912)
"The Burnt Dancer" (1914)
"Oh Little Voices of the Throats of Men" (1914)
"The Love Song of St. Sebastian" (1914)
"Paysage Triste" (1914)
"Suppressed Complex" (1914)

"Afternoon" (1914)
"Introspection" (19??)
"While you were absent in the lavatory" (19??)

The Waste Land Facsimile

"So through the evening" (1914)
"After the turning" (1914)
"I am the Resurrection" (1914)
"The Death of Saint Narcissus" (1915)

Knowledge and Experience in the Philosophy of F.H. Bradley (1916)

♦ PART IV ♦

The Beginning of Wisdom
(1915–1920)

There is for each time, for each artist, a kind of alloy required to make the metal workable into art.

— T.S. Eliot

Vivienne

In early 1915, Eliot was at a crossroads. He could return to the States, finish his degree and pursue an assistant professorship at Harvard, or he could remain in London and pursue the life of an artist. On February 2, he wrote to Ezra Pound that he was tormented by his own indecision: Should he return to America, to become a professor and start a family? Or should he embrace the solitary life of an artist? Neither option seemed very appealing.[1] Eliot, who had spent the last several years formulating questions, was impatient for answers — so much so that he was willing to entrust the biggest decision of his life to someone else.

In March, a mutual friend introduced Eliot to Vivienne Haigh-Wood, an English woman of comparable age, who (according to her biographer) was known to be "mercurial, intense, albeit immature,"[2] "child-like, artistic and vulnerable."[3] Vivienne was particularly restless because she recently had been abandoned by her longtime beau. Her impulsive, even brash, personality appealed to Eliot, who was paralytic by comparison. Likewise, his quiet, debonair attitude was attractive to her. Each saw the other as a socially legitimizing and emotionally stabilizing influence. After a handful of meetings over the next three months, they were married.

Feeling empowered by this decision — a symbolic initiation into adulthood — Eliot decided to remain in London and pursue his future as a writer. To show his support, Pound convinced his friend Harriet Monroe to publish "The Love Song of J. Alfred Prufrock" in her literary journal *Poetry* in June 1915. "Preludes," "Rhapsody on a Windy Night" and "Portrait of a Lady" followed soon after. Publication boosted Eliot's confidence, but the monetary rewards were less reassuring. With a new wife to consider, he started thinking seriously about the financial shortcomings of his chosen profession. Immediately after the marriage, he and Vivienne went to live with her parents in Hampstead, and Eliot had to write home to ask his parents for an allowance to help him get started in his new life.

There is a slightly defensive tone in Eliot's July 15 letter to his father, in which he attempts

69

to explain the hasty marriage. No doubt his tone would have been defensive regardless of the success of that first month of Eliot's marriage — he had, after all, just eloped — but there is also a hint of desperation, as if Eliot is feeling overburdened by his new responsibilities as a husband. He seems unsure of his ability to care for his wife, and eager to share some of the responsibility with his family.[4]

From the beginning, there were bigger problems in the marriage than money. On July 9, the newlyweds accepted an invitation to dinner with Bertrand Russell, Eliot's former professor at Oxford. After the meeting, Russell wrote to a friend that Vivienne had confided in him about intimacy problems in her new marriage. She was hurt by her inability to "stimulate" her husband.[5] Already, Eliot had emotionally withdrawn. The next day he set sail — alone — for America, to convince his parents that his decision to get married and settle abroad was the right one. Vivienne remained in London, where she was consoled by Bertrand Russell. During her husband's absence, the jilted wife angrily wrote to a friend, "Rather unwise to leave so attractive a wife alone to her own devices!"[6] Russell took advantage of her vulnerability.

Eliot returned to London at the end of the summer, having convinced his parents to grant him an allowance for the upcoming months. In return, he had promised them that he would complete his Harvard thesis and submit it for his doctoral degree. Despite their support (or perhaps because he needed it so badly), Eliot felt like a failure in his parents' eyes. They had given him all the educational opportunities of America's elite, yet he had chosen a life that showed no promise of financial security, social acceptance or emotional fulfillment. His belief that he had disappointed his parents only heightened Eliot's anxieties about his new marriage.

His attempt at reconciliation with Vivienne did not go well. In September, the couple vacationed in Eastbourne, on the southeastern coast of England, a belated honeymoon. If we are to believe Bertrand Russell's account, Vivienne was suicidal by the time they returned to London.[7] The all-too-generous professor had offered the young couple a room in his London flat, which the Eliots accepted as a temporary solution to their financial problems. Whether Eliot knew about his wife's affair with their benefactor is questionable. In September, he wrote a letter to Russell, in which he — perhaps too eagerly — insisted that Russell stay in the flat with Vivienne while Eliot himself was away. There is also a suggestion of impropriety in Vivienne's October 24 letter to her friend Scofield Thayer: "We have been more or less of a triple ménage. Bertie Russell has taken us to his bosom."[8]

Whatever the specific details of this arrangement, it took a heavy psychological toll on the newlyweds. In the following months, Vivienne began suffering intense migraines and intestinal problems. In a short prose piece called "Hysteria," the poet described his own internal nerve storms — brought on by the maddening sound of his wife's laughter. Decades later, Eliot would reflect on the beginnings of the marriage:

> I think that all I wanted of Vivienne was a flirtation or a mild affair. [...] I believe that I came to persuade myself that I was in love with her simply because I wanted to burn my boats and commit myself to staying in England.

For all the suffering the decision caused both him and his wife, he concedes that the marriage created the state of mind out of which came his masterpiece *The Waste Land*.[9] Marriage, clearly, was not the stabilizing influenced he hoped it would be. If anything, the couple's incompatibility had amplified their individual anxieties.

The Education of Henry Adams

In October 1915, Eliot wrote a series of poems inspired by his recent family reunion. In each poem — "The Boston Evening Transcript," "Aunt Helen," "Cousin Nancy" — he renounces the life that he has left behind, mocking the habits of friends and relatives in New England. Despite the problems of his new marriage, Eliot embraced his role as an American expat, identifying himself with other expatriate writers like novelist Henry James (1843–1916). He was particularly fond of James's early novels — *The American, The Europeans, Washington Square* and *Daisy Miller*—which take the perspective of outsiders in a foreign culture.[10]

Another literary idol was a distant cousin whom Eliot had never met — a New England man of letters named Henry Adams (1838–1918), who recorded his own life as an expat in a 1907 autobiography. Adams writes in the third person about the stigma of being born into one of the most prominent families in Boston society, a family that had already produced two U.S. presidents: "Had he been born in Jerusalem under the shadow of the Temple and circumcised in the Synagogue by his uncle the high priest, under the name of Israel Cohen, he would scarcely have been more distinctly branded."[11] From an early age, Adams was painfully aware of expectations that he would follow in the footsteps of his ancestors, many of whom were among America's wealthiest and most influential policy-makers.

Adams went to Harvard and pursued a career in law. In the years afterwards, he realized that his formal education had poorly prepared him for life in the early 20th century. Harvard had exposed him to a broad range of cultures and traditions but simultaneously prevented him from embracing any one in particular — including the traditions of his own family and country. "The Harvard graduate," he writes in his autobiography, "was neither American nor European, nor even wholly Yankee; his admirers were few, and his critics many; perhaps his worst weakness was his self-criticism and self-consciousness."[12] Accordingly, Adams designed a curriculum for his own self-education. Reflecting on his first trip to London — the start of his informal "education" — he writes about himself in the third person, as if he's writing about a stranger:

> Adams, still a boy, could not guess how intensely intimate this London grime was to become to him as a man, but he could still less conceive himself returning to it fifty years afterwards, noting at each turn how the great city grew smaller as it doubled in size; cheaper as it quadrupled its wealth; less imperial as its empire widened; less dignified as it tried to be civil. He liked it best when he hated it. Education began at the end, or perhaps would end at the beginning.[13]

From London, he traveled relentlessly and pursued multiple careers — in law, politics, journalism, education, social reform; he was also a historian and a novelist. At the end of his life, however, he remained unfulfilled. In his final years Adams was overcome with longing for the simpler days of his youth — days when he went to church twice every Sunday and believed in the mild deism of the Unitarian church. He believed that he had lost something vital during the course of his education:

> The religious instinct had vanished, and could not be revived, although one made in later life many efforts to recover it. That the most powerful emotion of man, next to the sexual, should disappear, might be a personal defect of his own; but that the most intelligent society, led by the most intelligent clergy, in the most moral conditions he ever knew, should have solved all the problems of the universe so thoroughly as to have quite ceased making itself anxious about past or future, and should have persuaded itself that all the problems, which had convulsed human thought from earliest recorded time, were not worth discussing, seemed to him the most curious social phenomenon he had to account for in a long life.[14]

Too much information had left Adams without a heartfelt faith in anything; too many travels had left him without a home.

In 1915, Eliot was struggling with fears of the same fate. So far, his American education had left him with no substitute for the religious tradition of his youth (Unitarianism), no country to call his own and only one immediate job prospect. That autumn, he reluctantly took a teaching position at Wycombe Grammar School, teaching French, math, history, drawing and swimming. Like Adams, he began to design his own curriculum for postgraduate study, though he would now be doing so in the role of teacher rather than student. In February 1916, he applied to the Oxford University Extension Delegacy; the following autumn, he began giving nighttime lectures in the English countryside on topics of his choosing.

Around the same time, Eliot started teaching at the Highgate Junior School in Hampstead and Bertrand Russell completely withdrew from the lives of the Eliots. Vivienne's biographer suggests that this marked the beginning of the end of the couple's marriage.[15] For his part, Eliot continued to retreat into the world of his imagination. He wrote "Mr. Apollinax," a poem in which he cryptically vented his contempt for Russell, casting him as a sly, horny devil with aspects of Priapus (a minor Greek god with a frighteningly large phallus) and Proteus, Homer's crafty "old man of the sea" who could foretell the future but frequently concealed his identity so that he would not have to. In the poem, the speaker looks "for the head of Mr. Apollinax rolling under a chair."[16]

Four poems, including "Mr. Apollinax," were published in Harriet Monroe's journal *Poetry* in September 1916, but Eliot remained pessimistic about his future as a poet. Around the same time, he turned to writing book reviews — focusing on works of theology — at a furious pace, hoping that he might be able to quit teaching and make a living as a literary critic. One imagines Eliot struggling to compose his reviews by candlelight, his nerves frayed by constant fears of German Zeppelin raids on the city of London. On October 2, he received a summons for showing too much light through his curtains during an enforced nightly blackout.[17]

Eliot's first series of weekly nighttime lectures, delivered between October and December 1916, was a survey of modern French literature. His syllabus shows that he began with an examination of French romanticism, arguing that all "contemporary" intellectual movements in France have sought to define themselves in relation to romanticism. Notes for the second lecture assert that the modern age is experiencing a revival of the ideals of classicism, which he defines as "*form* and *restraint* in art, *discipline* and *authority* in religion, *centralization* in government (either as socialism or monarchy)."[18] It seems that Eliot was not merely making an observation, but seeking to clarify his own personal beliefs. It would be ten years before he declared himself a classicist in literature, a royalist in politics and an "Anglo-Catholic" in religion,[19] but he was already honing his beliefs, trying to synthesize them into a coherent system. In his notes, he writes that in the French mind "no theory ever remains merely a theory of art, or a theory of religion, or a theory of politics. Any theory which commences in one of these spheres inevitably extends to the others." He goes on to say that a "classicist in art and literature" will be "likely to adhere to a monarchical form of government, and to the Catholic Church."[20] For the time being, he continued to develop his own theories of religion and politics through works of literary criticism.

The second series of lectures, which also began in the fall of 1916, turned to the subject of modern English literature. Eliot again started with an overview of the Romantic period, setting up an understanding of Victorian literature as a reaction against the literature of the previous era. In a 16-part series designed to get right to the heart of the culture of his new homeland, Eliot explored the works of revered poets like Alfred, Lord Tennyson (1809–1892) and Robert Browning (1812–1889), and novelists like Charles Dickens (1812–1870). One lecture focused entirely on the works of Matthew Arnold (1822–1888), the dominant figure in English literary criticism.

Matthew Arnold: The Function of Criticism

Arnold began his literary career as a poet, inspired by the works of William Wordsworth. His earliest poetry shows a kinship with the Romantic poets who, in the face of England's Industrial Revolution, longed for the serenity of Nature. Later Arnold went beyond the yearnings of the Romantics — his poetry conveyed a sense of despair, suggesting that the beautiful world of the Romantic poets was unrecoverable. Romanticism for Arnold was useless nostalgia, rendered impotent by the "strange disease of modern life."[21] In 1852, he wrote:

> But often, in the world's most crowded streets,
> But often, in the din of strife,
> There arises an unspeakable desire
> After the knowledge of our buried life;
> A thirst to spend our fire and restless force
> In tracking out our true, original course;
> A longing to inquire
> Into the mystery of this heart which beats
> So wild, so deep in us — to know
> Whence our lives come and where they go.
> And many a man in his own breast then delves,
> But deep enough, alas! none ever mines.
> ["The Buried Life"]

Arnold regarded himself as a thinker at odds with the culture into which he was born, and appointed himself as a champion of lost ideals. He turned to literary criticism and, later, social criticism. As a literary critic, he undertook a full evaluation of the whole body of Western literature — beginning with Homer, "the most important poetical monument existing."[22] Arnold contrasts the magic of Homer's "grand simple style" with the more intellectual "grand style severe" of Milton, and praises Dante for "affording admirable examples of both styles."[23] In the Elizabethans, he says, English literature reached its apex: "Whatever be the defects of Elizabethan literature (and they are great), we have no development of our literature to compare with it for vigour and richness."[24] In his essay "The Function of Criticism at the Present Time," Arnold attributes much of this "vigour and richness" to the zeitgeist of the Elizabethan era. "In the England of Shakespeare," he says, "the poet lived in a current of ideas in the highest degree animating and nourishing to the creative power; society was, in the fullest measure, permeated by fresh thought, intelligent and alive."[25]

By comparison, Arnold finds no such intellectual vitality in the literature of his own times: "The English poetry of the first quarter of this century, with plenty of energy, plenty of creative force, did not know enough. This makes Byron so empty of matter, Shelley so incoherent, Wordsworth even, profound as he is, yet so wanting in completeness and variety."[26] Arnold anticipates no works of genius from his peers — not because they lack talent but because they lack *perspective*. At the heart of Matthew Arnold's role as a critic is his argument that "the grand work of literary genius is a work of synthesis and exposition, not of analysis and discovery."[27] He says that the only way a poet in modern times can create a grand work of art is through a long, arduous study and critical evaluation of what has come before him. Despite his own lifelong commitment to the study of culture, Arnold's poetry was hardly revolutionary. T.S. Eliot opined that Arnold's best work was "too honest to employ any but his genuine feelings of unrest, loneliness and dissatisfaction."[28] Hence Arnold's most often cited contribution to the English literary canon is "Dover Beach" (1867), which includes the following passage:

> The Sea of Faith
> Was once, too, at the full, and round earth's shore
> Lay like the folds of a bright girdle furled.
> But now I only hear
> Its melancholy, long, withdrawing roar,
> Retreating, to the breath
> Of the night wind, down the vast edges drear
> And naked shingles of the world.

Predicting an ongoing cultural drought in England's immediate future, Arnold devoted the rest of his life to criticism — a crusade for what he called "sweetness and light." In 1867, he stated his goal as follows: "He who works for sweetness and light, works to make reason and the will of God prevail. He who works for machinery, who works for hatred, works only for confusion. Culture looks beyond machinery, culture hates hatred; culture has only one great passion, the passion for sweetness and light."[29] In Arnold's later writings, we can find the roots of Irving Babbit's humanism and George Santayana's Life of Reason,[30] Josiah Royce's prescriptions for 20th-century Christianity[31] and T.S. Eliot's budding career as a literary and social critic.

Like Arthur Symons and W.B. Yeats, Matthew Arnold argued that poetry could take up the mantle of religion, replacing dogma with a living truth: "Our religion has materialized itself in the fact, in the supposed fact; it has attached its emotion to the fact, and now the fact is failing it. But for poetry the idea is everything; the rest is a world of illusion, of divine illusion. Poetry attaches its emotion to the idea; the idea is the fact. The strongest part of our religion today is its unconscious poetry."[32] The young poet T.S. Eliot surely would have agreed with this last statement. Nevertheless, as a teacher and lecturer, Eliot was eager to point out Arnold's shortcomings. Initially, he attacked the effectiveness of Arnold's cultural criticism: "If he were our exact contemporary, he would find all his labour to perform again. A moderate number of persons have engaged in what is called 'critical' writing, but no conclusion is any more solidly established than it was in 1865."[33] This was the perfect justification for Eliot to tackle a career as a literary critic — he gradually decided to attempt the first full reevaluation of Western literature since Arnold. In 1916, Eliot began developing literary opinions and theories that would provide the foundation for his 1933 Harvard lectures, published as *The Use of Poetry and the Use of Criticism*. The lectures are a direct descendant of Arnold's essay "The Function of Criticism at the Present Time." In them, Eliot says that it is necessary, "every hundred years or so," for a critic to review and "readjust" the popular conception of the history of literature.[34] Just as Arnold insisted that any great modern poet would have to shape his art through intense critical evaluation of his predecessors, Eliot came into his own by filling that prescription — by evaluating Arnold and surpassing him.

Four Jacobean Dramatists

Eliot, like Arnold before him, held Elizabethan and Jacobean literature in high regard. Several of Eliot's earliest critical essays, published between 1918 and 1932, focused the dramatic poets who often get lost in the shadow of William Shakespeare. In 1924, Eliot made plans to write a book (never completed) about the works of four such poets: George Chapman (c. 1559–1634), Cyril Tourneur (1575–1626), Thomas Middleton (1580–1627) and John Webster (c. 1580–c. 1634).

While he grants that none of these poets has given us a body of work with the kind of thematic unity that we find in Shakespeare, Eliot declares that in each of these dramatists "there is the essential, as well as the superficies, of poetry; they give the pattern, or we may say the undertone, of the personal emotion, the personal drama and struggle, which no biography, however full and intimate, could give us; which nothing can give us but our experience of the plays themselves."[35] His analysis of their work draws attention to the successful fusion of thought and feeling in the poetry of the time period. The subject of these plays and the politics of their authors also may have had an influence on Eliot's developing system of beliefs.

George Chapman's greatest tragic plays take their subject matter from French politics and history, and their rhetorical bombast from the classic tragedies of Greco-Roman antiquity, but their theme of civil unrest is undoubtedly a reflection of the political climate of Jacobean England. Chapman's acknowledged masterpiece *Bussy D'Ambois*— about a maniacally corrupt aristocrat — is believed to have been written around the time that King James I succeeded Queen Elizabeth I on the throne of England. King James was not as popular with the people as Elizabeth had been, and in 1605 a group of Catholic extremists plotted to blow up the House of Lords and kill him. The plot was uncovered and one of the conspirators, Guy Fawkes, was burned alive.

Shakespeare responded to the political turmoil of the Jacobean era in a more conservative Elizabethan fashion. Whereas his younger contemporaries were apt to focus their stories on the rebellious common man and his disgust with a corrupt, decadent monarchy, Shakespeare focuses on the tragedy of the doomed monarch in his play *Coriolanus*. By contrast, *The Revenger's Tragedy* (alternately attributed to Jacobean dramatists Cyril Tourneur and Thomas Middleton) romanticizes the heroism of a knave named Vendice, whose action brings about the downfall of a royal court characterized by perverse lust and power. Lacking the intellectual hesitancy of Shakespeare's Hamlet, Vendice gleefully murders the duke, and quips, "Alas! poor lecher: in the hands of knaves, / A slavish duke is baser than his slaves" [III.iv]. More shocking still, Vendice gets away with the murder. T.S. Eliot marvels at the intensity of *The Revenger's Tragedy*— a play "in which the horror of life ... finds exactly the right words and rhythms."[36] Like Arthur Symons before him, he also praises *Coriolanus,* ranking it with *Antony and Cleopatra* as "Shakespeare's most assured artistic success."[37]

Perhaps Eliot, like Shakespeare, was fearful of the alternative to aristocracy: an uncertain future for the British Empire. In his criticism, he points out that other writers illustrated the sadness of a culture in chaos. Thomas Middleton pined for a prerevolutionary golden era, while John Webster revealed "the last ripeness" of Elizabethan drama.[38] Like the author of *The Revenger's Tragedy*, each of these poets blamed the same thing for the rapid decline of a noble aristocracy: the corrupting influence of lust within the royal court.

Thomas Middleton: A Game of Chess

In Middleton's play *Women Beware Women*, the female characters exist only as property to be bartered — by men, and by each other. Livia, a power-hungry widow, orchestrates a love triangle that threatens to destroy the dukedom. In order to win the political favor of the Duke of Florence, she arranges for him to satisfy his lust for a young newlywed named Bianca. First, she convinces Bianca that she has married her husband, Leantio, for the wrong reason: love rather than power. She suggests that Bianca spurn her inconsequential husband and seduce the rich and influential duke. "She that can place her man well," Livia advises, "can never lose her game" [II.i]. The naïve young girl, only just beginning to realize the power of lust, puts her feminine wiles to work.

Leantio responds with the full range of emotions of a scorned lover. When he first learns of the affair, it fuels his cynicism about the "fairer sex." Anger turns to disgust, and he likens his wife's body to a "goodly Temple / That's built on Vaults where Carkasses lie rotting" [III.i]. Later, self-pity and remorse lead to forgiveness. When he sees his wife again, his love for her overwhelms his anger:

> Branch! Now I miss thee; Oh return!
> And save the faith of woman; I nev'r felt
> The loss of thee till now; 'tis an affection
> Of greater weight, than youth was made to bear. [III.ii]

The damage, however, is done. One suspects that Leantio will never be able to forget his wife's infidelity. Bianca realizes her mistake but can do nothing to rectify it. The marriage has been destroyed. Leantio's feelings toward the duke are more consistent, as are the playwright's. Early in the play, Leantio says:

> ... love that's wanton, must be rul'd a while
> By that that's careful, or all goes to ruine,
> As fitting is a Government in Love,
> As in a Kingdom; where 'tis all meer Lust,
> 'Tis like an insurrection in the people
> That rais'd in Self-wil, wars against all Reason. [I.iii]

At the end of the play, the Lord Cardinal reiterates this message to the Duke himself: "Where lust raigns, that Prince cannot raign long" [V.ii].

T.S. Eliot, who knew something of the maddening outcome of infidelity, argues that the playwright was more concerned with portraying the complexity of human emotions than with delivering a political message. Of the play he writes: "The wickedness of the personages in *Women Beware Women* is conventional wickedness of the stage at the time; yet slowly the exasperation of Bianca, the wife who married beneath her, beneath the ambitions to which she was entitled, emerges from the negative; slowly the real human passions emerge from the mesh of interest in which they begin." Middleton, he concludes, ultimately succeeds in capturing "permanent human feelings."[39]

Middleton's *The Changeling* is another tragic tale of wanton lust that leads to murder. In the final act, the characters reflect — with utter amazement — on how thoroughly desire has transformed each of them, and transformed the way they see each other. One character speaks as if he has just awakened from a dream:

> What an opacous body had that moon
> That last chang'd on us! Here's beauty chang'd
> To ugly whoredom, here servant obedience
> To a master sin, imperious murder.
> I, a suppos'd husband, chang'd embraces
> With wantonness, but that was paid before;
> Your change is come too, from an ignorant wrath
> To knowing friendship. Are there any more on's? [V.iii]

There is no coda in *The Changeling* comparable to the Lord Cardinal's admonition to the duke in *Women Beware Women*. Here, the playwright seems less concerned about presenting a thematic message than presenting complex characters. Eliot criticizes Middleton for the lack of thematic unity in his plays, but he nevertheless admires the playwright's ability to record human nature "without fear, without sentiment, without prejudice."[40]

John Webster: The Skull Beneath the Skin

At the end of Middleton's *Women Beware Women*, the Lord Cardinal issues the following speech to warn the duke about his affair with Bianca:

> ... Is she a thing
> Whom sickness dare not visit, or age look on,
> Or death resist, does the worm shun her grave?
> If not (as your soul knows it) why should Lust
> Bring man to lasting pain, for rotten dust? [IV.i]

Middleton's contemporary John Webster employs similarly haunting imagery of the physicality of death, to give immediacy to the theme of moral decay. In Webster's *The White Devil*, believed to have been written around 1607, Cardinal Monticelso delivers an equally horrid depiction of the trappings of lust. After the death of his sister Isabella, Monticelso visits his brother-in-law Brachiano and accuses Brachiano's mistress Vittoria of the murder. The cardinal is merciless in his condemnation, comparing Vittoria to "sweetmeats which rot the eater," "poisoned perfumes," "cold Russian winters, that appear so barren," and calling her "Worse than dead bodies which are begged at gallows, / And wrought upon by surgeons, to teach man / Wherein he is imperfect" [III.i]. When he has debased her enough, Monticelso sends Vittoria to a convent for penitent whores.

The cardinal is not the only character whose speech reveals an obsession with the physicality of death. Vittoria's brother Flamineo worries that his role in Isabella's murder will lead to his own untimely demise: "Knaves turn informers, as maggots turn to flies" [III.i]. Another character assures us that "treason, like spiders weaving nets for flies / By her foul work is found, and in it dies" [III.ii]. The message is clear: Murder will out. When it does, the murderer faces a fate that is more horrible than the death itself. Flamineo's dread of postmortem decay is reinforced by the ramblings of his insane mother, who sings an incoherent dirge over the corpse of her son Marcello:

> Call for the robin-red-breast and the wren,
> Since o'er shady groves they hover,
> And with leaves and flowers do cover

> The friendless bodies of unburied men.
> Call unto his funeral dole
> The ant, the field-mouse, and the mole,
> To rear him hillocks that shall keep him warm,
> And (when gay tombs are robbed) sustain no harm:
> But keep the wolf far thence, that's foe to men,
> For with his nails he'll dig them up again [V.iv].

Afterwards, Flamineo can find no joy in life. "We think caged birds sing," he says, "when indeed they cry" [V.iv]. Moments later, he is confronted by Branchiano's ghost, who carries a skull in a pot of lily-flowers. Flamineo, acutely aware that he is going to die, confronts the ghost with questions, like Odysseus or Aeneas among the shades in Hades. But Flamineo is no hero, and the ghost offers no reassurance.

Later, Vittoria urges him to remember the Bible's promise of a resurrection to eternal life. Flamineo says he is too tired to go on struggling with the possibility of belief; he wants nothing but a quick death. At this point, he is willing to accept whatever fate awaits him, whether it is the fate promised in Christian teachings or the afterlife of older religions: "Whether I resolve to fire, earth, water, air, / Or all the elements by scruples, I know not, / Nor greatly care" [V.vi] After he dies, Vittoria goes to her own death with the same uncertainty: "My soul, like a ship in a black storm, / Is driven, I know not whither" [V.vi].

Webster's *The Duchess of Malfi*, believed to have been written around 1614, seems only slightly more optimistic because the title character has faith. In *Malfi*, the Duchess is virtuous, while her brother the Cardinal is corrupt — a "white devil," hiding his own immorality behind the walls of the Catholic Church. After the Duchess secretly gets married, the Cardinal and his brother Ferdinand plot to kill their sister, so that they can keep her dowry. At her execution, the Duchess faces death without fear: "Who would be afraid on't, / Knowing to meet such excellent company / In the other world?" [IV.ii]. Ferdinand, however, is tormented by the murder of his sister, and of her maid and two children. The cardinal finds him in a state of madness, chanting: "O, I'll tell thee; / The wolf shall find her grave, and scrape it up, / Not to devour the corpse, but to discover / The horrid murder" [IV.ii]. A doctor explains his rhyme as a symptom of "a very pestilent disease" called lycanthropia:

> In those that are possessed with't there o'erflows
> Such melancholy humour they imagine
> Themselves to be transformed into wolves;
> Steal forth to churchyards in the dead of night,
> And dig dead bodies up... [V.ii].

Here too we see the roots of the English Gothic tale in the idea that there are supernatural forces at work in the natural world to insure moral justice. Even the cardinal begins to imagine that there is a beast on his back: "When I look into the fish-ponds in my garden, / Methinks I see a thing armed with a rake, / That seems to strike at me" [V.v]. In this case, the supernatural force takes a shape similar to that of the Furies of Greco-Roman mythology.

In the end, the cardinal and Ferdinand get their comeuppance — though there is no indication that supernatural powers played a part in their fates. Only the duchess's widower remains to give perspective on the entire tragedy: "Integrity of life is fame's best friend, / Which nobly, beyond death, shall crown the end" [V.v]. Webster, who left his audience in the wilderness of sin at the end of *The White Devil*, plucks us out at the end of *The Duchess of Malfi*. T.S. Eliot, however, was apparently unsatisfied with *Malfi*'s ending. In the 1924 preface to his unwritten book, he argues that Webster's work, and the work of his contemporaries, suffered from a "defect of realism": the "meaning" presented in the works of the Jacobean playwrights appeared as nothing more than the subjective realities of "the most commonplace mind," the beliefs of a variety of unintellectual men and women living in that era.[41] What Eliot wanted was for the playwright to offer, within the context of the play, more order and objectivity.

Eliot concludes, "The case of John Webster, and in particular *The Duchess of Malfy* [sic], will provide an interesting example of a very great literary and dramatic genius directed toward chaos."[42] With regard to the golden era of English drama: "The art of the Elizabethans is an impure art."[43] Eliot never completed his book on the four dramatists who managed — like the French Symbolists — to capture the boredom, the horror and the glory of their world, but he makes his point about playwrights of the time period in a series of short essays that span more than a decade. (In 1934, these were collected and published as *Elizabethan Essays*.) Furthermore, just as Eliot had outlined his own beliefs as a literary critic by criticizing the critic Matthew Arnold, he predicts his future as a playwright through his criticism of the great playwrights.

Saving Tom

In December 1916, Eliot quit his daytime teaching job out of frustration. Before long, Vivienne's parents were forced to come to the couple's financial aid. Quickly realizing the impracticality of his decision, Eliot took a new job in March 1917 as a clerk at Lloyds Bank in the City of London. Ezra Pound balked, and quickly concocted a "Saving Tom" campaign. He hoped to raise enough money so that Eliot could avoid menial "day jobs" and concentrate on his art. Eliot refused this kind of support; he was trying to become self-sufficient. In April, Vivienne wrote to Eliot's sister Charlotte, indicating that the bank job seemed to be doing quite a bit of good for her husband's emotional stability. In the same letter, she writes about the demoralizing effect of the war.[44]

Around the same time, Eliot composed a rare prose piece about a sexually ambiguous bank clerk named Eeldrop and his roommate Appleplex (who some critics say is based on Ezra Pound). The two men live in an "evil neighborhood of silence," thriving on degenerate observations of miscreant neighbors. Eliot writes:

> There was a common motive which led Eeldrop and Appleplex thus to separate themselves from time to time, from the fields of their daily employment and their ordinarily social activities. Both were endeavoring not the commonplace, respectable or even the domestic, but the too well pigeonholed, too taken-for-granted, too highly systemized areas, and — in the language of those whom they sought to avoid — they wished "to apprehend the human soul in its concrete individuality."[45]

Searching for inspiration, he also wrote the uncharacteristically lighthearted satire "The Hippopotamus," and a series of verses in French. In "Mélange Adultère de Tout," Eliot muses on the many hats he wears — as professor, journalist, lecturer, philosopher, poet — and proposes an escape to Africa, à la Rimbaud. In "Lune de Miel," he presents a couple on honeymoon in Europe, and juxtaposes their cultural discoveries with more carnal discoveries behind the bedroom door. In "Le Directeur," he pokes fun at the editor of a London periodical called

The Spectator. Appropriately, Eliot would soon become the editor of a competing periodical, *The Egoist*; he was persuaded by an admiration for the journal's mission to assert the importance of things other than the war.[46] Eliot himself, of course, was struggling to do the same thing.

In June 1917, The Egoist Limited published Eliot's first book of poetry, *Prufrock and Other Observations.* For Eliot, it was a major validation; he felt that the publication of *Prufrock* gave him permission to put those old poems behind him and start something new. In December, he wrote to his father with a guarded sense of optimism for his future as a poet.[47] For the time being, however, the Great War was consuming the minds and bodies of Europe; Eliot had little energy for art.

By August 1918, America had been engaged in the war for over a year, and Eliot belatedly applied for active military service. Perhaps his mental exhaustion was so overwhelming that part of him longed for the peace of death — the way Flamineo longed for it in *The White Devil.* Ezra Pound was quick to protest; just as he had tried to raise money to save Eliot from the bank job, he protested at the American Embassy in London that there was no sense in sacrificing the one American who might be capable of securing the future for democracy.[48] In November, Eliot was called up by the U.S. Navy. Amidst a great deal of confusion about where he was to be assigned, the armistice was declared.

The end of the war did not end the problems in Eliot's marriage, which may have been the inspiration for four new quatrains that appeared in the *Little Review* in September 1918. "Sweeney among the Nightingales," "Mr. Eliot's Sunday Morning Service," "Dans le Restaurant" and "Whispers of Immortality" dwell on images of sex and violence, showing Eliot's affinity with the Jacobean dramatists and their righteous indictments of obsessive lust. The first two poems introduce Sweeney, a character who later reappeared in "Sweeney Erect" (written 1919), *The Waste Land* (written in 1921) and an abandoned play originally called *Wanna Go Home, Baby?* and later retitled *Sweeney Agonistes* (written between 1924 and 1926). This makes Sweeney the most persistent character in Eliot's entire oeuvre, but the recurrence doesn't make him any less enigmatic.

Saving Sweeney

The name *Sweeney* is perhaps derived from the urban legend of Sweeney Todd, a Scottish barber who committed a series of murders with a straight razor in the early 1800s and baked the remains of his victims into delicious meat pies. The Demon Barber of Fleet Street is comparable to real-life serial killer Jack the Ripper, whose East End murder spree had taken place only three decades before Eliot invented Sweeney. In 1919, the Whitechapel murders still haunted the thoughts of many Londoners, and Sweeney became Eliot's fictional reminder.

In "Sweeney among the Nightingales," the title character appears primal, even subhuman: ape-necked, knees spread, arms hanging down like a monkey. He is Robert Louis Stevenson's Dr. Jekyll. Sweeney keeps company with two lascivious ladies: an unidentified woman in a Spanish cape, and a Jewish woman named Rachel with "murderous paws." The poem suggests that the two women are conspiring to assassinate Sweeney, which reminds the poet of the Greek warrior Agamemnon, who was murdered by his wife in the *Oresteia.* The only apparent similarity between Sweeney and Agamemnon is the fate they have created for themselves: Murder begets murder. In the final stanza, Agamemnon's death cry mixes with the song of nightingales in the "bloody wood."[49] Four decades after he wrote the poem, Eliot explained that "the wood I had in mind was the grove of the Furies at Colonus; I called it 'bloody' because of the blood of Agamemnon in Argos."[50] As literary critic Ronald Schuchard points out, it is with this invocation of the Furies that Eliot "begins to trace the psychological transformation of promiscuous characters possessed by moral agents."[51]

Sweeney reappears briefly in "Mr. Eliot's Sunday Morning Service," in which the poet denounces parasitic religious types who have neutered the Word of the God for modern man. Literary critic Elizabeth Drew suggests that Sweeney's appearance in the final stanza is the coup de grâce of the poem: "The final degrading 'offence' is the contrast of Sweeney wallowing in his bath with the figure of the Baptized God; with the further irony that there is a parallel between the movement of his body, shifting from ham to ham and stirring the water, and the 'controversial' antics of the learned theologians."[52] Sweeney remains a symbol of uncivilized man, while embodying Eliot's disgust with modern-day religious figures. The specific details of Eliot's disgust are unclear; only the cleverness of his contempt is preserved in the poem.

In "Sweeney Erect," Eliot again transplants his modern-day caveman onto a mythological story. After sex with a whore, Sweeney stands naked, shaving with a straight razor. When the whore on the bed suffers an epileptic seizure, Sweeney dismisses the sight. This reminds the poet of the Greek hero Theseus, dismissing his lover Ariadne, who subsequently hung herself. The poet's description of the seizure betrays his own contempt for the woman and what she represents. He describes her genitalia as "this oval O cropped out with teeth."[53]

In *The Waste Land*, both Sweeney and the nightingales reappear. This time, Eliot inserts his character into the mythological story of Philomel, the princess of Athens who was brutally raped by her sister's husband, King Tereus. According to Ovid's *Metamorphoses*, when Philomel threatened to tell her sister Procne what had happened, Tereus cut out her tongue. Philomel then wove a tapestry that told Procne what had happened. Procne took her revenge by killing her son and feeding him to her husband in a meat pie. Ultimately, the gods transformed all three characters into nightingales, whose song appears, condensed, in "The Fire Sermon" of *The Waste Land*:

> Twit twit twit
> Jug jug jug jug jug jug
> So rudely forc'd.
> Tereu[54]

In the same poem, Sweeney is tormented by thoughts of death. In his fear, Eliot humanizes the character for the first time, making him more like a character in a John Webster play. Eliot borrows a line from metaphysical poet Andrew Marvell (about "Time's winged chariot") to convey Sweeney's anxiety. Sweeney himself tries to dispel his morbid thoughts by mindlessly chanting:

> O the moon shone bright on Mrs. Porter
> And on her daughter
> They wash their feet in soda water.[55]

In due time, there is a reckoning for Sweeney. It occurs in "Fragment of an Agon," from Eliot's unfinished play *Sweeney Agonistes*. Previous to this, Sweeney has been an unthinking character — the opposite of Prufrock, whose anxieties stemmed from too much thinking. That changes in this poem, when Eliot gives Sweeney a voice. Suddenly, the uncivilized man, the serial killer, offers coded insight into his own warped mind.

First, Sweeney taunts a woman named Doris, promising to carry her off to a cannibal isle. Of course, she thinks he's kidding. For the time being, she plays along, offering to be the missionary to his cannibal. Sweeney continues, but his description of the cannibal island sucks the fun out of the joke. There will be, he says, only "birth, copulation, and death" on the island.[56] Doris thinks that sounds like a frightfully dull life: "Why I'd just as soon be dead." This statement sets Sweeney's imagination to work. "I knew a man once did a girl in," he confesses. Doris protests that it is an inappropriate subject for conversation, but the other men around her disagree. They want to hear more. Sweeney continues his lurid tale, implicating the male listeners in his confession:

> Any man might do a girl in
> Any man has to, needs to, wants to
> Once in a lifetime, do a girl in."[57]

Then he tells them about a murder that he presumably committed himself. When the men asked if the murderer got "pinched," Sweeney says the murderer got away with it — for a while. After a few months, he began to lose touch with reality. Now he doesn't know if he's alive or dead, or if there's a difference. He lives in constant fear — fear of the hangman and of something worse: the boogeyman, the "hoo-ha's," the Furies on his trail. *Dread* is the chief subject of the play — dread related to horrible things that have already taken place, dread of things to come and dread of the death-in-life that results. Going one step beyond Prufrock, who hesitated on the edge of the abyss, Sweeney is a character who has surrendered to his primal urges and fallen.

Eliot regarded the Sweeney cycle as a milestone in his writing. In 1922, before he began "Fragment of an Agon," he wrote to his brother Henry that he considered his Sweeney poems to be among his most serious and mature works.[58] At the same time, however, he seemed unsure of where Sweeney would lead him. In December 1918, when Eliot was starting the Sweeney cycle, Vivienne wrote to Eliot's sister Charlotte that her husband was worried that his mind was "not acting as it used to do."[59] It may well be that Eliot's mind was *not* "acting as it used to do." Looking at the Sweeney poems within the context of Eliot's personal and professional life, it is clear that he was on the verge of a nervous breakdown and a creative breakthrough.

John Donne: Whispers of Immortality

If surviving manuscripts are an accurate indication, the composition of the poem "Whispers of Immortality" (first published in September 1918) may have troubled Eliot more than any poem prior to *The Waste Land*. He was struggling to craft new poetry in the style of metaphysical poet John Donne (1572–1631), who had strived to fuse thought and feeling. Although the first two stanzas, reflecting on the achievements of Webster, remained intact through several revisions, the section on Donne was entirely rewritten at least twice. In the earliest manuscript, we see Eliot trying to extend the imagery that he has applied to Webster, who "saw the skull beneath the skin," to give an impression of Donne's achievements:

> He found no substitute for death
> But toothed the sweetness of the bone.[60]

The images are compelling, but perhaps too imprecise for Eliot. Subsequent attempts lacked the striking imagery of the first.[61] It was only by combining thoughts and phrases present in these early drafts that Eliot arrived at the final poem:

> Donne, I suppose, was such another
> Who found no substitute for sense,
> To seize and clutch and penetrate;
> Expert beyond experience.
>
> He knew the anguish of the marrow
> The ague of the skeleton;
> No contact possible to flesh
> Allayed the fever of the bone.[62]

Eliot is most precise in his appraisal of the Jacobeans in a discarded passage from one of the earlier drafts that refers to Donne and Webster's "Ethics of the Dust."[63]

With the phrase "Ethics of the Dust," Eliot praises the ability of Webster and Donne to present morality as more than a concept — to give it the immediacy of sensory perception. With the line that appears in the final version of the poem, he praises their ability to do the same for metaphysics. Eliot also articulated this praise in his critical writings. Not long after "Whispers of Immortality" was published, he wrote an essay on Shakespeare, Chapman, Tourneur, Marlowe, Webster and Donne, saying, "They had a quality of sensuous thought, or of thinking through the senses, or of the senses thinking."[64] He then spent the next decade trying to clarify this statement.

In 1921, his essay on the metaphysical poets of the 18th century attempts an explanation: "When a poet's mind is perfectly equipped for its work, it is constantly amalgamating disparate experience; the ordinary man's experience is chaotic, irregular, fragmentary. The latter falls in love, or reads Spinoza, and these two experiences have nothing to do with each other, or with the noise of the typewriter or the smell of cooking; in the mind of the poet these experiences are always forming new wholes."[65] No poet serves as a better illustration of this statement than John Donne, who was the master of the metaphysical conceit — an extended metaphor combining two vastly different ideas into a single image. In his early love poems, he compares his beloved to fishing bait,[66] and the two of them together to the feet of a compass.[67] Elsewhere, he equates the exploration of his beloved's body to the discovery of America,[68] and elaborates on the sexual connotations of the intermingling of his blood with the blood of his beloved ... in the body of a flea.[69] Just as Webster sought to illustrate the horror of death with concrete images of physical decay, so Donne tries to convey the spiritual union of two souls through images of physical union. His goal is to convey a sense that the union cannot be unmade, even by death. In "The Canonization" he writes:

> Call us what you will, we are made by such love;
>   Call her one, me another fly,
> We are tapers too, and at our own cost die,
>   And we in us find the eagle and the dove,
>   The phoenix riddle hath more wit
>   By us; we two being one, are it.
> So to one neutral thing both sexes fit
>   We die and rise the same, and prove
>   Mysterious by this love.[70]

More than anything, the poet was trying to surprise the reader — forcing us to consider the bonding power of love as if for the first time, by appealing to the immediacy of our senses with bold new imagery. Eliot was particularly impressed with the image of "a bracelet of bright hair about the bone" in Donne's poem "The Relic," showing how a lover clings even in the grave.[71]

After his conversion to Anglicanism, Donne tried to do the same thing for religion. In a 1919 review of a book of Donne's sermons, Eliot points to a particular sermon[72] in which Donne brings a "fresh emotional tone" to a familiar message: "The method is a vivid figure of speech, an image developed with point by point reference to spiritual truth. The world is a sea, has ebbs and flows, storms and tempests, the greater fish devour the less; it is like the sea, no place of habitation, but a passage to our habitations. We fish in this sea for the souls of men; we fish with the Gospel of Christ Jesus. The net has leads, the denouncing of God's judgments, and corks, the power of absolution."[73] Eliot applauds the method of the sermon, comparing Donne's use of analogy and repetition to the Buddha's Fire Sermon.

In the years to come, however, Eliot expressed the opinion that Donne was confused in his beliefs — even going so far as to suggest that he had no beliefs. Donne's most metaphysical poem, "An Anatomy of the World," illustrates this point with its chaotic structure and the blunt, hopeless confession that "'Tis all in pieces, all coherence gone."[74] In the 1926 Clark lectures at Trinity College, Cambridge, Eliot made a case for Donne as the first modern poet, arguing that he is "capable of experiencing and setting down many super-sensuous feelings, only these feelings are of a mind in chaos, not of a mind in order. The immediate experience passes into thought; and this thought, far from attaining *belief*, is immediately the object of another feeling."[75] He says that this is not a reflection of insincerity on Donne's part, but an inevitable outcome of the culture in which Donne lived: "It seemed as if, at that time, the world was filled with broken fragments of systems, and that a man like Donne merely picked up, like a magpie, various shining fragments of ideas as they struck his eye, and stuck them about here and there in his verse."[76] The criticism of Donne is also a self-criticism.

In his essay "The Metaphysical Poets," written while *The Waste Land* was taking shape in his mind, Eliot essentially defines modern poetry in his praise of John Donne: "The poet must be more and more comprehensive, more allusive, more indirect, in order to force, to dislocate if necessary, language into his meaning."[77] Based on Eliot's comments about the revolutionary nature of poetry, we may conclude that he regarded modern poetry as a revolt against Victorian poetry, a mutant strain of the English literary tradition that grew out of the post–Jacobean "dissociation of sensibility"[78] and lack of visual imagination, embodied in the writings of John Dryden (1631–1700) and John Milton (1608–1674).

This brings us to Alfred, Lord Tennyson (1809–1892) and Robert Browning (1812–1889), Romantic poets who "do not feel their thought as immediately as the odour of a rose"[79]; and to Victorian poet William Morris (1834–1896), whose emotion is "not more refined nor more spiritual," only "more vague"[80]; and finally to Victorian poet Algernon Charles Swinburne (1837–1909), whose words are "all suggestions and no detonation."[81] Their poetry suffers the same defects that Eliot finds in the vast majority of English poetry going back to the Jacobeans. Despite his critical dismissal of these poets, however, there is no doubt that their works influenced Eliot's own poetry. Like John Donne's poetry, Eliot's poetry reflects a world "filled with broken fragments" of systems and ideas. Eliot saw it as his duty to set these fragments in order.

William Wordsworth: Intimations of Immortality

What Eliot explicitly *didn't* want to do was get lost in the world of romanticism, which he regarded as vague and immature. In 1926, he says that, although the English Romantic poets saw themselves as a new literary movement, they "seem merely to prolong with more excitement the language and sentiments of the latter half of the eighteenth."[82] In a sense, Eliot was revolting against his own early poetry, which had been Romantic in tendency. Without a solid system of beliefs, he could hardly create the systematic poetry of belief that he wanted. He could only develop his poetry in conscious opposition to the Romantic tradition, which necessitated a thorough understanding of it.

The Romantic period of English literature was inaugurated by the 1798 publication of *Lyrical Ballads*, a collection of poems by William Wordsworth (1770–1850) and Samuel Taylor Coleridge, two poets with very different backgrounds. Wordsworth was raised in the rural Lake District of northwestern England, but he became a poet only after he took an extensive tour of Europe during his third year of college. He was particularly affected by the frantic pace of life in cities like London and Paris. In his poetry, Wordsworth referred to London as a "too busy world," where he struggled to find the mental peace that he had known throughout his childhood in rural West Cumberland. Only on rare occasions was he able to recover his sense of calm and see "the parts / As parts, but with a feeling of the whole."[83] He recalled one such experience — taking in the view from Westminster Bridge by the light of early morning — in an early sonnet:

> Never did sun more beautifully steep
> In his first splendor, valley, rock, or hill;
> Ne'er saw I, never felt, a calm so deep![84]

Wordsworth was much happier in Paris, where he claimed to have become a patriot during the time of the French Revolution.[85] When England declared war on the government of France, he felt his loyalties divided. This precipitated an emotional collapse, forcing Wordsworth to return to his home in the Lake District where he experienced a spiritual revival. Soon after, he met Samuel Taylor Coleridge, and the two men spearheaded the literary equivalent of the French Revolution.

Wordsworth's poetry presents a stark contrast between rural and urban life. Upon his return home, he became convinced that the ideal life was to be found in rural settings, where man has a more intimate relationship with Nature and therefore greater opportunities for reflection, peace and joy. He defined Romantic poetry according his own personal experiences, saying that "it takes its origin from emotion recollected in tranquility."[86] Many of his poems in *Lyrical Ballads* take their inspiration from rural locations where he had such profound experiences of peace and joy: "Lines Left upon a Seat in a Yew-Tree Which Stands near the Lake of Esthwaite, on a Desolate Part of the Shore, Yet Commanding a Beautiful Prospect"; "Lines Written near Richmond, upon the Thames, at Evening"; "Lines Composed a Few Miles above Tintern Abbey on Revisiting the Banks of the Wye during a Tour. July 13, 1798."

In this last poem he concludes the *Lyrical Ballads* with a reflection on the restorative spirit that reveals itself through Nature:

> ... I have felt
> A presence that disturbs me with the joy
> Of elevated thoughts; a sense sublime

> Of something far more deeply interfused,
> Whose dwelling is the light of setting suns,
> And the round ocean, and the living air,
> And the blue sky, and in the mind of man,
> A motion and a spirit, that impels
> All thinking things, all objects of all thought,
> And rolls through all things....[87]

This is Wordsworth's attempt to identify the impetus for Romantic poetry — for *all* poetry with a sense of grandeur and awe. He is writing about the same mysterious force that pervades Edgar Allan Poe's "Al Aaraaf," or Fitzgerald's *Rubaiyat*, Rimbaud's "Eternity" and T.S. Eliot's 1910 poem "Silence." In his 1919 essay "Tradition and the Individual Talent," however, Eliot rejected Wordsworth's assertion that poetry originated in "emotion recollected in tranquility," proposing instead an impersonal theory of poetry. Nevertheless, some of Eliot's later poems, particularly his landscape poetry, bear a strong resemblance to Wordsworth's pastorals. For the younger Eliot, still grappling with the chaos of city life, the common theme was dread. As in the examples by Poe, Fitzgerald and Rimbaud, Eliot's early poetry thrives on a complex fear that is born in chaos: the fear of something incomprehensibly larger than oneself.

We find the same presence in an early passage of Wordsworth's autobiographical *The Prelude*, in which the poet recalls an evening when he took a small shepherd's boat out on a lake at night. The passage is so vividly descriptive that the reader can easily imagine himself floating inside a rocky cave, and hear the echoes of every little sound that occurs within. As the boat drifts forward, the poet sees a huge cliff come into view. With every passing moment, it looms larger until it eclipses the moon and the stars. With trembling hands, the poet turns the boat around and returns to the shore and a willow tree that provides the illusion of safety. "After I had seen that spectacle," Wordsworth writes,

> ...for many days my brain
> Worked with a dim and undetermined sense
> Of unknown modes of being. In my thoughts
> There was a darkness — call it solitude
> Or blank desertion — no familiar shapes
> Of hourly objects, images of trees,
> Of sea or sky, no colours of green fields,
> But huge and mighty forms that do not live
> Like living men moved slowly through my mind
> By day, and were the trouble of my dreams.[88]

Here, Wordsworth has strayed into the territory of dread that was more thoroughly explored by his friend Samuel Coleridge. In his autobiography *Biographia Literaria*, Coleridge recalls the initial plan for the composition of the *Lyrical Ballads*: "The thought had suggested itself (to which of us I do not recollect) that a series of poems might be composed of two sorts. In the one, the incidents and the agents were to be, in part at least, supernatural.... For the second class, subjects were to be chosen from ordinary life." Coleridge goes on to explain that the two poets agreed that Coleridge would concentrate on the supernatural ("or at least romantic"), while Wordsworth concentrated on Nature, the "things of everyday."[89] Wordsworth set out to capture intimations of immortality in the "little things" that often go overlooked in ordinary life, while Coleridge sought to capture intimations of immortality in the unseen and unknown.

Samuel Taylor Coleridge: The Secondary Imagination

The early life of Samuel Coleridge (1772–1834) stands in stark contrast to that of Wordsworth. When he was nine years old, Coleridge's father died and the boy was sent to live in a strict boarding school at Christ's Hospital in London. The following years were solitary ones, and it has been suggested that this environment — so unlike that of his fellow poet — cultivated a sense of despair in the young poet's mind. Like Wordsworth, Coleridge takes Nature as his main subject, but one cannot imagine Wordsworth writing many of the horrific passages in Coleridge's most famous contribution, "The Rime of the Ancient Mariner":

> The very deep did rot: O Christ!
> That ever this should be!
> Yea, slimy things did crawl with legs
> Upon the slimy sea.[90]

or

> O Wedding Guest! This soul hath been
> Alone on a wide wide sea:
> So lonely 'twas, that God himself
> Scarce seemed there to be.[91]

For the most part, Wordsworth's writings on Nature and the sublime are characterized by overwhelming peace and joy which he regarded as a reflection of the world around him. Coleridge's writings are characterized by overwhelming anxiety.

"The Rime of the Ancient Mariner" is the spiritual odyssey of a man who finds himself at odds with Nature after he witnesses one of his shipmates murdering an albatross. Wordsworth, in his "Lines Left upon a Seat in a Yew-Tree," warns us against human pride, and instructs us that "true knowledge leads to love" of the natural world. Coleridge's mariner agrees that "he prayeth best, who loveth best / All things both great and small." Unlike Wordsworth, Coleridge explored Nature's wrathful side, with all the fearfulness of an Old Testament prophet.

We know from Romantic poet William Hazlitt's personal recollection "My First Acquaintance with Poets" that Coleridge briefly served as a Unitarian minister. Hazlitt shows, however, that Coleridge was never self-righteous. He saw the darkness as well as the light — even in the church. In response to a sermon that Coleridge gave in Shrewsbury in January 1798, Hazlitt wrote:

> The sermon was upon peace and war; upon church and state — not their alliance but their separation — on the spirit of the world and the spirit of Christianity, not as the same, but as opposed to one another. He talked of those who had "inscribed the cross of Christ on banners dripping with human gore." He made a poetical and pastoral excursion — and to show the fatal effects of war, drew a striking contrast between the simple shepherd boy, driving his team afield, or sitting under the hawthorn, piping to his flock, "as though he should never be old," and the same poor country lad, crimped, kidnapped, brought into town, made drunk, at an alehouse, turned into a wretched drummer boy, with his hair sticking on end with powder and pomatum, a long cue at his back, and tricked out in the loathsome finery of the profession of blood.[92]

This passage suggests that Coleridge was perhaps better at pointing out the shortcomings of religious institutions than at championing their causes. Though he later became a devout Anglican, the young Coleridge was apparently very conflicted in his beliefs. His poetry offers further proof.

After "Ancient Mariner," Coleridge is best known for two equally unsettling poems written in his youth: "Kubla Khan" and "Christabel." Coleridge tells us that "Kubla Khan" was the product of a dream that he had while under the influence of a prescribed drug (presumably an opiate). When he awoke, he recorded the first half of the dream exactly as he remembered it. The existing fragment paints a vivid portrait of a seemingly mythological location on the banks of a "sacred river" that runs through ancient "caverns measureless to man / Down to a sunless sea." There are only vague hints about what actually occurs in this seemingly idyllic spot, inside a "stately pleasure dome" that the poet calls

> A savage place! as holy and enchanted
> As e'er beneath a waning moon was haunted
> By woman wailing for her demon lover!
> This natural paradise seems as if it might be built on the gateway to hell.

"Christabel" is set in an equally enchanting world — the "midnight wood" of a faraway kingdom. There, a virginal lady meets a mysterious woman in white, who says she has been recently attacked by a band of villains. The lady, Christabel, brings the apparent victim home to meet her father Sir Leoline, but she soon realizes that there is something profoundly unnatural about their guest. The woman in white introduces herself as Geraldine, daughter of Lord Roland de Vaux of Tryermaine — a long-lost friend of Sir Leoline. Despite Christabel's intuition that their guest is not to be trusted, Sir Leoline sees only an opportunity to reconcile with his friend. He vows to avenge the attack on Geraldine, and to take her home safely to her father.

"Christabel" is less about the thrust of its narrative than about its sense of foreboding. The poet hints that Geraldine's woeful story should not be accepted at face value any more than the beauty of Kubla Khan. When Christabel recounts a dream in which a wounded bird is accompanied by a snake, we understand instinctively that Geraldine is the snake — and something much worse. It remains unclear exactly what kind of threat Geraldine poses to Christabel. Since Coleridge left the poem unfinished, this question can be answered only in the reader's imagination. The effect of the poem is to create a sense of *dread without object*.

It is possible that Coleridge himself could not have consciously identified the source of his heroine's dread — for, when he wrote "Christabel," he was relying on his intuitive powers of storytelling, what he called *the secondary imagination*. In *Biographia Literaria*, Coleridge explains: "The primary IMAGINATION I hold to be the living power and prime agent of all human perception.... The secondary I consider as an echo of the former.... It dissolves, diffuses, dissipates, in order to recreate; or where this process is rendered impossible, yet still, at all events, it struggles to idealize and to unify."[93] Coleridge's definition is admittedly confusing. Nevertheless, his theory that the "secondary imagination" goes through a process of abstraction in an effort to achieve unity is familiar — linking Coleridge with the ancient philosophers of the Far East, who believed that such paradoxes could help one to understand the true nature of the world.

Just as Wordsworth saw "the parts as parts, but with a feeling of the whole," and as Eliot would later attempt a "unity of belief," Coleridge's poetry is an attempt at *fusion*. In his autobiography Coleridge writes: "The poet, described in ideal perfection, brings the whole soul of man into activity, with the subordination of its faculties to each other, according to their relative worth and dignity. He diffuses a tone of spirit of unity and blends (as it were *fuses*) each into each, by that synthetic and magical power to which we have exclusively appropriated the name of imagination."[94] Perhaps nothing says more about the young poet's perspective on Imagination than a single line from his poem "Dejection: An Ode," in which he writes "that which suits a part infects the whole." This line captures not only the similarity between the philosophies of Wordsworth and Coleridge, but also their main difference: Coleridge's choice of the word *infects* carries negative connotations that one would never expect to find in Wordsworth. Wordsworth embraces Nature in all its complexity; the young Coleridge fears what he can't fully understand.

Eventually, Coleridge joined the Anglican Church. Afterwards, he never again wrote the kind of morbid, impressionistic poetry for which he's famous, so we may wonder if this conversion helped him to conquer some of his fears. Whether it did or not, he continued to champion the role of Imagination on the poet's path to understanding a higher power, be it God or Nature. In 1825, Coleridge wrote a religious tract on the importance of Reflection and Novelty in religious instruction. In his *Aids to Reflection*, he argues that it is necessary for poets, philosophers and clergymen to rescue the universally admitted truths of Christianity from "the neglect caused by the very circumstance of their universal admission." This requires the religious instructor to give "freshness and importance to the most common-place maxims."[95]

Coleridge attempts to do this by reflecting on the "phantasms" that filled the "hours of darkness" in his youth:

> The bodings inspired by the long habit of selfishness, and self-seeking cunning,
> though they are now commencing the process of their purification into that fear
> which is the *beginning* of wisdom, and which, as such, is ordained to be our guide
> and safeguard, till the sun of love, the perfect law of liberty, is fully arisen — these
> bodings will set the fancy at work, and haply, for a time, transform the mists of
> dim and imperfect knowledge into determinate superstitions.[96]

It is obvious, from the tone of his writing, that the fear associated with these "bodings" no longer has the urgency it did when Coleridge wrote his early poetry. What he once called "the supernatural" he now refers to as "spiritual." For him, the phantasms have become part of the whole, and there is no more fear.

Supernatural Horror in Shelley and Browning

In *The Use of Poetry and the Use of Criticism* (1933), Eliot writes that after he discovered *Omar Khayyam* and the horror stories of Edgar Allan Poe he began reading works by Romantic poets like Percy Bysshe Shelley (1792–1822), Lord Byron (1788–1824), John Keats (1795–1821), Dante Gabriel Rossetti (1828–1882) and Algernon Swinburne (1837–1909). Each of these poets, following in the footsteps of Coleridge, had a strong preoccupation with supernatural horror — as did Eliot. From the confines of his haunted abbey in the 1905 poem "A Fable for Feasters" to the tormenting Furies of his mature play *The Family Reunion*, Eliot's fictional world is frequently populated with moral agents from the supernatural realm. Those supernatural agents fulfill a key function in his work, as they do in the works of several Romantic and Victorian poets who came before him.

In the introduction to his 1927 survey of this oft-maligned genre, H.P. Lovecraft writes that "atmosphere is the all-important thing" for works of sustained supernatural horror:

A certain atmosphere of breathless and unexplainable dread of outer, unknown forces must be present; and there must be a hint, expressed with a seriousness and portentousness becoming its subject, of that most terrible conception of the human brain — a malign and particular suspension or defeat of those fixed laws of Nature which are our only safeguard against the assaults of chaos and the daeligmons [demons] of unplumbed space.[97]

Lovecraft traces the origins of the supernatural horror story back to English Gothic novelists and classic examples such as Horace Walpole's *The Castle of Otranto* (1765), Ann Radcliffe's *The Mysteries of Udolpho* (1794) and Matthew Lewis's *The Monk* (1796), which established a long list of genre conventions. Perhaps none of those conventions is more important than a setting that conveys an atmosphere of death and decay. Medieval settings were especially popular, and many of the Romantic poets used medieval imagery in their poems. Keats's "La Belle Dame sans Merci," like Coleridge's "Christabel," is set in the world of valorous knights and seemingly innocent maidens.

Other poets used very different settings to effect an atmosphere of cosmic dread. In an 1816 Dante-esque allegory entitled "Alastor, or The Spirit of Solitude," Percy Bysshe Shelley writes of an idealistic youth who embarks on a spiritual quest to discover universal truths. The youth's journey leads him through

> ... the awful ruins of the days of old:
> Athens, and Tyre, and Balbec, and the waste
> Where stood Jerusalem, the fallen towers
> Of Babylon....[98]

At the end of his journey, the traveler is devastated by the sights he has seen, culminating in the discovery of "a wide and melancholy waste of putrid marshes" in the place of a vast ocean. The youth expects to meet Death there, knowing that the "mighty Shadow loves / The slimy caverns of the populous deep."[99] In a preface to the poem, Shelley explains the meaning of the youth's quest: "He seeks in vain for a prototype of his conception. Blasted by his disappointment, he descends to an untimely grave."[100] Although the tone is predominantly one of melancholy rather than fear, Shelley conveys a sense of overwhelming awe with his imagery of a vast waste land and the great ruined civilizations of antiquity.

Robert Browning's poem "Childe Roland to the Dark Tower Came" features similar imagery. This dream-like narrative revolves around Roland, a knight on a long, perilous journey through a barren gray land, in search of an elusive "Dark Tower." Filled with doubt, he continues his quest only out of habit. He has traveled too far to go back, and yet he has no reason to hope that he is near his destination. The road ahead appears lifeless and hopeless; even Nature muses, "'Tis the Last Judgment's fire must cure this place."[101] At the end of the poem, Roland finally comes within view of the Dark Tower and suffers a ghostly vision of "all the lost adventurers my peers."[102] After a life spent training for the sight, he suddenly seems delirious. The poem ends there, and the reader cannot help sensing that Roland's quest is far from over. So many questions remain: Is the tower real or is it just an illusion? If real, is it a place of rest or a place of battle? If a place of battle, can the battle be won or has Roland undertaken his quest in vain? Browning gives us no answers, only foreboding. His reference to "the Last Judgment," however, suggests a Christian interpretation of the poem's pervasive sense of doom. The Dark Tower fills the knight with an intense awareness of his own mortality and an intense dread of something more powerful than Nature. Roland's success, like that of the land itself, is based entirely on God's judgment.

William Blake: The Religion of Art

No English Romantic poet created a more elaborate world of Imagination than William Blake (1757–1827). Modern scholars rank him with Wordsworth and Coleridge as one of the innovators of modern poetry. Most of Blake's contemporaries, however, dismissed him as an obscure mystic and madman. Blake's literary contributions remained in doubt until an 1863 biography revived interest in his work. The biography prompted essays by eminent Victorian writers like Dante Rossetti and Algernon Swinburne. At the dawn of the 20th century, W.B. Yeats was not alone in his enthusiastic assertion that it was Blake who first "announced the religion of art."[103]

Blake's first collection, *Poetical Sketches* (1783), features several poems that reflect the spirit of his age and the age of his predecessors: a quartet of Wordsworthian poems that personify the four seasons, as well as a timely gothic experiment ("Fair Elenor") and a series of imitations of the 18th century's "poets of sensibility," who followed the literary tradition of Shakespeare and Milton. Around 1788, Blake produced two poems that announced his unique genius. In "All Religions Are One," he speaks in the voice of a lonely artist crying in the wilderness — "the Poetic Genius, the true Man," whose powers of Imagination offer quasi-mystical redemption to mankind:

> To see the World in a Grain of Sand
> And a Heaven in a Wild Flower
> Hold Infinity in the palm of your hand
> And Eternity in an hour[104]

Blake's mature belief — articulated more fully in "The Marriage of Heaven and Hell" — is that man possesses the innate ability to transcend the natural world and his five senses. Imagination, Blake says, will allow us to see God as He truly is: Infinite. Blake believed that it was the job of the Poetic Genius, rather than sectarian religious leaders, to lead mankind into the future: "If it were not for the Poetic or Prophetic character. the Philosophic & Experimental would soon be at the ratio of all things & stand still, unable to do other than repeat the same dull round over again."[105]

In his *Songs of Innocence and of Experience* (1789 and 1794), Blake continues to develop his philosophy by illustrating the difference between "the two contrary states of the human soul." The state of innocence is reflected in the pastoral imagery of Wordsworthian poetry; the state of experience is reflected in the post-industrial waste land of London — where joy is "unnaturally" suppressed, and leads the Poetic Genius to melancholy:

> I wander thro' each charter'd street,
> Near where the charter'd Thames does flow.
> And mark in every face I meet
> Marks of weakness, marks of woe.[106]

In poems like "London," "The Chimney Sweeper" and "The Garden of Love," Blake portrays the churches of London as corrupting institutions rather than redeeming forces that will return man to his state of innocence. The poet's problem with organized religion is simple; he preaches tolerance of other beliefs and respect for life. In "The Divine Image" (from *Songs of Innocence*), he writes:

> And all must love the human form,
> In heathen, turk or jew.

> Where Mercy, Love & Pity dwell,
> There God is dwelling too[107]

As he further developed his personal mythology, beginning with "The Book of Thel" in 1789, Blake's philosophy becomes more complicated. In "The Marriage of Heaven and Hell," he envisions a universe that is not characterized by opposing forces of Good and Evil but by "Attraction and Repulsion, Reason and Energy, Love and Hate"—all of which are "necessary to Human existence." He explains: "From these contraries spring what the religious call Good & Evil. Good is the passive that obeys Reason. Evil is the active springing from Energy."[108] Therefore, in *Songs of Experience* (1794), Christ the Lamb becomes Christ the Tyger—a fear-inducing creature of fiery Energy, "burning bright." In "The Poison Tree," the tree of knowledge from the biblical Garden of Eden appears as a product of man's wrath rather than the cause of his fall.

Elements of Blake's seemingly un–Christian worldview may be traced to certain strains of ancient Eastern thought as well as to Greco-Roman philosophy, in which God is an all-pervading, rather than purely benevolent, influence. Nevertheless, Blake chooses to deliver his message in the recognizable style of Old Testament Hebrew prophets, through symbolism and allegory and sometimes even the personas of the prophets themselves. At the end of "The Marriage of Heaven and Hell," Isaiah speaks directly to Blake, validating the poet's vision: "I saw no God, nor heard any, in a finite organical perception; but my senses discover'd the infinite in every thing."[109] Ezekiel adds, "The philosophy of the east taught the first principles of human perception. some nations held one principle for the origin & some another, we of Israel taught that the Poetic Genius (as you now call it) was the first principle and all the others merely derivative, which was the cause of our despising the Priests & Philosophers of other countries, and prophecying that all Gods would at last be proved to originate in ours & to be the tributaries of the Poetic Genius."[110]

Blake's meaning is oblique, and at times this complexity serves his aim. Blake, like many of his peers, is a poet of the 18th-century aesthetic of the sublime. His visions are intended to conjure feelings of fear and awe, rather than lead to simple understanding. One goal is implicit in all of Blake's writings — transcendence through imagination: "If the doors of perception were cleansed every thing would appear to man as it is: infinite."[111]

In later years, Blake continued to develop his personal mythology, incorporating it into works of political allegory and moral prophecy. "America: A Prophecy" (1793) introduces the leaders of the American Revolution ("Washington, Franklin, Paine & Warren, Gates, Hancock & Green") into Blake's imaginative world of angels and demons, tigers and dragons, and mysterious god-like figures (Albion, Orc, Urizen) who orchestrate events on a global scale. Blake obliquely alludes to the Old Testament's Ten Commandments and the myth of the lost city of Atlantis, and builds toward an apocalyptic vision of the future, in which the American continent is ravaged by fire and plague.

"Europe: A Prophecy," written on the eve of England's war with France, continues to develop the author's philosophy that man can transcend his natural senses — beginning with a passage that is reminiscent of the Buddha's Fire Sermon. Blake also continues to use imagery from earlier poems: the changing seasons and the industrial city of London. The poem culminates with a war to end all wars, prophesying doom for eighteen centuries of Christian civilization. His vision of Judgment comes not from the Bible (which he calls a "brazen Book"), but out of his own personal mythology: the giant god-like figure Albion casts a "bleak, dark, abrupt" shadow over the city, and sounds "the trump of the last doom."

Although modern scholars recognize Blake as a key figure in Romantic literature, it is easy to understand why his contemporaries dismissed him: His is a world of brilliant imagination, inaccessible to the casual reader. T.S. Eliot, hardly a casual reader, was not as intimidated by Blake's obscurity; he focused his criticism of Blake on the question of literary merit, aware that great art often has a touch of madness. Eliot writes that Blake's poetry "has the unpleasantness of great poetry," but that it exhibits "nothing that can be called morbid or abnormal or perverse, none of the things which exemplify the sickness of an epoch or a fashion ... only those things which, by some extraordinary labour of simplification, exhibit the essential sickness or strength of the human soul."[112]

In Eliot's view, Blake's early poems show "immense powers of assimilation," found lacking in the later work.[113] Eliot suggests that the fault stemmed from the culture of Blake's place and time, which "failed to provide what such a poet needed." "Perhaps," he says, "the poet required the philosopher and the mythologist."[114] Forced to create his own philosophy and mythology to support his poetry, Blake became "eccentric," and his art "inclined to formlessness."[115] As a result, the mature Blake is simply "too much preoccupied with ideas."[116] This diagnosis fits neatly into Eliot's theory (summarized in his influential 1919 essay "Tradition and the Individual Talent") that great poets are largely the products of the culture in which they live and write. When Eliot calls Blake "eccentric," he is noting that Blake's ideas lack continuity with the religious and literary traditions of England. Blake exists in a cultural vacuum, and that — according to Eliot — is what limits his greatness. In contrast, Eliot himself had spent years studying Eastern and Western cultures, carving out his own place in the tradition of world literature. He would allow himself no such limitation.

Lines for an Old Man

In January 1919, T.S. Eliot's father died suddenly. Just a few days before, Eliot had written to publisher John Quinn about the publication of some of his literary criticism in the States because he was desperate for his parents to see what he was doing.[117] When Henry Ware Eliot died, he probably regarded his youngest son's future as, at best, uncertain. In a despairing letter to his mother, T.S. Eliot writes, "If I can think at the end of my life that I have been worthy to be his son I shall be happy."[118]

Over the course of the following year, some of Eliot's most influential essays and two collections of new poetry were published. In July, Eliot sent a new poem entitled "Gerontion" to John Rodker, who was making plans to publish a comprehensive collection. "Gerontion" — Greek for "little old man" — begins as a monologue, not unlike "The Love Song of J. Alfred Prufrock." Its speaker, however, is older and less anxious. Critic F.O. Mathiessen tells us that the opening section of the poem is paraphrased from a 1905 biography of Edward Fitzgerald, whose epic poem *The Rubaiyat of Omar Khayyam* had been an early influence on Eliot. The biography sets the scene for a quotation from one of Fitzgerald's letters: "Here he sits, in a dry month, old and blind, being read to by a country boy, longing for rain:—'Last night ... we heard a Splash of Rain, and I had the book shut up, and sat listening to the Shower by myself— till it blew over, I am sorry to say, and no more of the sort all night. But we are thankful for that small mercy.'"[119] Eliot's poem revolves around this evocative image.

Eliot, who as a young man cast himself in the role of the middle-aged Prufrock, now casts himself in the role of an old man reflecting on the life behind him and all of its unfulfilled promise. He is weary, but the weariness has been caused by time, not by action:

> I was neither at the hot gates
> Nor fought in the warm rain
> Nor knee deep in the salt marsh, heaving a cutlass,
> Bitten by flies, fought.

Here, Eliot is possibly thinking of the war. Though it had claimed an entire generation of men of action, Eliot himself had avoided service — a fact that made him feel guilty. He imagines himself as Gerontion, in the twilight of his life, with no memories of action — only listless observations of his surroundings and idle speculations about *how things might have been.* In the wake of his father's death, Eliot was imagining what he himself would be thinking if he were on the verge of death. Such thoughts urge a man to faith ... but, the poem asks, faith in what?

The next section of the poem insists, like the Jewish unbelievers to Jesus, "We would see a sign!" and invokes Christ the Tiger — a reference to Blake's emblem for energy. Some critics have also noted references to a Nativity sermon delivered by the Anglican priest Lancelot Andrewes, and interpreted this poem as an indication of Eliot's religious conversion. Eliot himself offered the same interpretation, later in life. At the time of composition, however, Eliot was not a practicing Christian, and his allusions to Blake suggest that he was struggling with belief in good and evil. The poem equates Christ the Tiger with springtime that mocks the speaker's "reconsidered passion," and the presence of a "wrath-bearing tree" is reminiscent of Blake's "A Poison Tree." The implication of the latter is that the tree of knowledge is the true source of the speaker's conflict of belief, for he asks: "After such knowledge, what forgiveness?"

In the sixth stanza of the poem, the Tiger devours "us," and the speaker subsequently addresses an unidentified "you." In the final lines of this section, he ruminates on the possibility of "closer contact" with this mysterious Other: "I have lost my sight, smell, hearing, taste and touch: / How should I use them for your closer contact?" In a sense, Eliot may have been addressing his father or his friend Jean Verdenal. Either way, it seems he is confronting death and questioning the existence of the God of Christianity. Receiving no response, Gerontion blames his own inability to follow faith instead of reason. The stalemate leaves the speaker in a "wilderness of mirrors." Too old to continue, he dismisses his reconsidered passion as hopeless "thoughts of a dry brain in a dry season," and waits to be blown away like white feathers in the snow.

This final image is reminiscent of the Sybil's plight in Virgil's *Aeneid.* The leaves that she uses to predict the future are always scattered by the wind, so her visions are fragmentary. The poem "Gerontion," unlike "Prufrock," is fragmented in the sense that the perspective changes, from that of the old man himself to a more objective narrative voice. Within this framework, the speaker at the end of the poem might easily have chosen to make direct reference to the Sybil, as Eliot did later in *The Waste Land.* Instead, he chose the image of white feathers in the snow, which conveys not only a sense of being at the mercy of harsh nature but also a sense of lightness and purity. Because the object is the same color as the snow, it disappears into the scene like a drop of water in the ocean. This image could be distressing or reassuring, depending on the reader's perspective. We might say that the old man has been swallowed by unthinking, unfeeling chaos. Alternatively, we might say that the old man, waiting without hope, is now truly receptive to a higher power.

The Alchemy of Words

By the summer of 1919, Eliot had concluded his lecturing engagements. In a July letter to his friend Mary Hutchinson, he writes with authority about a sort of conclusion to his own education: "It seems that one ought to *read* in two ways: 1) because of a particular and personal interest, which makes a thing one's own, regardless of what other people think of the book 2) *to a certain extent*, because it is something one 'ought to have read' but one must be quite clear that this is *why* one is reading. Although my education is very fragmentary I believe I shall do no more of this."[120] Confident that more than a decade of studying world literature and philosophy had prepared him to espouse his own literary theories, Eliot delved into an intense period of critical writing.

His seminal essay "Tradition and the Individual Talent" appeared in *The Criterion* in the fall of 1919. In the essay, Eliot rejects Wordsworth's definition of poetry as "emotion recollected in tranquility," contrasting it with his own Impersonal Theory of Poetry: "[Poetry] is neither emotion, nor recollection, nor, without distortion of meaning, tranquility. It is a concentration, and a new thing resulting from the concentration, of a very great number of experiences which to the practical and active person would not seem to be experiences at all; it is a concentration which does not happen consciously or of deliberation."[121] The essay uses examples from Dante as well as John Keats's "Ode to a Nightingale" to make a distinction between personal "emotion" (associated with real-life experience) and "feeling" (an effect of art). Eliot also makes a scientific analogy to illustrate his meaning, comparing poets to medieval alchemists:

> When the two gases previously mentioned [oxygen and sulfur dioxide] are mixed in the presence of a filament of platinum, they form sulphurous acid. This combination takes place only if the platinum is present; nevertheless the newly formed acid contains no trace of platinum, and the platinum itself is apparently unaffected; has remained inert, neutral, and unchanged. The mind of the poet is the shred of platinum. It may partly or exclusively operate upon the experience of the man himself; but, the more perfect the artist, the more completely separate in him will be the man who suffers and the mind which creates; the more perfectly will the mind digest and transmute the passions which are its material.[122]

Eliot does not stop here; his criticism of the Romantic writers is evident in his assertion that great art produces, not only feeling, but a synthesis of *thought* and feeling, in the reader. The created poem therefore exists completely independent of the poet.

Eliot was eager to distance his poems from the experiences that prompted them. He wanted to escape — or perhaps transcend — his own personality and experiences through art. "Poetry," Eliot writes, "is not a turning loose of emotion, but an escape from emotion; it is not the expression of personality, but an escape from personality."[123] Around the same time, he admitted to using his art to build a "hard exterior" around his emotions and personality, so that "nothing can touch what is inside."[124] In his essay "Hamlet and His Problems," written and published in September 1919, Eliot gives practical advice to artists seeking the same goal: "The only way of expressing emotion in the form of art is by finding an 'objective correlative'; in other words, a set of objects, a situation, a chain of events which shall be the formula of that *particular* emotion."[125]

During this period of time when Eliot was hermetically sealed, he was storing up numberless feelings, phrases, images — a vast collection of objective correlatives — that he would eventually put to use in *The Waste Land*. In December, he wrote to his mother that his New

Year's resolution was to write a long poem that he'd been thinking about for a long time.[126] In the meantime, he was working long hours at the bank, simply trying to survive a mind-numbing daily routine.

In March 1920, J.H. Woods wrote to Eliot about the possibility of a professorship at Harvard, but by then Eliot had no intention of ever returning to live in America. He was now well-entrenched in literary London, corresponding regularly with local artists like Virginia Woolf, Aldous Huxley, Richard Aldington and fellow American expat Conrad Aiken. Woolf may have based the character of Septimus Smith, in her stream-of-consciousness novel *Mrs. Dalloway* (1925), on Eliot. Eliot may have also provided inspiration for the character Denis in Huxley's first novel, *Crome Yellow* (1922). In a July 1920 letter to his mother, Eliot remarked that Huxley owed him a creative debt. He later made a similar statement about his friend Conrad Aiken's poem *The House of Dust* (1920), saying that the abode in question was built mostly by Swinburne and himself.[127] Richard Aldington later satirized Eliot's self-importance in a short story called "Stepping Heavenward" (1931).

Eliot was as frustrated with his own writing as he was with the writing of his peers. He felt stifled, like Gerontion, and was waiting with hope for a creative breakthrough — something that would elevate him to the level of the great poets. In March, he wrote an essay in praise of Dante, who was becoming more and more his literary idol. The essay explains Eliot's admiration in terms of the theories he laid down in "Tradition and the Individual Talent" about the fusion of thought and feeling: "Dante's is the most comprehensive, and the most *ordered* presentation of emotions that has ever been made.... More than any other poet, [he] has succeeded in dealing with his philosophy, not as a theory (in the modern and not the Greek sense of that word) or as his own comment or reflection, but in terms of something *perceived*."[128] In a letter to his friend Ottoline Morrell, he says that he believes himself to be so inferior to Dante that there is little he can say to illuminate the master's work.[129]

Just as Dante was an inspiration to him, Eliot hoped to be an inspiration for younger poets. Shortly after the publication of *The Sacred Wood*, his first collection of literary criticism, he admits to his brother that he used Matthew Arnold's literary criticism as a "cloak of invisibility-respectability,"[130] to give credence to his own work. He wanted desperately to reach the younger generation, and spur a major revival of classicism. His book aims to "rectify, so far as I can, the immense skew in public opinion"[131] about the Romantic writers, by revealing their philosophic shortcomings: "The vast accumulations of knowledge — or at least of information — deposited by the nineteenth century have been responsible for an equally vast ignorance. When there is so much to be known, when there are so many fields of knowledge in which the same words are used with different meanings, when every one knows a little about a great many things, it becomes increasingly difficult for anyone to know whether he knows what he is talking about or not."[132] What he wants, in the simplest terms, is *unity of thought and feeling*: "Every work of imagination must have a philosophy; and every philosophy must be a work of art."[133]

Breakdown

In a letter to his mother just a few days before the November 1920 publication of *The Sacred Wood*, Eliot continues to yearn for "a period of tranquility" in which to complete a poem.[134] The poem would have to wait. In October, Vivienne's father suffered a near-fatal collapse.

For months, Vivienne nursed him back to health, an imposition that proved destructive to her own health. In February, Eliot wrote to his friend Brigit Patmore that her pain was so extreme and so constant that she could no longer distinguish between reality and delusion.[135] A few months later, Vivienne herself confessed to her friend Scofield Thayer that she was becoming insane.[136]

In August 1921, Eliot's mother finally came to London for a visit, along with his brother Henry. Eliot, who had not seen any of his relatives for over six years, was extremely sentimental. He was suddenly overwhelmed by the realization that he could never return to the home he missed: his father was dead, and his mother had sold the house in Gloucester where his fondest memories of childhood were set. Vivienne, apparently, was just as emotional; she later wrote to Henry to apologize for her behavior.[137] After the visit, Tom was physically and emotionally exhausted, and more than a little embarrassed by his wife's behavior. His mental health became such a concern that he consulted a "nerve specialist" in London. The doctor advised an immediate, and solitary, vacation.

On October 3, Eliot wrote to his brother Henry about plans to go on a three-month, physician-supervised retreat: "I dread this enforced rest and solitude (I must be away completely among strangers with no one I know) and expect a period of great depression. It is very terrifying to stop after having gone on for so long. I am told that people always find the first part of such a cure very trying indeed."[138] Perhaps he was remembering the words of psychologist William James, whose 1902 book *Varieties of Religious Experience* made an impression on Eliot while he was studying mysticism. James writes about the "time of tension" preceding spiritual rebirth:

> There are only two ways in which it is possible to get rid of anger, worry, fear, despair, or other undesirable affections. One is that an opposite affection should overpoweringly break over us, and the other is by getting so exhausted with the struggle that we have to stop — so we drop down, give up, and DON'T CARE any longer. Our emotional brain-centres strike work, and we lapse into a temporary apathy. Now there is documentary proof that this state of temporary exhaustion not infrequently forms part of the conversion crisis. So long as the egoistic worry of the sick soul guards the door, the expansive confidence of the soul of faith gains no presence. But let the former faint away, even but for a moment, and the latter can profit by the opportunity, and, having once acquired possession, may retain it.[139]

Eliot understood that he had only two options: to move forward in life, or to disappear completely. According to James, he would have to go through the latter in order to achieve the former. On October 14, he departed for the Albemarle Hotel in Margate, on the southeastern coast of England.

Suggested Reading (1915–1920)

Prufrock and Other Observations

"The 'Boston Evening Transcript'" (1915)
"Aunt Helen" (1915)
"Cousin Nancy" (1915)
"Hysteria" (1915)
"Mr. Apollinax" (1915)

Poems (1920)

"The Hippopotamus" (1917)

"La Directeur" (1917)
"Mélange Adultère de Tout" (1917)
"Lune de Miel" (1917)
"Sweeney among the Nightingales" (1918)
"Mr. Eliot's Sunday Morning Service" (1918)
"Dans le Restaurant" (1918)
"Whispers of Immortality" (1918)
"A Cooking Egg" (1919)
"Burbank with a Baedeker: Bleinstein with a Cigar" (1919)
"Sweeney Erect" (1919)
"Gerontion" (1920)

Inventions of the March Hare

"In the Department Store" (1915)
"O lord, have patience" (19??)
"In Silent Corridors of Death" (19??)
"Airs of Palestine, No. 2" (1917?)
"Petit Epitre" (1917?)
"Tristan Corbiere" (1917?)

The Sacred Wood (1920)

♦ PART V ♦

Beyond Good and Evil (1920–1921)

> Every artist is a kind of pantheist.
> — T.E. Hulme

The Decline of the West

In his 1912 book *The Decline of the West*, German historian Oswald Spengler (1880–1936) examines the history of civilization in three phases: *ancient— medieval—modern*, correlating to *beginning—middle—end*. His "morphology" of world history is admittedly West-centric: "World-history is our world picture and not all mankind's. Indian and Classical [Greco-Roman] man formed no image of a world in progress."[1] Spengler cites the "Persian and Jewish religions ... notably the Gnostic systems"[2] as the beginning of civilization. As for the end of civilization, he writes that the modern period has "been stretched and stretched again to the elastic limit at which it will bear no more."[3]

Spengler marks the acme of the modern period just before 1800, prior to the French Revolution. Ever since, he says, Western civilization has been in a period of cultural decline: "The series 'ancient-medieval-modern history' has at last exhausted its usefulness ... the picture is beginning to dissolve into a chaotic blur."[4] He compares the modern decline of the West to the decline of Greek civilization. Noting that the conquering Romans emphasized law over philosophy and science over art, he argues that now is the time for "technics instead of lyrics, the sea instead of the paint-brush, and politics instead of epistemology."[5] After the conclusion of the Great War, the pessimistic tone of Spengler's message rang true among European intellectuals for whom the ideas of progress and God no longer seemed realistic.

For American intellectuals, life was not quite as bleak. In 1929, American philosopher Will Durant (1885–1981) looked beyond Spengler's prophecy of doom for Western civilization. Where Spengler writes about a world in which many strongly-defined Cultures[6] appear to be fundamentally at odds with each other, Durant suggests that we may cultivate hope for the postwar world by encouraging learning and tolerance of different cultures. During the 20th century, he predicts, individual cultures will no longer be self-sustaining, which should foster more open-minded exchanges between the great cultures of the world and prevent large-scale conflicts. Durant argues that philosophy and art should be the building blocks of the future. For the time being, he says, "We stand between two worlds — one dead, the other hardly born;

and our fate is chaos for a generation.... Everything must be rebuilt, even as if we had been cast into the wilderness and forced to begin civilization anew."[7] In 1920, T.S. Eliot — an American among the ruins of Europe — was piecing together the fragments of his own vision of the future, struggling to find hope in despair. *The Waste Land* would prove to be the culmination of modern theories about the fate of Europe; the prophecy of a cultural rebirth under the influences of the East dovetailed with Eliot's own personal longing for spiritual rebirth.

Goethe: Prelude to a Philosophy of the Future

Oswald Spengler claimed that his two main sources of inspiration for *The Decline of the West* were Johann Wolfgang von Goethe (1749–1832) and Friedrich Nietzsche (1844–1900). Nietzsche himself also cited Goethe as a major influence — particularly his masterpiece *Faust*, the tale of a young doctor who sells his soul to the devil. In the beginning of *Faust*, the title character is frustrated with the limitations of his education, complaining that "for all our science and art / We can know nothing."[8] Faust is Goethe's representative of modern man, who has replaced meaning with science, and wisdom with information. Years of restless study have left the young doctor with too much information but not enough wisdom to understand his place and purpose in the world, so he resorts to magic for answers to the cosmic questions. Mephistopheles responds, appearing to him in the flesh, and offers to grant Faust godlike powers in exchange for his immortal soul.

Faust considers this decision carefully, trying to sort out his religious beliefs. He struggles to translate the meaning of John's gospel into German: "In the beginning was the Word" becomes "In the beginning was the Mind," then "In the beginning there was Force" and finally "In the beginning was the Act."[9] For him, the message is lost in semantics. He has no clear understanding of the God that created the universe and, perhaps more importantly, he doesn't believe that God is at work in the modern world. As far as he can tell, God is an absentee landlord who lives only in the imagination. That is not enough, so he accepts the devil's offer as a way to bring God to life in the modern world, and to discover a new kind of knowledge on behalf of humanity:

> The time has come to prove by deeds that mortals
> Have as much dignity as any god,
> And not to tremble at that murky cave
> Where fantasy condemns itself to dwell
> In agony. The passage brave
> Whose narrow mouth is lit by all the flames of hell;
> And take this step with cheerful resolution,
> Though it involve the risk of utter dissolution.[10]

Mephistopheles's choir of invisible spirits cheers him on: "Rebuild it, you that are strong, / Build it again within! / And begin / A new life, a new way, / Lucid and gay, / And play / New songs."[11]

Mephistopheles gives Faust a tour of the modern world, and teaches him that vitality depends upon primordial urges for creation that have been repressed by the educated man. Religion calls these powers of creation "evil," but Mephistopheles argues that, without evil, there is no good. The devil explains: Without darkness for contrast, there is no light; without the primitive sea, no evolution of life. This prompts Faust to acknowledge his own duality: "Two souls, alas, are dwelling in my breast."[12] By realizing and acting upon his primal urge to create, Faust revives the godlike part of himself.

Faust never repents his decision, even though it eventually causes him as much pain as pleasure. Instead, he lives the life he has chosen to its fullest — taking the bad with the good. When asked if he still believes in God, he explains that his concept of God has changed:

> Call it bliss! heart! love! God!
> I do not have a name
> For this. Feeling is all;
> Names are but sound and smoke
> Befogging heaven's blazes.[13]

His travels have revealed to him a unifying life-force beyond good and evil, beyond dogma. He argues that his God, though infinitely more complex than the God of the Church, is nevertheless undeniable:

> Wherever you go,
> All hearts under the heavenly day
> Say it, each in its own way;
> Why not I in mine?[14]

Through his rebellion against traditional religion, Faust has discovered true vitality. His search has not been in vain. For that reason alone, he is prepared to accept servitude in the afterlife.

Goethe, however, cannot condemn him to that fate: Faust is rescued by a host of angels who explain that "Who ever strives with all his power, / We are allowed to save."[15] This is the author's way of validating his character's heroic rebelliousness and his vision of a God that encompasses life in all its complexity: Faust finds "impunity / in cosmic unity."[16] Like Dante's pilgrim at the conclusion of *The Divine Comedy*, Faust is guided to salvation by the saintly woman he loves, a representation of the Eternal-Feminine.

Friedrich Nietzsche: Beyond Good and Evil

Walter Kaufmann, who translated works by Goethe and Nietzsche into English, once remarked that, in Faust, "Goethe created a character who was accepted by his people [Germans] as their ideal prototype."[17] Literary critic Thomas Mann goes even further: "The whole Western world has accepted this valuation and recognized in the symbolism of the Faust-figure its own deepest essence."[18] In his first book, *The Birth of Tragedy* (1872), Friedrich Nietzsche agrees, saying, "Modern man is beginning to divine the limits of the Socratic love of knowledge and yearns for a coast in the wide waste of the ocean of knowledge.... We again have need of the wisdom of Goethe to discover that such a surprising form of existence is not only comprehensible, but even pardonable."[19] Nietzsche diagnoses the malady of Western civilization as an over-reliance on the Apollonian mindset; he argues that hope for the future lies in the Dionysian myth, which "saves all the powers of the imagination of the Apollinian dream from their aimless wanderings."[20] In his native Germany, Nietzsche detected the stirrings of a Dionysian revival — particularly in the music of composers like Johann Sebastian Bach, Ludwig van Beethoven and Wilhelm Richard Wagner.

Wagner's 1865 opera *Tristan and Isolde* strongly impressed Nietzsche. The tale can be traced back to Arthurian legend, with some details drawn from the *Metamorphose*s of Ovid. Wagner's version begins at sea, on a ship that is transporting the Irish healer Isolde to Cornwall, where she is to be married. On the way, Isolde overhears the sailors singing a disparaging song about her, and becomes angry. She demands to speak with Tristan, the knight who arranged her marriage with his uncle, King Marke, after the death of her fiancé. Isolde soon learns that Tristan murdered her fiancé, and she resolves to avenge that death by making Tristan drink a deadly potion. Isolde's handmaiden Brangaene concocts the potion, and both Tristan and Isolde drink it. Instead of dying, however, the two fall in love, and Brangaene reveals that she gave them a love potion in order to save their lives.

Upon arrival in Cornwall, Isolde marries Marke, but she and Tristan continue to meet under cover of darkness until their affair is revealed by one of Tristan's jealous friends. The same friend fatally wounds Tristan, who narrowly escapes to his home and lingers there in a state of progressive delirium. On the brink of death, he is haunted by a shepherd's tune, which reminds him of his youth and of Isolde's absence. He watches the sea closely, hoping to witness the arrival of Isolde's ship, but the sea remains empty, and the sight deepens Tristan's exquisite sorrow. When Isolde finally does arrive, he is so overwhelmed that his frail body expires. Soon after, King Marke arrives and announces that he has learned about the love potion and has decided to allow the union of the two lovers. Hearing this, Isolde dies from grief.

For Nietzsche, *Tristan and Isolde* illustrates the value of tragic myth: "However powerfully pity affects, it nevertheless saves us in a way from the primordial suffering of the world, just as the symbolic image of the myth saves us from the immediate perception of the highest world-idea, just as thought and word save us from the uninhibited effusion of the unconscious will."[21] Through our experience of Wagner's music, Nietzsche says, we may be awakened to the Dionysian side of life — life at its most awe-inspiring. Such an experience could well leave us helpless:

> Suppose a human being has thus put his ear, as it were, to the heart chamber of the world will and felt the roaring desire for existence pouring from there into all the veins of the world, as a thundering current or as the gentlest brook, dissolving into a mist — how could he fail to break suddenly? How could he endure to perceive the echo of innumerable shouts of pleasure and woe in the "wide space of the world night," enclosed in the wretched glass capsule of the human individual, without inexorably fleeing toward his primordial home, as he hears this shepherd's dance of metaphysics?[22]

Thankfully, Wagner does not leave us stranded. Our experience of the eternal is, in this instance, vicarious. Wagner soon draws us back to the tale of Tristan, for whom the moment has passed:

> Here the *Apollinian* power erupts to restore the almost shattered individual with the healing balm of blissful illusion: suddenly we imagine we see only Tristan, motionless, asking himself dully: "The old tune, why does it wake me?" And what once seemed to us like a hollow sigh from the core of being now merely wants to tell us how "desolate and empty the sea."[23]

T.S. Eliot's friend Jean Verdenal was equally moved by *Tristan and Isolde*, which may have inspired Eliot's 1910 poem "Opera." In a February 1912 letter to Eliot, Verdenal writes, "Music goes more directly to the core of my being, and I have been listening to it quite a lot recently (still mainly Wagner).... Tristan and Isolde is terribly moving at the first hearing, and leaves you prostrate with ecstasy and thirsting to get back to it again."[24] Eliot frequently described a similar frustration that he could not sustain such vigorous feelings, nor summon them at will. Nietzsche's writings, on the other hand, seem to suggest a constant state of rapture.

At the time that he wrote *The Birth of Tragedy*, Nietzsche believed that he was living in a culture that would soon produce a more highly evolved man — an artist strong enough to cast off the old religions and popular conceptions of morality, and allow humanity to achieve its full creative potential. *The Wanderer and His Shadow* (1880) reveals that he had become more pessimistic, and had begun to focus on cultural restraints that he believed were preventing the rebirth of Greek values. He aimed his sharpest criticisms at Pauline Christianity, which he called the most creatively stifling influence in Western civilization. One year later, the author of *The Dawn* (1881) seems to have lost faith in the ability of his fellow countrymen to live up to the ideal of the Greeks. The German people, he laments, have too thoroughly subscribed to the Christian concept of morality.

Nevertheless, he continued to wage his philosophical war against value systems that he regarded as misanthropic and life-negating. Midway through his career, Nietzsche argued that the notions of good and evil are nothing more than historical ideas employed by the Church to maintain the status quo. He yearned for the dawn of a new day when Western civilization no longer bows to the will of the Christian Church — a day when individuals embrace passion and progress and freedom from the past, follow their own wills and look to the future with new eyes.

Zarathustra: Nietzsche As Symbolist Poet

The central ideal of Nietzsche's philosophy is the *Übermensch* (often translated in English as "overman" or "superman"), the fully actualized human being whose every thought and action affirms the complexity of life beyond good and evil. In his autobiography, Nietzsche writes that the *Übermensch* first came to him in a vision: "One hears, one does not seek; one accepts, one does not ask who gives; like lightning, a thought flashes up, with necessity, without hesitation regarding its form — I never had any choice."[25] That vision became the focus of his literary masterpiece, *Thus Spake Zarathustra: A Book for All and None* (1883–1885).

Zarathustra is a poet and a self-proclaimed prophet, who emerges from a hermit-like existence to inform the masses that God and the afterlife are illusions invented by poets to make life bearable for the sick and lazy — those who are unable to give life meaning for themselves. Zarathustra beseeches modern man to "*remain faithful to the earth*, and do not believe those who speak to you of otherworldly hopes!"[26] Through this teaching, he hopes to stave off a future in which all men are slaves to historical ideologies. He addresses a world of "hollow" men who know only what is told to them, and who avoid genuine experience of life:

If one took the veils and wraps and colors away from you, just enough would be left to scare away the crows.... Rather would I be a day laborer in Hades among the shades of the past! Even the underworldly are plumper and fuller than you.... For thus you speak: "Real are we entirely, and without belief or superstition." Unbelievable: thus I call you, for all your pride in being real![27]

He diagnoses the malady of modern man in one succinct sentence: "You are sterile: that is why you lack faith."[28] The antithesis of this sterility is the dream of the *Übermensch*.

The *Übermensch* wants to "create beyond himself," and has the strength of will to avoid being ruled by thoughts of power, lust, revenge, punishment, reward and retribution. He reserves particular contempt for pity, and for petty thoughts such as original sin. He advises men to discover their own self-worth and rejoice in this life and in humanity rather than prostrate themselves before an illusory god in anticipation of an afterlife: "As long as there have been men, man has felt too little joy: that alone, my brothers, is our original sin. And learning better to feel joy, we learn best not to hurt others or to plan hurts for them."[29]

Zarathustra uses poetic symbolism to explain the stages of man along the road to self-actualization: "the spirit becomes a camel; and the camel, a lion; and the lion, finally, a child."[30] The camel, for Nietzsche, is a "beast of burden" that endures the harsh, lifeless desert. It represents man's earliest stage of experience, after he has cast off the otherworldly delusions of youthful innocence in order to seek truth. The symbol of the lion is reminiscent of Blake's emblem of experience, the Tyger. Both represent an awesome force of creation and destruction. This creature belongs, not to the desert, but to the jungle, where survival demands more than endurance. The final stage of spiritual rebirth is that of the child, "innocence and forgetting, a new beginning, a self-propelled wheel, a first movement, a sacred 'Yes.'"[31] Whereas Zarathustra associates the camel with the desert and the lion with the urban jungle, he associates this third stage of experience with the sea, which is vast and unconquered and always changing: "One must be a sea to be able to receive a polluted stream without becoming unclean. Behold, I teach you the overman: he is this sea."[32]

Here, the problem of Zarathustra's vision becomes apparent. The innocent creature has come full circle and returned to innocence; his end is his beginning. He wonders: *Must I not then go through the entire journey again? Have I not therefore done everything in vain?* For Nietzsche, this agonizing idea of eternal recurrence had first surfaced at the end of *The Gay Science*, when an imagined demon taunted him: "The eternal hourglass of existence is turned over and over, and you with it, a grain of dust."[33] Haunted by this thought, Zarathustra retreats solemnly to his cave, where he suffers the "stillest" and most frightening hour of his journey. He desperately hopes that this is simply another stage of development on his own path to becoming the overman. "It is the stillest words that bring on the storm,"[34] he reassures himself, and later, "It is out of the deepest depth that the highest must come to its height."[35]

In the final section of Nietzsche's book, Zarathustra is taunted by his own imaginary demon — a lame "half dwarf, half mole."[36] He struggles with the horrifying thought that "the will cannot will backwards; and that he cannot break time and time's covetousness."[37] After much self-torment, the seemingly defeated poet rediscovers Nature. The voices of the animals lure him away from thoughts of fear and melancholy to healthier songs. His lust for life renewed by Nature, Zarathustra embraces his destiny as the teacher of eternal recurrence: "If this is my alpha and omega, that all that is heavy and grave should become light; all that is body, danger; all that is spirit, bird — and verily, that is my alpha and omega: Oh, how should I not lust after eternity and after the nuptial ring of rings, the ring of recurrence?" He concludes, "*For I love you, O eternity!*"[38] Despite this enthusiasm, however, there is a sense that while Zarathustra the poet has conquered his devil, Nietzsche the philosopher has not quite conquered his.

In *The Wanderer and His Shadow*, Nietzsche says that "above the founder of Christianity, Socrates is distinguished by the gay kind of seriousness and that wisdom full of pranks which constitute the best state of the soul of man. Moreover, he had the greater intelligence."[39] Nietzsche believes that Zarathustra's life-affirming gaiety is a necessary component of "the best state of the soul of man." He therefore dismisses Christianity, proposing that the teachings of Jesus Christ, who suffered and died willingly, stem from an earlier stage of experience on the path of spiritual rebirth: "Would that he had remained in the wilderness and far from the good and the just! Perhaps he would have learned to live and to love earth — and laughter too.... He himself would have recanted his teaching, had he reached my age."[40] Elsewhere, Nietzsche writes about the limitations of two of his philosopher heroes — Plato and Arthur Schopenhauer (1788–1860). "Schopenhauer's philosophy," he says, "remains the reflection of ardent and melancholy youth — it is no way of thinking for older people. And Plato's philosophy recalls the middle thirties...."[41] In Nietzsche's estimation, *none* of the great thinkers were able to encompass the breadth and height of human spirituality in all of its seasons. And neither, Nietzsche admits, was his alter ego Zarathustra.

This is the end for Nietzsche as Symbolist poet. "I have grown weary of this spirit," he confesses, "and I foresee that it will grow weary of itself." Nietzsche knew that he must remain in flux and so, like a snake, he shed his skin. His next two books, *Beyond Good and Evil* (1886) and *On the Genealogy of Morals* (1888), attempted to systematize the teachings of Zarathustra as objective philosophy. For those who believe that Nietzsche achieved his greatest potential with *Thus Spake Zarathustra*, the final words of the philosopher's alter ego offer his greatest message: "'This is *my* way; where is yours?'— thus I answered those who asked me 'the way.' For *the* way — that does not exist."[42] Nietzsche continued to follow his own winding way until he suffered a mental collapse in 1889. Like Zarathustra, he walked "among men as among the fragments of the future"[43] and heralded a storm on the horizon of European civilization.

T.S. Eliot's opinion of Nietzsche is somewhat ambiguous. He rarely mentioned the philosopher in his published writings; when he did, he offered dismissive criticism of Nietzsche's philosophy ("his belief in violence is a confession of weakness"[44]) with faint praise for its literary qualities.[45] At first glance, the dismissal seems unfair — Nietzsche did not champion physical power so much as willpower — but it would not have been an uncommon view in the early 20th century. Eliot's peer William James was equally dismissive, claiming that Nietzsche "lacked the purgatorial note which religious sadness gives forth."[46] Eliot presumably agreed. Still, he might have taken note of the fact that Nietzsche used symbolism from Eastern religions in his masterpiece *Zarathustra*. Nietzsche seems to be alluding to Shiva, the Hindu god of changes, when he remarks that "I would believe only in a god who could dance.... Now a god dances through me."[47] His symbols of the man-lion and a river flowing into the sea are also frequently associated with Shiva. Eliot might also have noted similarities between Nietzsche and F.H. Bradley, who ended his masterpiece *Appearance and Reality* the same way that Nietzsche ended *Zarathustra*— by telling readers to find their own path. Eliot did just that, virtually ignoring Nietzsche's philosophy. In the years after World War I, however, the great minds of Europe began paying more and more attention to Nietzsche, who provided a voice to a civilization on the verge of a violent collapse.

Fyodor Dostoevsky: In Sight of Chaos

In his 1889 book *Twilight of the Idols*, Nietzsche refers to Russian novelist Fyodor Dostoevsky (1821–1881) as "the only psychologist from whom I have anything to learn."[48] Like Nietzsche, Dostoevsky was struggling to cope with a world in which science had stripped religion of its authority. In 1919, T.S. Eliot also expressed admiration for the novelist, whose writing transformed everyday ennui into "extremities of torture."[49] He proposes that Dostoevsky's strength as a writer stems from his physical frailty; the epileptic novelist had "the gift, a sign of genius in itself, for utilizing his weaknesses: so that epilepsy and hysteria cease to be the defects of an individual and become — as a fundamental weakness can, given the ability to face and study it — the entrance to a genuine and personal universe."[50] No doubt Eliot saw a bit of himself in Dostoevsky. They both suffered from "bad nerves" that sometimes made life unbearable, and both interpreted their neurological attacks as a symptom of modern life. In his 1864 novel *Notes from Underground*, Dostoevsky writes: "We've lost touch with life and we're all cripples to some degree. We've lost touch to such an extent that we feel disgust for life as it is really lived and cannot bear to be reminded of it. Why, we've reached a point where we consider real life as work — almost as painful labor — and we are secretly agreed that the way it is presented in literature is much better."[51]

Dostoevsky's final novel, *The Brothers Karamazov*, is a portrait of this crippled modern world. It revolves around three estranged brothers and the murder of their father. Each brother responds to the murder in a different way, owing to his religious beliefs. In the most famous chapter of the novel, the atheist brother Ivan shares a parable about the Christian Church with his devout brother Alyosha. In the parable, Jesus Christ has returned to earth sometime during the Spanish Inquisition. Although the common people rejoice at his return, they nevertheless submit to the Grand Inquisitor's decision to burn Jesus as a heretic. The Inquisitor explains to Jesus that, in the fifteen centuries since He produced "signs from heaven," the Roman Catholic Church has been forced to maintain order among His people on earth. Because the Church assumed responsibility during His absence, the Inquisitor instructs Jesus that he has no right to return. His presence would undermine the rigid authority of the church, and thereby undermine the complacency of the masses and the order of Christian society. "Today," the Inquisitor explains, "people are more persuaded than ever that they have perfect freedom, yet they have brought their freedom and laid it humbly at our feet."[52] By counteracting confusion and fear with mystery and authority, the Church has removed that unbearable freedom for the good of the people. The message of Ivan's parable is that the majority of men are natural-born followers; the Inquisitor assures Jesus that "man is weaker and baser by nature than Thou hast believed him!"[53]

Ivan's faithful brother Alyosha responds that this is "mere fantasy." If such an Inquisitor existed, Alyosha says, he would not be burning Jesus to protect the masses but to protect the system of control that satisfies his own lust for power. Ivan disagrees, presenting the Inquisitor as a lonely superman among weak-willed men:

> It is no great moral blessedness to attain perfection and freedom, if at the same time one gains the conviction that millions of God's creatures have been created as a mockery, that they will never be capable of using their freedom, that these poor rebels can never turn into giants to complete the tower, that it was not for such geese that the great idealist dreamt his dream of harmony.[54]

Here, Ivan sounds like the older Nietzsche, who lost faith in the people around him to achieve their full creative potential and rise above historical ideology. Though Ivan reassures his brother that "there is strength to endure everything," his frustration soon drives him mad.

In 1922 German novelist Herman Hesse (1877–1962) wrote that *The Brothers Karamazov* foretells and explains the downfall of Europe, which he defines as the yearning of a tired civilization for a "return home to the mother, a turning back to Asia, to the source."[55] European man, he says, is striving to rise above the historical ideologies of the Western Church and rediscover the primeval demiurge of ancient religions — a creative life-force that exists beyond good and evil:

> The urgent appeal ever rings out from these Karamazovs for the symbol after which their spirit is striving, a God who is also a Devil. Dostoevsky's "Russian man" is penetrated by that symbol.

The God-Devil, the primeval Demiurgus, he who was there from the beginning who alone stands the other side of the forbidden, who knows neither day nor night, neither good nor evil. He is the Nothingness and the All.[56]

Hesse acknowledges that there will be much resistance to a reevaluation of religious values in Western civilization. A few people will welcome a new beginning, but many will cling to the Church's traditional morality of good and evil and some, like the third brother, Dmitri Karamazov, will be violently irrational.

The Treaty of Versailles, which officially ended the Great War in June 1919, politically and economically crippled Germany. Within the year, critics like British economist John Maynard Keynes were arguing that the treaty would only perpetuate further conflict in Europe. Three and a half years later, Hesse wrote that the transformation of European culture was well underway, creating temporary chaos: "Already half Europe, at all events half Eastern Europe, is on the road to Chaos. In a state of drunken illusion she is reeling into the abyss and, as she reels, she sings a drunken hymn such as Dmitri Karamazov sang. The insulted citizen laughs that song to scorn, the saint and seer hear it with tears."[57]

Herman Hesse: The Journey to the East

Hesse had been skeptical about the war from the beginning. In November 1914, after he was found unfit for military service, he wrote to a friend that, although the war might be "worthwhile" for creating a "spirit of unity and self-sacrifice in Germany," he couldn't help thinking that "those who are rotting in the woods, those whose cities, villages, fields, and aspirations have been ravaged and destroyed do not agree."[58] In the following years, the author actively campaigned for peace above nationalism. In October 1915, he wrote to a local newspaper to remind the citizens of Germany of their "supranational obligations" — obligations to their fellow man that supersede obligations to country.[59]

Hesse's wartime dissent cost him many friends, and his literary work was blacklisted in Germany. At the same time, the writer struggled with a mentally ill spouse, who would later be committed to a sanatorium. By June 1917, his nerves were so frayed that he was unable to write, and could only idly speculate that "by the time my friends and the world at large begin pestering me with questions and reproaches, I shall probably have something to show them."[60] The novelist was trying to create his own vision of the future, but he needed time and perspective. In the summer of 1918, he formulated his thoughts in an essay entitled "War and Peace," which outlined his hopes for the future of Europe:

Like all human progress, the love of peace must come from knowledge.... Where that supreme knowledge is present (as in Jesus, Buddha, Plato, or Lao-tzu), a threshold is crossed beyond which miracles begin. There war and enmity cease. We can read of it in the New Testament and in the discourses of Gautama. Anyone who is so inclined can laugh at it and call it "introverted rubbish," but to one who has experienced it his enemy becomes a brother, death becomes birth, disgrace honor, calamity good fortune.[61]

In 1919, Hesse's fifth novel, *Demian*, was published pseudonymously. Like his earlier novels, *Demian* was a spiritual autobiography in the tradition of Goethe's *Wilhelm Meister* — a coming-of-age story of a rebellious youth who is trying to follow his unique destiny instead of following the crowd. Unlike the earlier novels, *Demian* was specifically tailored to the disillusioned youth of Germany in the aftermath of the Great War. The hero of Hesse's novel is

Emil Sinclair, a teenager whose innocent world is shattered when a classmate named Demian prompts him to question the meaning of the biblical story of Cain and Abel. Demian tells Sinclair, "Such age-old stories are always true but they aren't always properly recorded and aren't always given correct interpretations." Echoing Nietzsche, he suggests that the real story is that "the strong man slew a weaker one."[62] Because of his rebellious nature, Sinclair begins to think of himself as a descendant of Cain, and he comes to believe that his spiritual journey is not a matter of getting rid of this mark, but of understanding it. Sinclair knows that he is not evil, but also that he is not "good" in the traditional Christian sense. Therefore, he is receptive to Demian's proposal that such values are arbitrary, and that "we ought to consider everything sacred, the entire world, not merely this artificially separated half!"[63]

As Sinclair begins to look beyond good and evil, Demian removes himself from the younger man's life, forcing him to search within himself for his true path. When the two friends are finally reunited, on the eve of the German declaration of war against Russia, they plan to become soldiers, convinced that the war is the means to a better future: "It will reveal the bankruptcy of present-day ideals, there will be a sweeping away of Stone Age gods. The world, as it is now, wants to die, wants to perish — and it will."[64] Sinclair muses that it is the duty of the children of Cain to "arouse fear and hatred and drive men out of confining idyl into more dangerous reaches."[65] Demian concurs — he doesn't look forward to committing acts of violence against his fellow man, but he regards violence as a necessary "evil," leading to an eventual rebirth: "You will see, Sinclair, that this is only the beginning. Perhaps it will be a very big war, a war on a gigantic scale. But that, too, will only be the beginning. The new world has begun and the new world will be terrible for those clinging to the old."[66]

Through Sinclair's story, Hesse provided hope for postwar Germany. Whereas many Western thinkers opined that the progress of Western civilization had been halted or reversed by the war, Hesse regarded it as an evolutionary step. In 1922 he wrote about his frustration with two types of postwar poets: decadent imitators of the old German idealists and poets of chaos, who "feel, or seem to feel, that there must first be disintegration and chaos, the bitter way must first be gone to the end, before new settings, new forms and new affinities are created."[67] Hesse himself preferred the notion of a gradual change, requiring the discipline of patience rather than nostalgia or despair. After *Demian*, he turned toward the teachings of the Far East, finding there the perfect example of his prescriptive discipline. Hesse's subsequent novel, *Siddhartha* (1922), reformulated Indian philosophy for the modern age. That same year, T.S. Eliot encountered Hesse's essay "The Downfall of Europe," and wrote to Hesse that he was eager to introduce his work to the British public.[68]

Carl Jung and James George Frazer: Symbols of Transformation

In 1917, after the death of his father and the mental breakdown of his wife, Herman Hesse had undergone psychoanalysis with a pupil of psychologist Carl Jung (1875–1961). The experience was a major inspiration for Hesse's novel *Demian*, which illustrates the Jungian concept of "symbols of transformation." In the novel, Emil Sinclair produces a number of visionary paintings, in which the central figure morphs from Demian to Demian's mother to Beatrice (Dante's symbol of the Eternal Feminine) to Sinclair himself and, finally, to a bird escaping from an egg. Each vision brings Sinclair one step closer to realizing his own symbolic rebirth.

The symbolic mother figure, according to Jung, represents the individual's desire for personal growth: the child seeks, through union with the opposite-sex parent, to be figuratively reborn. Jung argues that the child's sexual longing is the key to individuation and self-realization. Therefore, he says, psychology should try to help people understand their desires as symbols of transformation.

With his 1912 book *Psychology of the Unconscious*, Jung departed from the teachings of his mentor Sigmund Freud. The key difference between Freud and Jung, at that point, lay in their understanding of the human libido. For Freud, the term designated the primitive instinct for sexual creation; for Jung — who had thoroughly absorbed the writings of Goethe and Nietzsche — libido was a more all-encompassing kind of creative impulse, psychic as well as sexual. Libido, Jung teaches, is in fact the key to understanding mankind's collective spiritual and intellectual development. As human consciousness evolved, he says, man began using dream imagery in an effort to understand his creative powers beyond the sexual. The symbols were overtly sexual — representing life-giving feminine fertility and masculine potency — but they also represented powers of creation which were confusing to primitive man. These symbols formed the basis of ancient mythology and man's earliest attempts at religion.

Jung's combination of psychology, ethnology, mythology and religion was partly inspired by *The Golden Bough: A Study in Magic and Religion* (first edition 1890; third edition 1906–1915), an enormously influential work by Scottish anthropologist Sir James George Frazer (1854–1951). Frazer's work examines beliefs and practices common to a diversity of ancient cultures, supporting the author's hypothesis that all world religions have a common ancestor in the fertility cults of the Middle East. Many of those cults feature an androgynous god-figure–Osiris (in ancient Egypt), Tammus (in ancient Sumerian-Babylonian civilization), Adonis (in Greece) and Attis (in Rome) — whose virility is connected to the fertility of the land. Frazer theorizes that those "dying gods" are part of a continuous tradition that ultimately produced Jesus Christ.

According to ancient myths, the autumnal deaths of the god-figures Tammus, Adonis and Attis brought infertility to the land and suffering to the people who lived off of it. The resurrection of those same gods renewed life in the springtime, when religious festivals were held to honor their return. Frazer proposes that the Christian Church "adapted" these myths "for the sake of winning souls to Christ."[69] He views Christ's resurrection as the latest incarnation of a symbolic tale older than the Hebrew culture itself, and Jesus as the archetypal "dying god" of ancient civilization. This suggests that the message of early Christianity is an expression of the cyclical nature of existence, from birth to death to rebirth.

Jung argues that "medieval" Christianity diverged from the message of the ancient fertility cults in one very significant aspect. It vilified the creative powers of the libido, teaching that "the power of the good and reasonable ruling the world wisely is threatened by the chaotic primitive power of passion; therefore passion must be exterminated."[70] Jung suggests that this may have been a necessary step for mankind, leading human thought to independence. However, this having been accomplished, he says that modern man has outgrown the effectiveness of the religious construct of good and evil. Modern man has achieved intellectual independence and now needs, like the hero of Herman Hesse's novel, to be figuratively reborn:

> In the past two thousand years, Christianity has done its work and has erected barriers of repression, which protect us from the sight of our own "sinfulness." The elementary emotions of the libido have come to be unknown to us, for they are carried on in the unconscious; therefore, the belief which combats them has become hollow and empty.[71]

Jung does not propose that Western civilization dispense with Christianity, only that we modify our way of thinking about it: "The stumbling block is the unhappy combination of *religion and morality*. That must be overcome."[72] He argues that the medieval ideal of "life for the sake of death" should be gradually "replaced by a natural conception of life."[73] In other words, we must recognize symbols as symbols, in order to restore the psychological efficacy of religion. Jung says, "I think *belief should be replaced by understanding*; then we would keep the beauty of the symbol, but still remain free from the depressing results of submission to belief. This would be the psychoanalytic cure for belief and disbelief."[74]

The Mythical Method

Through his "analytical psychology," Jung attempts to help troubled patients understand the unconscious symbols in their own lives. In *Psychology of the Unconscious*, Jung provides the example of a 20-year-old woman named Miss Frank Miller, who uses symbolic poetry as a means of self-analysis. Her writings begin, after an exhausting tour of Europe, with ruminations on the serenity of the sea. Jung suggests that it is an apt symbol of her introversion: she is submerging herself in the inner world of ideas, preparing for rebirth — like Zarathustra descending into his cave. In subsequent writings, Miss Miller makes allusions to the pre-Socratic cosmologist Anaxagoras, the German metaphysician Leibniz (1646–1716), Milton's *Paradise Lost*, Edmond Rostand's *Cyrano de Bergerac* and the Book of Job — all of which figure into Jung's explanation that she is confronting questions about her own natural creativity, striving toward a particular kind of transformation. Like Demian, she is coming of age, discovering her own unique place in the world. Jung refers to this as "the sublimation of the infantile personality, or, expressed mythologically, a sacrifice and rebirth of the infantile hero."[75] In his book *Modern Man in Search of a Soul* (1933), he elaborates on the individual's use of pre-existing mythology to come to terms with this transformation:

> The primordial experience is the source of his creativeness; it cannot be fathomed, and therefore requires mythological imagery to give it form.... It is like a whirlwind that seizes everything within reach and, by carrying it aloft, assumes a visible shape. Since the particular expression can never exhaust the possibilities of the vision, but fall far short of it in richness or content, the poet must have at his disposal a huge store of materials if he is to communicate even a few of his intimations. What is more, he must resort to an imagery that is difficult to handle and full of contradictions in order to express the weird paradoxicality of his vision.[76]

T.S. Eliot may have begun to grasp this truth as early as the fall of 1918, when he praised James Joyce's avant-garde novel *Ulysses*. Joyce's work imposes the loose narrative framework of Homer's *Odyssey* onto a contemporary stream-of-consciousness narrative about a young boy coming of age in Dublin. Years later, Eliot articulated his thoughts on the significance of this artistic form: "It is simply a way of controlling, of ordering, of giving a shape and significance to the immense panorama of futility and anarchy which is contemporary history.... Instead of narrative method, we may now use the mythical method. It is, I seriously believe, a step toward making the modern world possible for art."[77]

Arthurian Legend

Just prior to his nervous breakdown in the fall of 1921, Eliot found a similar framework for his own personal panorama of futility and anarchy, in Jessie Weston's 1920 book *From Ritual to Romance.* Weston's work interprets the legend of King Arthur and the quest for the Holy Grail through Frazer's belief that ancient fertility cults and Christianity are part of a single tradition. This interpretation leads one to conclude that the medieval romances, with their emphasis on the Christian virtue of chastity, are at odds with the legend as it originated in the fertility cults. Eliot, whose own personal transformation was characterized by inner conflict between sexual repression and intuition of cosmic unity, could appreciate the contradiction.

The Arthurian tradition in English literature is usually traced back to Sir Thomas Malory's *Le Morte d'Arthur* (1485), a collection of traditional folk tales that had already existed for centuries. In the Welsh tradition, Arthur was a Christian warrior who helped to lead the rebellion against Saxon invaders on the British Isles around 5th century B.C.E. Outside of Wales, he was called the first king of the Britons, and legend has it that his rule restored the land to its earlier dignity, peace and prosperity.

For hundreds of years, Arthur's legend spread throughout England, Germany and France, where it was recorded in fragments. Different tales introduced Arthur's Knights of the Round Table: Sir Gawain was first mentioned in William of Malmesbury's *Acts of the Kings of the English* (c. 1125); Sir Perceval appeared in the German epic *Parzival* (early 13th century); Sir Lancelot and his son Sir Galahad seem to be products of the 13th-century French romances of Chretien de Troyes and Robert de Boron.[78] These knights, despite their personal flaws, maintained the safety and security of Arthur's kingdom until they were lured away by the quest for the Holy Grail. According to legend, the cup — used by Christ at the Last Supper — fell into the hands of Joseph of Arimathea, who brought it to the Vales of Avalon (future site of Glastonbury) in southern England, where it has remained hidden ever since. For him who finds it, the Grail promises eternal life.

In Malory's telling, the quest begins when a mysterious hermit notices an empty chair at the Round Table. The hermit prophesies that "he that shall sit there is unborn and ungotten, and this same year he shall be gotten that shall sit there in that Siege Perilous [the Perilous Seat], and he shall win the Sangreal."[79] Soon after, Sir Lancelot and Lady Elaine (a descendant of Joseph of Arimathea) bear a son named Galahad. When Galahad comes of age he is knighted — exactly 450 years after the Passion, on Pentecost. He then sits in the Perilous Seat, and the Knights of the Round Table share a fleeting vision of the Grail. Sir Gawain, unable to get a good look at it because it is so luminous, vows to seek it out: "Never shall I return again unto the court till I have seen it more openly than it hath been seen here."[80] Many of his fellow knights make the same pledge, despite the warning of King Arthur that it will destroy the bond of the Knights of the Round Table.

Before the knights leave, Queen Guenever remembers the words of the hermit: "He that is not clean of his sins he shall not see the mysteries of our Lord Jesus Christ."[81] As promised, the quest proves to be a test of spiritual purity for each of the knights. Sir Perceval travels through a marshy waste land, where he meets the ailing 300-year-old King Evelake. The king's followers believe that Perceval can heal the king and restore the land, but the chaste knight is led astray by a seductive woman, whom he later calls "a master fiend of hell."[82] Several other knights face temptations in the same form. Their greatest collective weakness seems to be lust. Only Galahad is able to complete the quest. He too wanders through a waste land, but he eventually restores its vitality by healing the maimed King Pelles. In this moment, Christ appears to Galahad in the likeness of a child, and Galahad vanishes from the mortal world.

Alfred, Lord Tennyson (1809–1892) retold the tale in his epic poem *Idylls of the King*, maintaining emphasis on the Christian virtue of chastity. In Tennyson's version, Sir Perceval is the main storyteller; having given up his knighthood for a monastic life, he recounts the tale to a fellow monk. He remembers the day when Galahad sat on the Siege Perilous: Merlin warned him that "no man could sit but he should lose himself," and Galahad responded, echoing the words of Christ from the Gospel of Matthew, "If I lose myself, I save myself!"[83] Galahad did just that, though his fellow knights succumbed to temptation. Perceval himself fell victim to despair, haunted by the warning of King Arthur:

> ...The dark warning of our King,
> That most of us would follow wandering fires,
> Came like a driving gloom across my mind.
> Then every evil word I had spoken once,
> And every evil thought I had thought of old,
> And every evil deed I ever did,
> Awoke and cried, "This Quest is not for thee."
> And lifting up mine eyes, I found myself
> Alone, and in a land of sand and thorns,
> And I was thirsty even unto death....[84]

Perceval claims he saw visions of an apple tree, a woman and a house, and a vision of the Rapture, in which Jesus Christ appeared to embrace him. All of these things crumbled into dust, convincing him of the futility of his quest: "Lo, if I find the Holy Grail itself / And touch it, it will crumble into dust."[85] A hermit finally explains that he lacks the true humility of Galahad.

When the knights return to Camelot, King Arthur explains that he avoided going on the quest himself because a king "must guard / that which he rules" and "may not wander from the allotted field / but his work be done." Only then, he says, can he welcome visions of the earth that "seems not earth," the light that "is not light," the air that "is not air" and "moments when he feels he cannot die." Perceval admits that he does not fully understand the king's words.[86] Arthur understands things that Perceval himself cannot.

In *The Golden Bough* Frazer writes that ancient kings were sometimes revered "not merely as priests, that is, as intercessors between man and god, but as themselves gods, able to bestow upon their subjects and worshippers those blessings which are commonly supposed to be beyond the reach of mortals."[87] Carl Jung makes the same observation, alluding to the mythology of Indra, the Hindu god of weather and war, whose marriage to Urvara (literally "the fertile land") guaranteed a bountiful spring harvest in that god's chosen land. "In a similar way," Jung says, "the occupancy of a country by the king was understood as marriage with the ploughed land. Similar representations must have prevailed in Europe as well."[88] Such kings were deemed responsible for changes in nature — the fertility of the land, the presence or absence of sun and rain. Some cultures believed that a king could exert power over nature through "definite acts of will" (Frazer calls this "sympathetic magic"), while others simply believed that the vitality of the king was inextricably linked to the vitality of nature, through a kind of "homeopathic magic." For this reason, Frazer says that the king may be regarded as "the lineal successor of the old magician or medicine-man," bridging the gap between ancient fertility cults and medieval Christianity as the culture "tends gradually to exchange the practice of magic for the priestly functions of prayer and sacrifice."[89]

From Ritual to Romance

In *From Ritual to Romance*, Jessie Weston writes that ancient fertility cults relied not on kings but on "mysterious rituals" to appease Mother Nature and ensure the revival of nature in the springtime. In India, for example, worshippers performed a ritualistic sword dance intended to stimulate the reproductive energies of the god Indra. Weston explains, "Dance holds a position equivalent to that which, in more advanced communities, is assigned to Prayer."[90] We find comparable rituals in the Greek festival of Dionysus, and in the nature cults of ancient Europe: the spirit of vegetation is sometimes burned in effigy; Dionysus is dismembered and consumed; Adonis is dismembered and thrown into water. Through this symbolic sacrifice, these gods of fertility are reborn, and their rebirth stimulates the regeneration of the land. The ritual suggests that if the god does not die abruptly the land will die slowly, entering a semi-permanent season of wither.

Jessie Weston finds the same symbolism in Arthurian legend, in which the prolonged illness of King Pelles, the "fisher king," is deemed responsible for the infertility of his lands. Only the Holy Grail — that cup blessed by the "dying god" who is resurrected in the spring — can restore life. In this Christianized version of the myth, magic gives way to prayer and sacrifice, but Weston argues that the key symbol — the Holy Grail — predates Christianity: "Students of the Grail literature have been too prone to treat the question on the Christian basis alone, oblivious of the fact that Christianity did no more than take over, and adapt to its own use, a symbolism already endowed with a deeply rooted prestige and importance."[91] According to her, the symbol of the sacred life-giving cup has its origin in the Tarot, an ancient system of magic symbols which the Egyptians used "to predict the rise and fall of the waters [of the Nile River] which brought fertility to the land."[92] In the ancient Tarot system, the Cup and the Lance were prominent symbols of the female and male elements of reproductive energy. It follows that the Holy Grail may be regarded as a symbol of the Eternal Feminine through which the hero seeks transformation or rebirth.

One questions remains: Which incarnation of the "dying god" myth — Christian or pagan — should the modern-day hero embrace? Helen Gardner, one of T.S. Eliot's most perceptive critics, writes that "there appears to be something in the Grail legend, as in Arthurian material generally, that resists ordering of plot. The 'meanings' are always overflowing the narrative and overwhelming the design."[93] The same might be said of much of Eliot's early poetry. Perhaps for that reason Eliot regarded Weston's interpretation of the Grail legend as a continuous tradition "which has never found final and supreme artistic expression"[94] as an appropriate template for his own tangled heap of recurring images and contradictory ideas.

Breakthrough

In November 1921, Eliot traveled to Lausanne, Switzerland, to be treated by Dr. Roger Vittoz (1863–1925), a student of Jungian psychology who had been recommended to Eliot by his friend Ottoline Morrell. According to Vittoz, all nervous disorders stem from the patient's inability to reconcile the activities of the conscious mind (reason, judgment, willpower) and the unconscious mind (originating ideas and sensations). In his 1911 book *Treatment of the Psychoneuroses by the Rehabilitation of Cerebral Control*, he writes that most nervous persons overemphasize the subconscious and are "troubled by a feeling of being only half awake, as if they were living in a kind of semi-dream state which they cannot break out of, a condition which can cause significant anxiety."[95] This reads like a diagnosis of Eliot's J. Alfred Prufrock — the poet's literary persona in 1911. Over time, Vittoz says, the symptoms increase until "patients no longer suffer from a vague sense of unease but rather from a very pronounced sense of confusion, where ideas become all mixed up, and have no logical sequence or direction."[96] We find this level of confusion in the voice(s) of Eliot's *The Waste Land*, much of which was written in 1921 while the author was under the care of Vittoz. Eliot's letters from his time in Lausanne offer few details about the treatment he received, but he does stipulate that the doctor is not a psychoanalyst.[97] Eliot's biographer Lyndall Gordon writes that the doctor's "cure was to concentrate on a simple word with a view to 'calm' and 'control.'" She adds that "for Vittoz, simplicity was based on religious belief."[98] Vivienne Eliot's biographer Carole Seymour-Jones says that "the psychiatrist urged his patients to follow the model of Christ, to take a path of sainthood and self-control."[99] Eliot could not help turning the experience into art. In early November, he wrote to a friend that he was channeling his thoughts into a scatter-shot poem.

During this period of withdrawal from normal activity, Eliot came to understand his nervous breakdown as the result of a lifelong "*aboulie.*" Vittoz defines the term as "a fear of wanting anything," caused when "patients believe that making any kind of effort is painful, and every action results in anxiety."[100] Eliot's fears had finally caused him to seal himself off from the world. He had become like a ghost among the living, reserving all thought and emotion for the imaginary world that existed only in his mind and through his writing. Dr. Vittoz helped him to return to the everyday world by teaching him how to control his thoughts.

That same month Eliot wrote to his brother, "The great thing I am trying to learn is how to use all my energy without waste, to be *calm* when there is nothing to be gained by worry, and to concentrate without effort."[101] A few days later, he wrote to another friend about his progress: "I was aware that the principal trouble was that I have been losing power of concentration and attention, as well as becoming a prey to habitual worry and dread of the future.... I *think* I am getting over that."[102] Around the same time, he finished his first draft of *The Waste Land*—which charts his progress by cobbling together poetic fragments from fellow intellectual journeymen, past and present. The poem is a portrait of a man trapped inside his own mind. For Eliot, writing the poem was also a way out.

The Waste Land: The Burial of the Dead (Part I)

Eliot's first draft of *The Waste Land* was entitled *He Do the Police in Different Voices*, and it began with a lengthy narrative about a group of lascivious barflies on a wild night in the red light district of Dickensian London. On the advice of Ezra Pound, Eliot began instead with what might have originally appeared to be thoughts of a sobering dawn, a reawakening to mundane life. It is spring and the lilacs are in bloom, but for the speaker there is nothing new under the sun — these false signs of new life are only painful reminders of the past.

Eliot remembers his time in Germany, before the outbreak of the war, when he met the Austrian countess Marie Larisch, who shared memories of her childhood, when she stayed with her cousin in the mountains. She also told him about her most famous relative, King Ludwig II of Bavaria — an eccentric ruler, alternately known as the "mad king" and the "fairy-tale king," who drowned in Starnberger Lake in 1886. In her biography, published in 1913, the countess writes that Ludwig's ghost once appeared to her mother, Empress Elisabeth of Austria. Dripping wet and hung with seaweed, the apparition warned Elisabeth of two impending deaths: the death of her sister by fire and the comparatively quick and painless death of Elisabeth herself. Elisabeth's sister died in a house fire in Paris in 1897. Elisabeth was assassinated in 1898 in Switzerland as she was boarding a steamboat on the shores of Lake Geneva, known to the French as Lac Leman.[103] T.S. Eliot found himself on these same shores in the fall of 1921, ruminating on fears of "death by water."

"Death by Water" is arguably the central theme of the poem. Water is both the potential cure for the sterility of the waste land and the means of baptizing the poet into a new religious life. For the speaker, however, this symbolic death and destruction seems to be a source of fear rather than hope. Eliot reworks an old poem, "The Death of Saint Narcissus," to convey his fear of transformation. In that poem, the title character underwent a startling metamorphosis from tree to fish to a young girl "caught in the woods by a drunken old man." Finally, he became a "dancer to God," who welcomed the burning arrows with a distinctly sexual satisfaction and ended "with the shadow in his mouth."[104] Eliot could not have provided a more apt illustration of Carl Jung's statement that, in depictions of martyrdom, "it is our *own repressed and unrecognized desires which fester like arrows in our flesh.*"[105] The title character's desire is to transcend his sexuality and his humanity: Narcissus becomes both male and female, like the "dying god" of the fertility cults, and he welcomes the arrows as the method of transcendence.

In this section, the poet also refers to "roots that clutch."[106] With this image, he seems to be following the martyr into the afterlife. Roots and branches are part of a specific mythical setting — the "sacred wood" from which Aeneas retrieves the golden bough. The existing epigraph to *The Waste Land* makes explicit reference to the Cumaean Sybil, who receives the golden bough from Aeneas in exchange for passage into the underworld. In Virgil's tale, the Sybil is a tragic character — she records her visions of the future on oak leaves, but the wind always blows them away, leaving her with only fragmented knowledge. The epigraph of Eliot's poem comes from the *Satyricon* of Petronius, which gives us an image of the Sybil in a cage, wishing for death.

Eliot soon turns from the sacred wood to a desert setting, in a passage that is reminiscent of the prophecies of the Old Testament figures Ezekiel (whom God repeatedly addresses as "son of man") and Isaiah, who sees a vision of the kingdom of God on earth:

> Behold, a king shall reign in righteousness, and princes shall rule in judgment. And a man shall be as an hiding place from the wind, and a covert from the tempest; as rivers of water in a dry place, as the shadow of a great rock in a weary land.... [Isaiah 32: 1–2]

"There is shadow under this red rock,"[107] Eliot says, but the shadow induces fear. Jung says that the shadow represents the *dark half* of man's soul — "the pathological aspect of life."[108] He urges us to strive for understanding of our dark half, rather than responding with fear, because "the shadow belongs to the light as the evil belongs to the good, and vice versa."[109] Eliot is struggling to integrate the shadow into the light, the evil into the good, but he hesitates at the crucial moment, when he shows us "fear in a handful of dust." Throughout "The Burial of the Dead," Eliot seems to be struggling with the Christian belief in the resurrection of the body into eternal life. His title is a reference to funeral rites from the Anglican Book of Common Prayer, which stipulates that the bodies of the deceased shall be committed to the ground, "earth to earth, ashes to ashes, dust to dust, in sure and certain hope of resurrection to eternal life, through our Lord Jesus Christ."

The next passage makes repeated reference to Wagner's opera *Tristan and Isolde*. The speaker is confronted by the "hyacinth girl," who appears "arms full" and "hair wet" like a confused vision of "la figlia che piange" and the ghost of King Ludwig. His response: "I could not / Speak, and my eyes failed."[110] The sight leaves him, like Tristan, desolate and empty as the sea.

The Waste Land: The Burial of the Dead (Part II)

Despite this initial failure, there is still a future for the speaker. We see it in the Tarot cards of Madame Sosostris. The name (spelled differently) also appears in Aldous Huxley's early novel *Crome Yellow* (1921), in which a group of eccentric modern artists gather to exchange ideas at a country manor called Crome. Huxley's main character, Denis Stone, is a self-conscious intellectual gleefully characterized as a walking contradiction: "Wild inside; raging, writhing — yes, 'writhing' was the word, writhing with desire. But outwardly he was hopelessly tame; outwardly — baa, baa, baa."[111] Denis is socially maladjusted, able to communicate only through other people's words. He says, "Things somehow seem more real and vivid when one can apply somebody else's ready-made phrase about them."[112] In the end, Denis simply cannot get out from under his books long enough to get a foothold in the real world, and so he imagines himself like a tragic figure in a work of fiction:

> In the world of ideas everything was clear; in life all was obscure, embroiled. Was it surprising that one was miserable, horribly unhappy? Denis came to a halt in front of the bench, and as he asked this last question he stretched out his arms and stood for an instant in an attitude of crucifixion, then let them fall to his sides.[113]

Toward the end of the novel, the group of artists participates in a carnival, and the incorrigible Mr. Scogan — a character allegedly modeled on Bertrand Russell[114] — assumes the role of gypsy fortune teller. Dressed up "like the Bohemian hag of Frith's Derby Day," he calls himself "Sesostris, the Sorceress of Ecbatana." Carnival-goers soon learn that Sesostris *never* makes good predictions about the future.

In *The Waste Land* the fortune teller looks into the speaker's future by using a "wicked pack of cards." Some of the cards he/she produces are authentic members of the Tarot deck and some are Eliot's own invention. (In the endnotes, Eliot confesses that he knows no more about Tarot than Mr. Scogan does.) The first card is the "drowned Phoenician Sailor," indicative of the speaker's fear of death by water. The aside — *Those are pearls that were his eyes* — comes from Shakespeare's *The Tempest*. The words are sung by Ariel as a lamentation for shipwrecked sailors in their watery graves:

> Full fathom five thy father lies;
> Of his bones are coral made;
> Those are pearls that were his eyes:
> Nothing of him that doth fade
> But doth suffer a sea-change
> Into something rich and strange.
> Sea-nymphs hourly ring his knell [I.ii].

The other false cards, which seem to represent something personal for the poet, are the Belladonna (symbolic of a troubling woman), the one-eyed merchant and a blank card (both symbolic of limited "vision"). The authentic cards are the man with three staves, the Wheel and the Hanged Man. Jessie Weston identifies the man with three staves as the Pope, who "shows the influence of the Orthodox Eastern Faith."[115] Eliot notes that he associates the Pope with the Fisher King, and the Hanged Man with the dying god of Frazer.[116] The Wheel is a more distinctly eastern symbol. Literary critic A.N. Dwivedi notes its repeated use in the *Bhagavad Gita*, in which it stands for birth, death and rebirth — the "eternally decreed pattern of suffering."[117] Eliot's use of the symbol, Dwivedi says, is consistent with that in Hindu mythology.

Significantly, the Wheel is part of the speaker's fortune while the Hanged Man is not. For that reason, Sesostris advises him to "fear death by water" — for him, the death will only perpetuate the eternally decreed pattern of suffering rather than provide an escape. In response to this revelation, the speaker becomes despondent — focusing on a mental image of the aimless souls in Dante's *Inferno*: "I see crowds of people, walking round in a ring."[118] This mental image is duplicated in Eliot's everyday world when he sees a crowd of workers streaming across London Bridge and down King William Street into the City on a winter morning. Again, he echoes Dante: "I had not thought death had undone so many."[119]

Jung's patient Miss Frank Miller was also haunted by images of European cities, which symbolized her own overwhelming anxiety. Jung writes:

> We know from psychopathology that certain mental disturbances exist which are first manifested by the individuals shutting themselves off slowly, more and more, from reality and sinking into their phantasies, during which process, in proportion as the reality loses its hold, the inner world gains in reality and determining power. This process leads to a certain point (which varies with the individual) when the patients suddenly become more or less conscious of their separation from reality. The event which then enters is the pathological excitation: that is to say, the patients begin to turn towards the environment, with diseased view (to be sure) which, however, still represent the compensating, although unsuccessful, attempt at transference.[120]

Dr. Vittoz elaborates:

> They seek out the dream state, and are soon unable to get out of it, reluctant even to try since the effort becomes so difficult. They start living more and more inside themselves, distancing themselves from the outside world; and this results in a kind of unhealthy, self-centered egoism, which affects their entire behavior, and makes them such a burden to other people. They lose all contact with the people and things around them, they cannot see further than the thick veil which crowds their minds; they have no sense of "self," and often end up hating themselves, without being able to escape from their own mental prison.... The return to normalcy can only be achieved after a kind of painful rupture has taken place, and patients are often fearful of the process.[121]

Unable to cope with normalcy, Eliot returns to the world of his imagination at the close of "The Burial of the Dead." Through allusions to other works, the poet refutes the notion of resurrection with a morbid image from John Webster's *The White Devil*, in which a dog unearths a corpse. That, Eliot's poem indicates, is the only form of resurrection that a fallen soldier can expect. In the final line, with a quote from Baudelaire, the poet not-so-gently reminds the reader — *my twin, my brother* — that the same applies to us.

The Waste Land: A Game of Chess / In the Cage

The original title of Eliot's second section of *The Waste Land* was "In the Cage" — a reference to Henry James's short story of the same name. The story is about an unnamed London telegraphist who lives vicariously through the imagined affairs of strangers she encounters at work. Though exhilarated by the world of her imagination, she ultimately embraces a comparatively humdrum, real-life romance. Eliot later retitled the section "A Game of Chess," apparently preferring the visual metaphor of Thomas Middleton's play *Women Beware Women*, which symbolizes a ruthless power struggle in which sex is the main weapon. The completed section juxtaposes modern dialogue — such as we might find in a Henry James novel — and Shakespearean imagery.

Its first line mimics a description of the exquisite Queen Cleopatra from *Antony and Cleopatra* (Act 2, Scene 2) and segues into a description of Princess Imogene's bedchamber in *Cymbeline* (Act 2, Scene 2), and her reference to the rape of Princess Philomel, taken from Ovid's *Metamorphoses* (Book 4). The entire passage draws us into an ancient, fairy tale world of enchanting women, who are at once powerful and tragic. In his endnotes, Eliot says that "all the women are one woman."[122] For the poet, this may well have seemed true at the time. The invisible figure who dominates this section is almost certainly inspired by his wife Vivienne, and it is presumably her voice that sharply disrupts the enchanting world of imagination:

> "My nerves are bad to-night. Yes, bad. Stay with me.
> Speak to me. Why do you never speak. Speak.
> What are you thinking of? What thinking? What?
> I never know what you are thinking. Think."[123]

A year after publication, Vivienne told friends that she felt her identity had become inextricably intertwined with *The Waste Land* in the past year.[124] This is nowhere more apparent than in "A Game of Chess," in which her voice antagonizes the poet, as he tries desperately to return to his interior world of confused symbols ("I remember / Those are pearls that were his eyes"[125]).

The third and final passage in "A Game of Chess" reads like a scene from a much more modern play. Similar to the opening passage of "The Burial of the Dead" which was excised by Ezra Pound, it is a snapshot of the mundane everyday world of Eliot's postwar London. A group of friends converse at the local pub about one woman's tryst with a recently returned soldier of war. She says she hasn't been the same ever since she had an abortion. This world, too, is interrupted. The bartender repeatedly makes his last call, trying to push them out the door: "HURRY UP PLEASE ITS TIME." As the group disperses, the poet conveys the sense that the time has already passed. The damage is done.

The repeated warning, however, suggests a beginning as well as an end. In Sir Edwin Arnold's *The Light of Asia*, on the night before the historical Buddha leaves "to wander lone, / Crownless and homeless, that the world be helped," his wife has a nightmare, and cries out in her sleep; "The time! The time is come!"[126] Her husband responds:

> My chariot shall not roll with bloody wheels
> From victory to victory, till earth
> Wears the red record of my name. I choose
> To tread its paths with patient, stainless feet,
> Making its dust my bed, its loneliest wastes
> My dwelling....[127]

Later, to a servant, he adds:

> For now the hour is come when I should quit
> This golden prison where my heart lives caged
> To find the truth; which henceforth I will seek,
> For all men's sake, until the truth be found.[128]

The following section of Eliot's poem, named for the historical Buddha's most famous sermon, finds the speaker at the beginning of his wandering. Here, it is worth repeating Stephen Spender's oft-quoted statement that he once overheard Eliot say that, while writing *The Waste Land*, he was seriously considering becoming a Buddhist.[129]

The Waste Land: The Fire Sermon

The third section of *The Waste Land* is entitled "The Fire Sermon," but the dominant imagery is of water — specifically, the water of the Thames River that runs through the heart of London. Like Ernest Dowson before him, Eliot evokes a dreary urban landscape, symbolic of moral decay. Whereas Dowson longed for an escape into "Hollow Lands, where just men and unjust / Find end of labor," Eliot imagines a continuous cycle of suffering beyond death. In an early draft of the section, Eliot repeats his sweeping indictment of the city's inhabitants: "London, your people is bound upon the wheel!"[130]

In earlier drafts, a sexually promiscuous character named Fresca served as the main example of moral decay. In the final draft, the Thames itself is the dominant symbol, reflecting the impurities of the city and its people. At the beginning of the section, the river appears polluted and stagnant. Eliot contrasts his image of the pollution-choked river with the glorious, free-flowing river of Edmund Spenser's "Prothalamion." In Spenser's poem, the Thames is a serene setting visited by mythic creatures; in Eliot's Waste Land, "the nymphs are departed."[131] The poet mourns the inevitability of death and decay, invoking the English metaphysical poet Andrew Marvell ("But at my back from time to time I hear") and Jacobean dramatist John Webster ("The rattle of the bones, and chuckle spread from ear to ear") on the shores of Lac Leman.[132]

This section is particularly dense with literary allusions. The action begins with a lone fisherman, no doubt intended to recall the Fisher King of the Grail mythology. The fisherman's thoughts — "Musing upon the king my brother's wreck / And on the king my father's death before him"[133] — are taken from Shakespeare's *The Tempest*, when the shipwrecked Ferdinand finds himself on an enchanted tropical island and believes that he is the only surviving member of the ship's crew. The setting of Eliot's poem — a "dull canal" plagued by rats and littered with bones — may be partly inspired by the Hades episode of Joyce's *Ulysses*.[134] These allusions juxtapose a magical, mythological world and Eliot's London, which is home to lascivious characters like Fresca and Sweeney. At the end of this passage, Sweeney is jokingly compared to the virtuous knight Perceval, by way of allusion to Paul Verlaine's sonnet "Parsifal." This is Eliot's way of pointing out the modern world's failure to live up to literary ideals.

Perhaps the most important allusion of all is a reference to Baudelaire. In his appended notes on *The Waste Land*, Eliot cites Baudelaire's poem "Les Sept Vieillards" ("The Seven Old Men") as the source of his key image of an "Unreal City," swarming with spectral figures. Just as Baudelaire's speaker is approached by a broken old man in yellow fog on the banks of the Seine, so Eliot's speaker is approached "under the brown fog of a winter noon" by "Mr.

Eugenides, the Smyrna merchant."[135] Literary critic Grover Smith suggests the meaning of this character: "The merchant is from a city in turmoil, another 'Unreal City,' perhaps connoting the decay of the Hellenic fertility cults and the Seven Churches of Asia."[136] In his endnotes, Eliot tells us that Mr. Eugenides is the one-eyed merchant of the Tarot reading, and "not wholly distinct from Ferdinand Prince of Naples."[137] This aligns him with the Fisher King.

Neither the king nor the knight, however, is the main focus of the poem. That honor goes to the blind prophet Tiresias, in whom the male and female characters, past and present, unite. His vision, Eliot tells us in the endnotes, is "the substance of the poem."[138] So what does Tiresias see? He sees the artless seduction of a bored typist (Fresca) by a crude, unattractive young man. When the deed is done, the woman puts a record on the gramophone, and the music — like a eulogy — drifts down the Thames, following the speaker from the city, where Mr. Eugenides dines with his "clients," to the north bank of the Thames River, where poor fishmongers work beside the white walls of the church of St. Magnus Martyr, and then down the polluted Thames, past the Tower of London, past Greenwich, past the Isle of Dogs, into obscurity.

The most significant sight, it seems, is that of St. Magnus Martyr on the banks of the Thames. The church, designed by Christopher Wren and completed in 1687, stands on the north side of London Bridge. Today, it is eclipsed by surrounding buildings, but at the time its spire would have loomed high above them. In *Landscape As Symbol in the Poetry of T.S. Eliot*, Nancy Duvall Hargrove contrasts the dazzling sight of St. Magnus Martyr with St. Mary Woolnoth, which was mentioned in "The Burial of the Dead."[139] The latter sits in the heart of the financial district, above the Moorgate tube stop and across the street from Lloyds Bank, where Eliot worked. Unlike St. Magnus Martyr, St. Mary Woolnoth appears boxy and unimposing. Whereas St. Mary Woolnoth serves only as a dreadful reminder of the beginning of the work day, St. Magnus Martyr inspires the poet with its "inexplicable splendour of Ionian white and gold."[140] It is one of the few bright spots in the dark, dingy city. In a June 1921 article in *The Dial*, Eliot had protested the proposed demolition of nineteen of the city's chapels, including St. Magnus Martyr: "To one who, like the present writer, passes his days in the City of London ... the loss of these towers, to meet the eye down a grimy lane, and of these empty naves, to receive the solitary visitor at noon from the dust and tumult of Lombard Street, will be irreparable and unforgotten."[141] Two months later, he wrote another public letter, contrasting the "natural disasters" of a "fine hot rainless spring" in the city with "towers and steeples of uncontaminated white." The tone of the letter is nearly apocalyptic, owing to its focus on ominous current events: "the comet, the sun-spots, the poisonous jellyfish and octopus at Margate" and the discovery of "a new form of influenza ... which leaves extreme dryness and a bitter taste in the mouth."[142]

Beyond St. Magnus Martyr, the speaker dwells only on the polluted river, imagining another harsh juxtaposition of beautiful myth and ugly reality: The three "Thames-daughters," counterparts of the Rhine-daughters in the disastrous conclusion of Wagner's *The Ring of the Nibelung*, are here defiled on the waters of the Thames. The first of the three daughters appears west of London, submitting to crude sex in a "narrow canoe" near Richmond and Kew. The second daughter appears near Moorgate, with an apologetic lover who promises a new start. The third daughter appears on Margate Sands, the seaside resort where Eliot escaped after his nervous breakdown. Like the poet, the third daughter "can connect / Nothing with nothing."[143] After much exploring, the sea remains desolate and empty.

The poet — in a moment of weakness — might have concluded this poem the way he concluded "The Love Song of J. Alfred Prufrock" in 1911. He has replaced Prufrock's mermaids with the Rhine-daughters, and "human voices" have destroyed the magic of them all. Like Prufrock, the speaker fears imminent death by water. In the final lines of this section, however, the imagery suddenly changes. Two new voices interrupt. The first voice — "To Carthage then I came"[144] — is that of St. Augustine. Carthage was the city of sin that nearly destroyed his soul. The second voice is that of the historical Buddha, taken from his "fire sermon." In his notes, Eliot tells us that "the collocation of these two representatives of eastern and western asceticism, as the culmination of this part of the poem, is not an accident." The poet seems to be trying to find his own religious path, favoring the traditions of Christianity and Buddhism.

The Waste Land: Death by Water

The fourth section of *The Waste Land*, "Death by Water," is a variation on the end of Eliot's "Dans le Restaurant," and a eulogy for the drowned Phoenician sailor referenced in "The Burial of the Dead." Literary critic James E. Miller has suggested that this section reveals the deepest personal meaning of the poem. Like several critics before him (beginning with John Peter in 1952), he sees this as Eliot's confession of love for his dead friend Jean Verdenal. Alternatively, we might associate the Phoenician sailor with St. Paul, who was reborn through baptism, and whose letter to the Romans is evoked by the phrase "Gentile or Jew." The poet humbly remembers that the Phoenician sailor was once "handsome and tall" as us, acknowledging that he too — like Perceval, like Paul — must lose himself in order to save himself.

Earlier drafts of the section made specific reference to the Dry Salvages, a cluster of dangerous rocks off the coast of Cape Ann, Massachusetts, where Eliot spent his childhood summers. Eliot compared the seafaring adventures of Gloucester fishermen with the mythic adventures of Odysseus/Ulysses. The poet speaks in the first person about a vision of "three women leaning forward, with white hair," who might be Homer's Sirens or Wagner's Rhine-daughters or Prufrock's mermaids. They leave the speaker with the feeling that "now, when I like, I can wake up and end the dream."[145] Eliot, it seems, was foreshadowing his own personal salvation.

Ezra Pound advised Eliot to trim this section drastically, leaving only the image of the Phoenician sailor, drowned in a whirlpool. The implication in the published poem is that there is no escape. With "What the Thunder Said," the fifth and final section of *The Waste Land*, Eliot finally surrenders — for better or worse.

The Waste Land: What the Thunder Said (Part I)

According to an October 1923 letter, the lines that Eliot himself liked best in the poem appear at the beginning of "What the Thunder Said," building upon a passage from "The Burial of the Dead." In that first section, the speaker found himself seeking shelter in the shadow of a great red rock. Now, at the end, he finds himself on a winding road among dry rocks of a dead mountain, suffering nightmare visions of "red sullen faces" in the "doors of mudcracked houses." His desire for water becomes a hallucinatory chant, answered only by "dry sterile thunder without rain."[146]

Here, as Eliot points out in his endnotes, the poem focuses on three themes: "the journey to Emmaus, the approach to the Chapel Perilous (see Miss Weston's book) and the present decay of eastern Europe."[147] The first seems to be a continuation of the early imagery of the shadow. In "The Burial of the Dead," the speaker promises to show us "something different from either / Your shadow at morning striding behind you / Or your shadow at evening rising to meet you."[148] In "What the Thunder Said," he makes good on his promise by pointing out the presence of a "third who walks always beside you," and describes him in terms befitting the androgynous "dying god" of the ancient fertility cults and of Christianity: "Gliding wrapt in a brown mantle, hooded / I do not know whether a man or a woman."[149] The Gospel of Luke says that two travelers met a similar figure on the road from Jerusalem to Emmaus, who told them the whole history of salvation. Convinced that they had seen the risen Christ, they returned to Jerusalem and spread the news.

After this, the poet turns his attention toward the air: "hooded hordes swarming / Over endless plains."[150] Since this apocalyptic vision ends with the destruction of five major historic cities in Eurasia (Jerusalem, Athens, Alexandria, Vienna, London) we may assume that Eliot is remarking on the postwar devastation of eastern Europe. Nancy Duvall Hargrove points out that the first four cities were "destroyed or partially destroyed by a force considered at the time to be barbarian, and thus brutalizing and bestializing" and that "by including London in the list, Eliot suggests — and indeed warns — that this modern city and the civilization which she represents are heading for a similar destruction of cultural, moral, and spiritual attainments, not by literal barbarians as in the past but by the barbarian attitudes (materialism, selfishness, physical lust) of contemporary man as revealed in the poem."[151] In his endnotes, Eliot refers to Herman Hesse's statement, in his essay on *The Brothers Karamazov*, that Europe is already on the road to chaos. Eliot, like Hesse, hoped this madness was a necessary stage in the process of rebirth. He therefore interprets the sound of "those hooded hordes swarming" as a murmur of maternal lamentation, and the unreal city on the verge of destruction becomes a symbol of faith.

Finally, Eliot turns back to the Grail legend and recounts one of the most frightening tales of tested faith. His immediate source for the story was probably Tennyson's *Idylls of the King*, which follows Sir Lancelot and Sir Gareth to the Chapel Perilous where they must rescue the Lady Lyonors from the Black Knight. The chapel appears to them under stormy skies. Sir Gareth grasps a black horn and blows, like the knight in Robert Browning's "Childe Roland to the Dark Tower Came," steeling himself for a forthcoming battle with unimaginable horrors. The horn summons the Black Knight, who emerges from the castle "high on a nightblack horse, in nightblack arms, / With white breast-bone, and barren ribs of Death, / And crown'd with fleshless laughter."[152] This ghastly creature — like something out of a Gothic horror novel — charges Lancelot, who casts him to the ground. Without hesitation, Gareth splits the knight's helmet. Beneath it appears the face of an unthreatening young boy, who begs them to spare his life. The knights are amazed to find that fear was their only true enemy.

Jessie Weston points out that the details of the tale of the Chapel Perilous vary from one telling to another: Sometimes the hero (or heroine) enters the castle and finds a dead body; sometimes a Black Hand extinguishes the lights; sometimes there are spectral voices. "The general impression," she sums up, "is that this is an adventure in which supernatural, and evil, forces are engaged."[153] In Tennyson's version, the supernatural proves to be an illusion. The same seems to be true in Eliot's version; he tells us that "dry bones can harm no one."[154]

The Waste Land: What the Thunder Said (Part II)

The final passage in *The Waste Land* begins with the coming of water that the speaker has longed for since the beginning of his quest. The rain falls on the Ganga and Himavant, personifications of the river Ganges and the Himalayan mountains. In conjunction with the rain comes the voice of the Thunder, delivering the final message of the *Brihadaranyaka Upanishad*: Datta, Dayadhvam, Damyata. In his endnotes, Eliot translates: "Give, sympathize, control."[155] In the *Upanishad*, these words appear in a reverse order: Damyata, Dyadhvam, Datta, or "Control, Sympathize, Give." A.N. Dwivedi points out that the *Upanishad* "mentions that self-control must come first in the development of an individual, since other virtues follow it automatically. Eliot seems to suggest that only the heart capable of love and generosity at the outset can achieve the kind of quiet self-mastery which is the goal of the sage."[156]

Eliot's quest at this point in his life was a quest for self-discipline. That is precisely what Dr. Vittoz was trying to teach him: that "normal cerebral control" depends on awareness, concentration and willpower.[157] For Vittoz, concentration meant that the brain should be aware *and* receptive, emitting *and* receiving energy.[158] He urged patients to practice concentrating on images, ideas, sensations in order to learn how to focus their thoughts, and thereby control their actions. Eliot followed his doctor's advice.

In *The Waste Land*, he concentrates on images, ideas and sensations that had appeared in his poetry for years. He concentrates on "the awful daring of a moment's surrender"—the giving-in to desire that Prufrock fears and Sweeney relishes. He concentrates on life "in his prison" (in the cage), and concludes that sympathy, in a world where two people cannot possibly understand each other, has produced a tragic hero, a "broken Coriolanus." Finally, he concentrates on the seacoast of New England. The sea was a constant reminder to Eliot of the light-heartedness of youth. At the end of *The Waste Land*, he imagines himself adrift on calm waters—the boat responding gaily to his "controlling hands."[159] For the time being, he has managed to escape into peaceful thoughts. In a November 30 letter to his friend Ottoline Morrell, Eliot writes that, at times, he feels more peaceful than he has since childhood.[160]

Eliot might have ended the poem here, with a reassuring image, but he doesn't. He returns to the plight of the Fisher King, still suffering. He returns to the image of London in ruins, and to the tormented soul of the poet Arnaut Daniel disappearing into the "purifying flames" of Dante's *Purgatory* (canto XXVII). Another fragment, from the mysterious Latin poem *Pervigilium Veneris* (probably written in the 2nd or 3rd century A.D.), expresses a longing for the springtime reawakening that has not come yet. This is followed by a reference to French romantic poet Gerard de Nerval's *The Disinherited One*, in which the banished prince faces captivity in a dark tower. Eliot makes one more allusion—to Hieronymo, the mad king of Thomas Kyd's *The Spanish Tragedy*. These two final allusions are perhaps meant to convey Eliot's mental state as one of defeat.

The speaker makes one final appeal to a power beyond reason, with a simple prayer repeating the word *shantih* three times. The prayer ends many of the Hindu Upanishads, and is intended to calm the three types of disturbances that can interfere with the listener's peace: disturbances from above (like thunder and rain), disturbances from the surrounding environment and disturbances within one's own mind. A.N. Dwivedi writes that "once such perfect peace is attained, man becomes liberated from all bonds for good. This is precisely the message of the Thunder, and this is unmistakably the exhortation of the poet to the erring modern man."[161] In his endnotes, Eliot defines the word as "The Peace which passeth understanding."[162]

With this definition, he equates the Eastern notion of cosmic unity with St. Paul's "peace of God, which passeth all understanding" (Philippians 4: 7). Many critics have pointed out that Eliot's definition is inaccurate, but the important thing to realize is that it demonstrates his desire to unite the worldviews of East and West.

In 1931, Eliot described his experience of composing this final section: "A piece of writing meditated, apparently without progress, for months or years, may suddenly take shape and word; and in this state long passages may be produced which require little or no retouch.... You may call it communion with the Divine, or you may call it a temporary crystallization of the mind."[163] If the composition of *The Waste Land* didn't bring the poet a lasting mental peace, Eliot's temporary crystallization of the mind nevertheless changed the course of his life. Before *The Waste Land*, he was a man striving for a sense of purpose. After *The Waste Land*, he was a man striving for strength of purpose.

Suggested Reading

The Waste Land (1922)

The Waste Land Facsimile (1974), ed. Valerie Eliot

The Annotated Waste Land with Eliot's Contemporary Prose (1995), ed. Lawrence Rainey

◆ PART VI ◆

Between Dying and Birth
(1922–1930)

What is important for us? ... The more personally we answer this question, it seems
to me, the more likely we are to vet a vital order out of the anarchy of the present.
— Van Wyck Brooks

Purgatory

In December 1921, T.S. Eliot visited Ezra Pound in Paris and gave him a copy of the sprawl-
ing 19-page poem *The Waste Land*. Pound, who had used the same exhaustingly allusive style
in his *Cantos*, suggested trimming several long sections, but his praise for the poem as a whole
could not have been more enthusiastic. Eliot returned to London in January and continued
to correspond with Pound about revisions to the manuscript while haggling with publishers
over placement of the finished poem. Though his letters show that both he and Vivienne were
suffering from prolonged illness and bouts of depression during this time, Eliot also felt
empowered by the completion of *The Waste Land* and immediately began making plans to
start his own quarterly review, *The Criterion*. The first issue appeared in October, featuring
a plan of a novel by Fyodor Dostoevsky, Herman Hesse's essay on recent German poetry, and
The Waste Land.

Soon after, Eliot bequeathed *The Waste Land* facsimile, along with a notebook of his
unpublished early poetry (later published as *Inventions of the March Hare*), to collector John
Quinn. It was his way of putting the poem — a collage of thoughts and feelings that had defined
his life for the past ten years — behind him. On November 15, he wrote to Richard Aldington that he was eager to start fresh, enthusiastically declaring that he was "feeling toward a
new form and style."[1] During that same month, he wrote a letter to his brother Henry, in
which he looked toward the future with hopeful resolve:

> I do not find that young people are capable of any real affection, just as they are incapable of any
> real understanding. They are interested only in themselves and they care only for people who
> affect them in the way they like to be affected. They enjoy their own feelings and are indifferent
> to the individuality of the people for whom they care. As one grows older one clings more and
> more — so I find — to the few genuine affections which it is possible to have.[2]

The letter is evidence of a major change in Eliot's outlook on life. He is attempting to shed
his tendency toward self-absorption, and to focus and control his thoughts and feelings in the

future. Having discarded the fragments of the past, he "feels toward" a way to understand, appreciate and express the "affections" that are truly important to him — in poetry and in life.

The years 1922 and 1923 were ones of germination for the renewed poet. They were also the most trying years of his codependent marriage. Upon his return to London and to his wife at the beginning of 1922, Eliot's health rapidly declined. In the spring, when he finally began to recover, Vivienne's health — which had always been unstable — deteriorated. She was often feverish and suffered symptoms of colitis, insomnia, neuralgia, eye trouble, migraines, skin rashes and physical and mental exhaustion. A specialist administered a violent treatment for glandular dysfunction, which left her completely exhausted.[3] By January 1923, her health was so poor that Eliot sent her to a private retreat in Eastbourne. At the same time, he rented a flat in Burleigh Mansions, where he could live and work alone.

During their time of separation, his health improved while her health continued to decline. Vivienne reached a point of a crisis in March, when she couldn't eat for days. For two months, she seemed close to death, her mental state approaching madness. In July, the couple sought the care of a new gland specialist in London. The following January, they turned to an orthopedic surgeon who specialized in spinal manipulation. Nothing helped.[4] For the marriage, it was a period of trial by fire. For consolation, Eliot turned — as he always had — to literature.

Dante II: The New Love

Lyndall Gordon writes that, during the period when T.S. Eliot was completing *The Waste Land*, he carried a dog-eared copy of Dante's poetry with him everywhere he went.[5] For that reason she suggests a parallel between Eliot's determination to start a new kind of life and Dante's revelation of a new kind of love. In the summer of 1923, Emily Hale — a young Bostonian with whom Eliot had fallen in love more than a decade earlier — visited London. It is unknown whether she met with her old friend while she was there, but her trip coincides with the earliest hints of his religious conversion. Gordon suggests that Emily Hale inadvertently played the role of holy muse to Eliot's pilgrim; a symbol of cosmic love comparable to Dante's Beatrice, leading the poet to a human understanding of God.

In his early autobiographical work *Vita Nuova* ("New Life"), Dante explains that both he and his muse were nine years old when he first saw her, and the image of Beatrice became "Love's assurance of holding me."[6] The poet was so overwhelmed by her beauty that he couldn't speak to her; he could only write about her. Soon, he became preoccupied with fears of her death, believing that this inevitable event would rob his life of all its meaning. Finally, the sight of Beatrice became such a source of emotional distress that the poet began to question his understanding of love. It was then that Love — communicating through the poet's own words — spoke to him, saying, "I am like the center of a circle equidistant from all points on the circumference; you, however, are not."[7] Dante took the lesson to heart, and began to put his faith in eternal, cosmic Love rather than temporal, human love. When Beatrice died, he understood that Love had not died, and afterwards wrote: "I still have hope that she will show me grace."[8]

Years later, in *The Divine Comedy*, Beatrice does just that. While in Purgatory, Dante's pilgrim reflects on the teachings of Thomas Aquinas, who suggests that earthly love is the soul's first inkling of God. In his *Summa Theologica*, Aquinas describes the steps that lead to cosmic Love:

There is, first, the love inclining toward the end; secondly, the desire which is a sort of emotion toward the end, and the actions issuing from such desire; thirdly, the form which the intellect receives; and fourthly, the resulting delight, which is nothing else than the repose of the will in the end as reached.

Aquinas adds that the goal of human life is the intellectual apprehension of cosmic love — "the direct vision of God." Like earthly love and desire, however, this is not "the ultimate end."[9] Dante echoes the teachings:

> It should be clear to you by now how blind
> > to truth these people are who make the claims
> > that every love is, in itself, good love.
> They think this, for love's substance, probably,
> > seems always good, but though the wax is good,
> > the impression made upon it may be bad.[10]

Realizing the limitations of earthly love, Dante looks higher. He resolves to wait for Beatrice to show him God's grace. In a similar fashion, T.S. Eliot aspired to a new love — beyond desire and intellect. Dr. Vittoz had taught him how to direct his thoughts and actions toward a higher purpose, and Dante had shown him the purpose.

At the end of *The Divine Comedy*, Dante's pilgrim comes face to face with Beatrice in the highest realm of Paradise. Once again, the poet struggles to understand Love's message. Neither his desire nor his intellect can make him "like the center of a circle." It is only through divine grace that he finally reaches the ultimate end of his journey:

> As the geometer who tries so hard
> > to square the circle, but cannot discover,
> > think as he may, the principle involved,
> so did I strive with this new mystery:
> > I learned to know how could our image fit
> > into that circle, how could it conform;
> but my own wings could not take me so high
> > then a great flash of understanding struck
> > my mind, and suddenly its wish was granted.
> At this point power failed high fantasy
> > but, like a wheel in perfect balance turning,
> > I felt my will and my desire impelled
> by the Love that moves the sun and the other stars.[11]

In a 1920 essay, Eliot says that Dante provides the experience of damnation, purgatory and grace not as "theory" but "in terms of something *perceived*."[12] Eliot believed that many of the other poets who had influenced him — Poe, Fitzgerald, Baudelaire, Laforgue — had fallen short of this range of emotion, expressing only the initial stage. Their visions were honest, he said, but incomplete; the same end is implicit in their writing, but they fail to recognize it and pursue it, dwelling instead on the experience of sin. Eliot writes, "The contemplation of the sordid or disgusting, by an artist, is the necessary and negative aspect of the impulse toward the pursuit of beauty. But not all succeed as Dante did in expressing the complete scale from negative to positive. The negative is the more importunate."[13] This realization became the basis for a series of lectures on metaphysical poetry, which he gave in early 1926 at Trinity College, Cambridge.

The Varieties of Metaphysical Poetry

The phrase "metaphysical poets" was first used by Samuel Johnson in his book *The Lives of the Poets* (1781), in reference to a loose-knit group of 17th-century British writers whose work is characterized by unlikely comparisons and elaborate philosophical/religious conceits. In 1926, Eliot applied the term to a larger poetic tradition, ranging from Dante to Laforgue. He defined metaphysical poetry as "that in which what is ordinarily apprehensible only by thought is brought within the grasp of feeling, or that in which what is ordinarily only felt is transformed into thought without ceasing to be feeling."[14]

Eliot says that certain cultures at certain times are more conducive to the production of metaphysical poetry than others; the metaphysical poet requires an environment in which human sensibility can be "momentarily *enlarged in certain directions*."[15] To illustrate his point, Eliot argues that Dante benefited from a culture that had a more "coherent system of thought"[16] than did the culture of Elizabethan and Jacobean England. In Eliot's opinion, the influence of Thomas Aquinas allowed Dante to achieve a greater poetic range — "deeper degrees of degradation and higher degrees of exaltation" — than Shakespeare ever achieved.[17] This allowed Dante to transform the "material of adolescence" in the *Vita Nuova* into something mature — "the contemplation of absolute beauty and goodness partially revealed through a limited though delightful human object."[18]

Eliot argues that this kind of transformation is absent from the writings of the 17th-century metaphysical poet John Donne. Donne, he says, is more of a modern poet than a medieval poet, because he emphasizes the modern conception of the separation of body and soul. Donne's recurring theme is "that of the union, the fusion and identification of souls in sexual love ... the *Word made Flesh*, so to speak."[19] Eliot regards this as "philosophically crude" and "emotionally limiting." He explains:

> This union in ecstasy is complete, is final; and two human beings, needing nothing beyond each other, rest on their emotion or enjoyment. But emotion cannot rest; desire must expand, or it will shrink. Donne, the modern man, is imprisoned in the embrace of his own feelings. There is little suggestion of adoration, of worship.[20]

Eliot concludes that Donne is a true poet but nevertheless a poet of intellectual disorder and emotional chaos who failed to realize the unity of thought and feeling that appears in Dante's work.

The same chaos, Eliot says, is apparent in many subsequent poets in the English literary tradition: Wordsworth, Shelley, Byron, Tennyson, Browning, Swinburne.[21] He might well have silently included himself in this list, as his own poetry (up to that point) was definitively modern, reflecting the "chaos" of the Jacobean playwrights and the French Symbolist poets, who were also subject to his new criticism. Eliot places Baudelaire's work at the forefront of metaphysical poets in recent times, but even Baudelaire falls far short of Dante — his work *implying* the existence of Paradise, but never looking beyond the Inferno. In a 1931 essay, Eliot examines the poet's work from the perspective of Catholicism:

> Baudelaire perceived that what really matters is Sin and Redemption. It is proof of his honesty that he went as far as he could honestly go and no further [...] the possibility of damnation is so immense a relief in a world of electoral reform, plebiscites, sex reform and dress reform, that damnation itself is an immediate form of salvation — of salvation from the ennui of modern life, because it at last gives some significance to the living.[22]

Eliot thus diagnoses Baudelaire's ennui, as he had diagnosed his own ennui, as a form of *acedia*, the sin of laziness or indifference in religious matters. What Baudelaire lacked was not belief, but *discipline*. Only through discipline, Eliot believed, could the suffering sinner hope to transcend the temporal world.

Laforgue's shortcomings were harder to diagnose. Eliot grudgingly admits that his biggest influence — the poet who helped him to find his own voice — is a lesser poet than Baudelaire. In Laforgue's defense, Eliot notes that his confusion was the confusion of the age: "For Laforgue, life was *consciously* divided into thought and feeling.... Hence the metaphysicality of Laforgue reaches in two directions: the intellectualising of the feeling and the emotionalising of the idea. Where they meet, they come into conflict, and Laforgue's irony, an irony always employed against himself, ensues."[23] Eliot concludes that what Laforgue needed was to write his own *Vita Nuova*, to "justify, dignify and integrate" his adolescent material into a mature philosophy that would allow him to think and feel at the same time.[24]

Eliot's interpretation of Laforgue's shortcomings was a prescription for his own future poetry. He believed that he was living in a "metaphysical period," when it was possible for art to enlarge the range of human sensibility. What Eliot, like his teacher George Santayana, required of modern poets was sensibility rather than confused sentiment; exactness rather than vague expression. Behind every poet, he said, there should be a mature philosophy. Eliot found his philosophy in the Church of England. In 1923, he met William Force Stead, a fellow American recently ordained in the church, and Stead encouraged him to study the sermons of 17th-century bishop Lancelot Andrewes. Gradually, Andrewes became something like an Aquinas to Eliot's Dante.

Lancelot Andrewes

The Church of England separated from the Roman Catholic Church in the early 16th century, during the reign of King Henry VIII. Henry's daughter Elizabeth became not only the first Protestant queen of England, but also the supreme head of the Church of England. During her reign, church leaders were attempting to distinguish their beliefs and practices from those of the Roman Catholic Church and from the beliefs and practices of the growing Puritan sect in England. Lancelot Andrewes (1555–1626) came of age during this period of formalization, and he helped to construct the ideology of the church according to his own convictions.

In his official capacity as a vicar, Andrewes was completely focused on establishing order and discipline in the Church of England. He spoke publicly about the shortcomings of the clergy during the final years of the Elizabethan era, calling them lazy and ignorant. In 1603 he found an ally in the new monarch, King James. Andrewes made a good first impression on James at a 1604 conference at Hampton Court, where he publicly rebuked Puritan rebels. Soon after, the king appointed him to help oversee a new translation of the Bible and consecrated him as bishop of Chichester. During his years as a bishop, Andrewes established strict rules for church ceremonies and practices and instructed church leaders and parishioners alike that every action of worship should be performed with the utmost focus, attention to detail and reverence. He was determined that, in his churches, there would be no casual actions or vague messages. Andrewes emphasized, above all, *strength of purpose.*

Foremost among his messages was the divine right of kings, which he believed was an important part of God's holy order. Andrewes became a bishop in the year of the Gunpow-der Plot in which Roman Catholic loyalists attempted to blow up the Houses of Parliament and assassinate the king. After Guy Fawkes and the other conspirators were caught, Andrewes preached a sermon in which he attributed the king's survival to divine intervention. He con-cluded that it was a day to remember in celebration: "This *Day* should not die, nor the memo-rial thereof perish, from our selfes or from our seed, but be consecrated to perpetual memory, by a yearly acknowledgement to be made of it through all generations."[25] For the remainder of his life, Andrewes continued to preach on the Gunpowder Plot and to assert the divine right of kings, even in his correspondence with the pope.

The assassination attempt prompted King James to demand that British subjects who remained loyal to Pope Bellarmine sign an oath of allegiance to the crown. When Bellarmine declared the king's authority invalid, Andrewes produced *Tortura Torti*, a scholarly work which sought to undermine the pope's authority and justify the king's. Andrewes asserted that the Church of England fulfilled the scriptural teaching of St. Peter, who said, "Be ye subject to the king as supreme; for this is the will of God."[26] In short, he empowered the Church of England by arguing that the king was not *innovating* beliefs, but *renovating* important teach-ings of the scriptures, which the Roman Catholic Church had reduced to "novelties."[27] By doing so, Andrewes distinguished the Church of England within the tradition of the ancient Christian Church — halfway between the extremes of Catholicism and radical Puritanism. In T.S. Eliot's words, Andrewes played a major role in making the English church "worthy of intellectual assent."[28]

Eliot was working out his own thoughts on Roman Catholicism and the Church of England during the year that he began studying Andrewes in earnest. In an essay entitled "The Function of Criticism," he reiterates literary critic Middleton Murray's association of Catholi-cism with classicism, emphasizing that "those of us who find ourselves supporting what Mr. Murray calls Classicism believe that men cannot get on without allegiance to something out-side ourselves."[29] Pressed to define that "something outside of ourselves," he ventures from the context of literature to the subject of religion and politics: "If [...] a man's interest is polit-ical, he must, I presume, profess an allegiance to principles, or to a form of government, or to a monarch; and if he is interested in religion, and has one, to a Church." For the time being, Eliot limits his own personal "interest" to literature, professing an allegiance to the complete above the fragmentary, the adult above the immature, the orderly above the chaotic.[30] He was not, however, oblivious to the fact that, for Lancelot Andrewes, allegiances to the Church of England, the king of England and literary tradition were inextricably intertwined. In 1927, Eliot followed Andrewes's lead, making an infamous announcement in the preface to his new book of essays (*For Lancelot Andrewes*) that he was an Anglo-Catholic in religion, a classicist in literature and a royalist in politics.

Death's Other Kingdom

In 1926, Eliot writes that "the English Church has no literary monument equal to that of Dante, no intellectual monument equal to that of St. Thomas, no devotional monument equal to that of St. John of the Cross, no building so beautiful as the Cathedral of Modena or the basilica of St. Zeno in Verona."[31] He praises the beauty of the Wren chapels in the City of London and the intellect of Lancelot Andrewes, but he is increasingly critical of the poets and dramatists who were writing during the early years of the English Church. The reason is simple: He wanted to succeed where they failed. In September 1923, Eliot began work on his first play, published (though unfinished) as *Sweeney Agonistes*. In it, he presented the worst impulses of his youth within the context of a higher moral order. It may be that he abandoned the play prior to completion because the moral order was not specifically that of his new faith.

In 1924, Eliot began a long process of personally embracing the moral order of the Church of England, as reflected in a series of poems called "Doris's Dream Songs." Doris is not named in the text of the poems themselves, but she appears as a character in *Sweeney Agonistes*. At the beginning of the play, we find her cutting a pack of cards, and — like Madame Sosostris in *The Waste Land*— interpreting one of the cards she draws as a premonition of death. A friend assures her that it may not be a premonition of *her* death, but Doris responds fearfully: "No it's mine. I'm sure it's mine. / I dreamt of weddings all last night."[32] Thereafter, the focus of the play shifts to Sweeney. Eliot explores Doris's fate in the dream songs.

Each of the three songs speaks of a vision of "death's other kingdom." Unlike the brutish life-in-death that the lustful Sweeney endures, Doris's fate is suggested by a "golden vision" of Paradise. For Eliot, as for Dante, vision is the initiator of love — the first hints of cosmic Love come to Doris and to us, the reader, through the eyes. In the first song, "Eyes that last I saw in tears," the eyes glimpse something beautiful, but they "hold us in derision,"[33] because the poet believes that humility is the first step toward a new life. The second song, "The wind sprang up at four o'clock," finds Doris "between life and death,"[34] in the hellish underworld of Greek mythology, on the edge of the River Styx. There she experiences a foreboding vision of what dreams may come: In Tartarus, an underworld dungeon of torment and suffering, monstrous horsemen violently shake their spears. A variation of this song was written for possible inclusion in *The Waste Land*, but removed at Ezra Pound's insistence. It was published in the spring of 1921 as "Song of the Opherian," serving instead as an informal prelude to *The Waste Land*—primarily, a vision of the Inferno. It serves the same function here, giving Doris's eyes a view of the first of Dante's three stages. The third song, "This is the dead land," places us back in the desert waste land of Eliot's earlier poem. He again evokes Percy Shelley's poem "Alastor," the "stone images" serving as reminders of great ruined civilizations. Eliot, however, makes a sharp distinction between the tone of *The Waste Land* and the tone of "This is the dead land." He writes:

> Here the stone images
> Are raised, here they receive
> The supplications of a dead man's hand
> Under the twinkle of a fading star.[35]

In the newer poem, Doris does not tremble with fear, but with tenderness — praying with utmost humility. Like the stone images, she is reaching for the sky, asking for God's grace.

"Doris's Dream Songs" were published in November 1924 in a literary journal, and never again republished as such. Eliot, who had compiled several years' worth of fragments to create the masterpiece *The Waste Land*, quickly came to regard the dream songs as fragments. He decided to eliminate all references to the identity of the speaker and reconfigure the most successful parts of the songs into something new. In January 1925, a slightly revised version of "Eyes that last I saw in tears" appeared in *The Criterion* as the first of "Three Poems." It was followed by "Eyes I dare not meet in dreams," which takes up the "stone images" of the previous cycle and turns them into a beatific vision — "more distant and more solemn / Than a fading star."[36]

The recurring image of a fading star seems to be Eliot's way of evoking the transitional passages in Dante's *Divine Comedy*. At the end of the *Inferno*, the pilgrim and his guide emerge from the underworld to see a star-filled sky. At the end of *Purgatory*, the pilgrim professes his readiness "for the stars." Eliot, by comparison, is not ready. Having seen the beatific vision, he hesitates at the bottom of Mount Purgatory. In the third poem, "The eyes are not here," we find Eliot's pilgrim there, in a "valley of dying stars,"[37] among a horde of blind, groping strangers gathered on the beach of a bulging river.

In *Purgatory*, Dante's pilgrim also hesitates on the edge of the River Lethe, which promises to wash away all memory of sin. For the hesitation, he is chastised by Beatrice, who uses harsh language reminiscent of the mad harpy in Eliot's *The Waste Land*: "Speak now, is this not true? Speak!" followed by "What are you thinking of?" / Answer me, now!"[38] (One can almost hear Eliot's dry response: "I think we are in rats' alley / Where the dead men lost their bones."[39]) Eliot's pilgrim awaits a mediator who can help him to begin his ascent — as Christ did for St. Augustine, as Beatrice did for Dante. Eliot here invokes the image of a "multifoliate rose," referring to it as the only star that will never fade. This symbol is also taken from Dante; at the end of *Paradise*, the pilgrim has a vision of the greatest saints in Heaven as a circle of petals in a beautiful white rose, and the center of the rose is the Virgin Mary. Mary, however, does not appear in Eliot's poem. The pilgrim believes that he must learn to wait without hope, believing that such a revelation will only come to him when he has completely surrendered all of his self-serving thoughts and emotions. At the end of the poem, he is still waiting among the hollow men.

With this final image, Eliot realized what his two triads ("Doris's Dream Songs" and "Three Poems") were striving for. In 1925, he again reconfigured them to create the five-part poem *The Hollow Men*. The sequence begins with a fragment that was published as "Poème Inédit" in the November 1924 issue of a French literary journal. Eliot may have chosen to write the poem in French because it was inspired by Paul Valéry's Symbolist poem "Cantique des Colonnes" ("Song of the Columns"), and includes two lines taken from that poem:

> Shape without form, shade without colour,
> Paralysed force, gesture without motion.[40]

These two lines, within the context of Eliot's poem, suggest that the movements of the hollow men — those shades hovering between life and death, Inferno and Purgatory — are as futile as the movements of the stone statues of ruined civilizations. This introduction is followed by slight variations on "Eyes I dare not meet in dreams," "This is the dead land" and "The eyes are not here" — charting the speaker's intellectual movement from beatific vision to tender prayer to a desire for pious emptiness. The pilgrim waits.

The final section of *The Hollow Men* returns to the nightmare world of the hollow men, as the speaker attempts to recite the Lord's Prayer while watching the futile procession of his fellow ghosts, endlessly circling a desert cactus. Only Eliot's mention of time — "at five o'clock in the morning" — suggests hope; Dante's pilgrim began his ascent of Mount Purgatory at dawn. Standing there, the speaker traces a lifetime of skepticism, which leads him to despair and indecision. Much of the thought and imagery in this section stemmed from Eliot's recent reading, particularly Valéry and Joseph Conrad.

Joseph Conrad: Heart of Darkness

Joseph Conrad (1857–1924) was a Polish-born writer who spent his early adult life in the Far East as a British merchant marine. His adventures during those years became the basis for his literary works, including his best-known novel, *Heart of Darkness* (1902). T.S. Eliot was already familiar with Conrad's work when he was an undergraduate; while he was in Paris in the summer of 1911, he recommended Conrad's short stories "Typhoon" and "Youth" to his teacher Alain-Fournier.[41] Both of these stories may have reminded Eliot of the tales that were told in the seaside fishing community of Gloucester, where he spent his summers as a child. Conrad was nostalgic about his own youthful affinity with the sea. In the short story "Youth," he reminisces in the voice of a seafarer named Marlow:

> I remember my youth and the feeling that will never come back anymore — the feeling that I could last forever, outlast the sea, the earth, and all men; the deceitful feeling that lures us on to joys, to perils, to love, to vain effort — to death; the triumphant conviction of strength, the heat of life in the handful of dust, the glow in the heart that with every year grows dim, grows cold, grows small, and expires — and expires, too soon, too soon — before life itself.[42]

Marlow has lost his enchantment with life. Unlike Eliot's characters, however, he has already lived a full, active life. He has seen it all and come away from his experiences with a deep melancholy. In *Heart of Darkness*, we find out why.

Marlow's narrative tone in *Heart of Darkness* is very different from his tone in "Youth." From the beginning, we know that he is not idly reminiscing; he is trying to reveal the transformative experience of his life, but the experience is so profound that he cannot find the words. The mere attempt to begin the story makes him acutely aware of his isolation from his companions and from the rest of humanity. Words, he believes, are insufficient to explain his thoughts and feelings. No one can ever know what he knows in exactly the way he knows it:

> It seems to me I am trying to tell you a dream — making a vain attempt, because no relation of a dream can convey the dream-sensation, the commingling of absurdity, surprise, and bewilderment in a tremor of struggling revolt, that notion of being captured by the incredible which is the very essence of dreams.... No, it is impossible; it is impossible to convey the life-sensation of any given epoch of one's existence — that which makes its truth, its meaning — its subtle and penetrating essence. It is impossible. We live, as we dream — alone....[43]

The story proper begins on the River Thames, as Marlow and his mates depart London and head south toward uncivilized wilderness (presumably the Congo, where Conrad had his own transformative experience). Along the way, they encounter a more primitive race of man and Marlow feels as if they are traveling back in time "to the earliest beginnings of the world."[44] In the heart of the African continent, he wonders if they haven't gone all the way to the "center of the earth ... into the gloomy circle of some Inferno."[45] There, in the oppressive silence and stillness of the primitive jungle, humanity appears in its ugliest forms. To Marlow, the natives appear subhuman: unthinking and violent. The "civilized" colonial leaders, white men like Marlow himself, are equally primitive in their violent efforts to control the natives. The uncivilized behavior of these leaders, Marlow explains, has destroyed something inside them and left them hollow. The company manager himself advises, "Men who come out here should have no entrails."[46] Here are Eliot's hollow men — not the natives, but the modern, supposedly civilized men who have willingly surrendered the better part of their humanity and given in to greed and lust for power. They have no intuition of a greater life force; no humility.

One of the company men, Kurtz, has become a full-blown megalomaniac, embracing the role of a pagan god among the natives. Conrad speculates that "all Europe contributed to the making of Kurtz."[47] Like Faust, Kurtz has cast off the reins of traditional morality and made himself the center of his universe. The result, according to Conrad, is the total collapse of civilization, the regression of humanity to its primitive state. For Kurtz, the result is a profound emptiness. Like the others, he is "hollow at the core."[48] Kurtz himself seems to realize this at the end of the novel, when — on his deathbed — he whispers four immortal words to his confessor: "The horror! The horror!" Marlow offers his own interpretation of Kurtz's death cry: "This was the expression of some sort of belief; it had candor, it had conviction, it had a vibrating note of revolt in its whisper, it had the appalling face of a glimpsed truth — the strange commingling of desire and hate."[49] One is reminded of Eliot's sympathetic reflection on Baudelaire: "It is proof of his honesty that he went as far as he could honestly go and no further." Afterwards, Marlow returns to London, but he can no longer look at civilized men and women in the same way — to him, they all look like primitive beasts. To him, they are hollow, because they go about their business in complete ignorance of the real dangers and the horrors inherent in human life. They are *unreal*, like the shades in Dante's Inferno, like the workers in Eliot's *The Waste Land*.

In an early draft of *The Waste Land*, Eliot used Kurtz's final words as an epigraph. On the advice of Ezra Pound, he removed them.[50] Having gained more confidence in his own judgment by the time he published *The Hollow Men*, Eliot references Conrad's revelatory moment ("Mistah Kurtz — he dead.") as an introduction to the five-part poem. Rejecting Pound's dismissal of Conrad may indicate that, with the new poem, Eliot intended to convey *consciously* what he had only *instinctively* revealed in the excised portions of *The Waste Land* (particularly in the "Death by Water" section): despair and death are merely early stages in the pilgrim's journey.

Eliot also added a second epigraph, which hinted at a related agenda in *The Hollow Men*. The first section is preceded by the phrase "a penny for the Old Guy" — a reference to the annual Guy Fawkes Day celebrations in England. Eliot was not oblivious to similarities between the modern-day Guy Fawkes festivities and ancient religious rituals described in James George Frazer's *The Golden Bough*:

> All over Europe the peasants have been accustomed from time immemorial to kindle bonfires on certain days of the year, and to dance round or leap over them. Customs of this kind can be traced back on historical evidence to the Middle Ages, and their analogy to similar customs observed in antiquity goes with strong internal evidence to prove that their origin must be sought in a period long prior to the spread of Christianity.[51]

By evoking these primitive rituals in conjunction with a reference to the primitive horrors of *Heart of Darkness*, Eliot is expressing an opinion about the nature and purpose of religious ritual in ordered society. In his mind, such rituals can only be a positive, civilizing influence when the object of worship is God and King ("Remember, remember, the fifth of November"). With this in mind, the speaker in the fifth section of *The Hollow Men* forsakes the dance of the savages — set to the tune of a children's rhyme — and prepares himself for earnest prayer.

The poet felt the mysterious allure of primitive rituals, just as Conrad did. In *Heart of Darkness*, when Marlow hears the drums of the natives, he is tempted to rush ashore and join them "for a howl and a dance," simply to overcome the anxieties of intellectual isolation. Kurtz knows this desire even better than Marlow, perhaps because Kurtz is a poet. In 1933, T.S. Eliot writes that "poetry begins, I dare say, with a savage beating a drum in a jungle, and it retains that essential of percussion and rhythm."[52] He explained his own use of incantatory rhythms to convey the primitive nature of the savages in the final section of *The Hollow Men* and of the lustful Sweeney in *Sweeney Agonistes*. He called his technique *auditory imagination*: "the feeling for syllable and rhythm, penetrating far below the conscious levels of thought and feeling, invigorating every word; sinking to the most primitive and forgotten, returning to the origin and bringing something back, seeking the beginning and the end."[53] Eliot uses the auditory imagination to convey his message that primitive thoughts and emotions have to be controlled through civilized reason and the power of the will. Only through such means can a man ascend the mountain of Purgatory.

Paul Valéry: Between the Motion and the Act

French poet Paul Valéry (1871–1945) held a similar theory about the technique of poetry. Comparing the effect of the poet's words to the effect of ancient rituals and magic, he says, "These words work on us (or at least on some of us) without telling us very much. [...] They act on us like a chord of music. The impression produced depends largely on resonance, rhythm, and the number of syllables; but it is also the result of the simple bringing together of meanings."[54] On the one hand, he says, there is the unintelligible meaning — the *feeling* produced by the poetry. On the other hand, there is the intelligible meaning — the *thoughts* that we take away. Like Eliot, he believed that the best poetry was a perfect combination of thought and feeling.

Because Valéry provided a precedent for Eliot's theory of poetry, Eliot writes that he is the "completion" and "explanation" of the Symbolist movement.[55] Whereas earlier poets like Charles Baudelaire, Arthur Rimbaud and Jules Laforgue provided only the unintelligible meaning, Valéry unifies unconscious feeling and conscious thought. He explains that his writing process begins with vague inspiration — a particular image or rhythm — but he stipulates that it must then be rigidly refined. Without reflection, decision, choice and combination, he says, the gifts of the Muse are only disordered fragments. The work must be willfully submitted to intellectual scrutiny if the poet is to achieve a sense of order.

Valéry illustrates the process in a valuable essay about his response to the mysterious beauty of a seashell. First, he tries to describe its graceful appearance. Unable to do so to his own satisfaction, he begins asking philosophical questions, starting with: *Who made this?* He answers first in a scientific manner — explaining to himself that pre-existing substances combined to create the materials of the shell, which took shape around a growing, living creature — but later concludes that this does not explain "what it may be that so miraculously harmonizes and adjusts the curves, and finishes the work with a boldness, an ease, a precision which the most graceful creations of the potter or bronze founder are far from equaling."[56] He asks the question again from the perspective of a naïve child, hoping to break the habitual state of the adult mind, which thinks more than it feels. In this state of innocence, he concludes that the shell was crafted according to a plan — "a pre-existing idea." Examining what might be regarded as a Bergsonian theory of art, he compares the creation of the sea shell with the creation of poetry:

> Our artists do not derive the material of their works from their own substance, and the form for which they strive springs from a specialized application of the mind, which can be *completely* disengaged from their being. Perhaps what we call perfection in art (which all do not strive for and

some disdain) is only a sense of desiring or finding in a human work the sureness of execution, the inner necessity, the indissoluble bond between form and material that are revealed to us by the humblest of shells.[57]

Valéry says that his poem "Le Cimitière marin" ("The Cemetery of the Sea") originated with an unintelligible rhythm and a few "hovering words."[58] Once he had determined the subject, he began the long, arduous process of selecting the right words to convey his intelligible meaning. The poet is frustrated by words like "Time" and "Life." These words mean something different for everyone, so the poet must be more precise — analyzing every word (much as Lancelot Andrewes did in his sermons) and finding new analogies that can convey the ever-elusive "dream world" to the reader. In this effort, Valéry says, the poet is always oscillating like a pendulum between *form* and *content*. A poem must, with its restless combination of words and sound, simultaneously illustrate what is transitory and what is permanent in life. Valéry concludes:

> So between the form and the content, between the sound and the sense, between the poem and the state of poetry, a symmetry is revealed, an equality between importance, value, and power, which does not exist in prose.... The essential principle of the mechanics of poetry — that is, of the conditions for producing the poetic state by words — seems to be this harmonious exchange between expression and impression.[59]

The completed "Le Cimitière marin" — which Eliot calls "one of Valéry's finest poems"[60] — illustrates the theory. The setting of the poem is reminiscent of those used by Edgar Allan Poe and Algernon Swinburne, two of Eliot's earliest influences. Poe's poem "Annabel Lee" is set in a sepulcher by the sea, where the speaker lies with his corpse bride, contemplating death. Swinburne's poem "By the North Sea" uses similar imagery — "a sea that is stranger than death" — to capture the poet's overwhelming fear of annihilation. In a few rare passages, the poem strays from feelings of overwhelming fear to feelings of peace:

> A land that is thirstier than ruin;
> A sea that is hungrier than death;
> Heaped hills that a tree never grew in;
> Wide sands where the wave draws breath;
> All solace is here for the spirit
> That ever for ever may be
> For the soul of thy son to inherit,
> My mother, my sea.[61]

In "Prufrock" and in *The Waste Land*, Eliot also fused the imagery of the sea with his fears of annihilation ("till human voices wake us and we drown" / "fear death by water"). The ending of each poem suggests desperation. Valéry's fear of annihilation, however, does not lead to a premature surrender. Contemplating the stillness of the sea, he writes that he can savor his "own future smoke" "as a fruit dissolves into taste."[62]

The sea, Valéry's most powerful symbol, is symbolic of an end and a beginning. It signals not the chaos and defeat of Prufrock's drowning, but the ordered reintegration of something small into something incomparably larger — like fuel added to a fire, a lump of salt dissolved in a glass of water, the Ganges River lost and found in the Indian Ocean. In his 1924 introduction to *Le Serpent*, Eliot makes reference to a passage in "Le Cimitière marin" that he found particularly affecting:

> Between emptiness and the pure event,
> I await my grandeur's echo from within....[63]

For Eliot, these lines summon to mind a passage from Shakespeare's *Julius Caesar* in which Brutus, betrayer of God and king, contemplates assassination:

> Between the acting of a dreadful thing
> And the first motion, all the interim is
> Like a phantasma or a hideous dream [II.i].

Valéry's poem has the haunting cadence and imagery — the unintelligible horror — of something by Edgar Allan Poe, John Webster or one of the Romantic poets. It incorporates familiar imagery of an empty skull and an insect scratching at the "dryness" of a grave. There is even a passage that suggests the presence of shades from the underworld: "An empty people among the tree roots / Have gradually come to take your side."[64] The subject of the poem, however, is not horror. Valéry believed that letting the poem rest on these fragments would be an overindulgence of his personal feelings, and a failure to grasp the unintelligible message inherent in them. Death beckons, and the poet answers without fear. His peaceful surrender, met with the "exhalation of the sea," is the static meaning, the intelligible message of the poem: despair and death are part of an ordered chaos, "a commotion that is silence's equal."[65]

Eliot, understanding the surrender, writes:

> One is prepared for art when one has ceased to be interested in one's own emotions and experiences except as material; and when one has reached this point of indifference one will pick and choose according to very different principles from the principles of those people who are still excited by their own feelings and passionately enthusiastic over their own passions.[66]

Eliot emulated Valéry's artistic achievement, which may be one reason that he became so disdainful of *The Waste Land*. The poem was prematurely ordered by Ezra Pound rather than by Eliot himself. At the time, of course, Eliot could not have done the work of ordering it himself; the message only gradually became clear to him later as he wrote *The Hollow Men*.

In the fifth and final section of *The Hollow Men*, Eliot contemplates the methodical approach of Valéry, oscillating between form and content. He is simultaneously contemplating religious conversion — oscillating between despair at the sight of the "hollow men" and fear of becoming hollow himself in the effort to ascend. In his essay "Poetry and Abstract Thought," Valéry tracks the pendulum as it swings between form and content, sound and sense, the poem and the state of poetry, Voice and Thought. Eventually, the Voice evolves, and the back-and-forth movement becomes a linear progression: going from Voice and Thought to "Thought and Voice," "Presence and Absence," "emptiness and the pure event." In the final section of *The Hollow Men*, Eliot charts the same progression inside his own poetic mind: from idea to reality, motion to act, conception to creation, emotion to response. Simultaneously, the pilgrim — clearly Eliot himself — attempts to recite the Lord's Prayer. At this point, the movement fails to evolve along a spiritual trajectory, becoming grossly physical instead: the pendulum swings between desire and spasm, potency and existence, essence and descent. There falls the Shadow — the oppressive phantasm that precedes the acting of a dreadful thing.

We might suppose that Eliot, like Valéry, has a precise meaning when he invokes the ominous presence of "the Shadow." In this case, however, the Shadow seems to be the symbol of everything that has prevented him from finding order in life and in his poetry: it is the symbol of his inability to be precise. The Shadow is a composite of the fears that he must overcome in order to go forward: phantasmagoric "shadowy sounds from visionary wings," the shadow of primitive humanity (our heart of darkness), illusory shadows of essential Reality on the walls of Plato's cave, the Biblical shadow of Death and the shadow of a great rock in a weary land, which is also the shadow of one who walks always beside you.

The ending of the poem is ambivalent. The speaker is unable to complete the Lord's Prayer, and a chorus of hollow men tells us that the world is ending "not with a bang but a whimper." Perhaps this whimper signifies failure, or perhaps it signifies the last breath before emptiness — Valéry's "exhalation of the sea." Whatever the case, it is clear that what Eliot aspired to was a higher order, uniting the Shadow with the perennial star.

Poetry and Belief

In January 1927, a few months before he was received by baptism as an Anglican, T.S. Eliot responded to an essay by I.A. Richards, who argued that poetry could and should be independent of belief. Eliot replies, "I cannot see that poetry can ever be separated from something that I should call belief," stipulating that it need not be "orthodox Christian belief, though that possibility can be entertained, since Christianity will probably continue to modify itself, as in the past, into something that can be believed in."[67] Here we see Eliot not only defending the new method of his poetry but defending his newfound faith as well. His comment about Christianity "modifying itself" recalls the teachings of his Harvard professor Josiah Royce.

For Royce, the question was not whether Christianity was a valid tradition but whether or not it could be effectively adapted to the modern age. In *The Problem of Christianity*, Royce offered two practical maxims for modification: 1) "Simplify your traditional Christology, in order thereby to enrich its spirit," and 2) "Look forward to the human and visible triumph of no form of the Christian church."[68] Royce proposes that the core Spirit of Christianity is not historical doctrine and dogma, but its more timeless aspects: "the Beloved Community, the work of grace, the atoning deed, and the saving power of the loyal life."[69] More important than the person of the religion's founder, he argues, is the Christian community that Christ created — because it is through loyalty to this community that individuals in the modern world may be saved.

Royce says that just as Christ's atonement for the sins of mankind created a community based on love for all mankind, so the Christian community ushers new members into the faith by loving them — sinners and saints, Jews and Gentiles, and Hindus and Buddhists alike. Love is the unifying force, not doctrine and dogma, and society is the medium for love. Royce's second suggestion for modification intends to prevent the sectarian mentality that has historically undermined the Christian community's love for all men. God, he says, does not call on us to *judge* those who are not members of the Christian community, but to *love* them — because God intends all men to become members of the Christian community. View your neighbor, Royce advises, "as the soldier views the comrade who serves the same flag as himself, and who dies for the same cause. In the Kingdom you, and your enemy, and yonder stranger, are one."[70]

Anticipating criticism from intellectual traditionalists, Royce cautions that what he proposes is not "vague humanitarianism."[71] The word had undesirable connotations among intellectuals of the day. Irving Babbitt had been careful to distinguish between humanitarianism and his philosophy of humanism, explaining that both types allow for sympathy, but only the humanist "insists that it be disciplined and tempered by judgment."[72] Babbitt criticizes the modern age for being too humanitarian, lacking the discipline and judgment that are necessary for the perfection of the individual. Unlike Babbitt, Royce is not focused on the perfection of the individual but on the perfection of a society, and his focus is less on tradition than on change. He argues that the Christian Church must evolve or perish:

> Religion must depend for its ability to resist change upon new weapons. Conservatism will no longer stand as its potent and natural defender. The human needs that it is to meet will be in a state of constant growth. The visible social organizations which have been its closest allies in the past can no longer be counted upon to preserve its visible forms.[73]

T.S. Eliot made the same distinction that Babbitt and Royce made between the perfection of the individual and the creation of a better world. Like Babbitt, he stresses the importance of reason and discipline. Like Royce, he also stresses the importance of society. In a series of essays following his religious conversion, Eliot criticized Babbitt, along with his ideological "forerunner" Matthew Arnold, for attempting to replace religion with secular belief. Eliot argues that humanism is a temporary worldview that will not last as Christianity has lasted because "it has never found anything to replace what it has destroyed."[74] He advises that we must use the *strength* of existing religious traditions, in combination with the disciplined judgment of humanism, to create a better world: "We cannot be aware solely of divine realities. We must be aware also of human realities."[75] When Eliot embraced Anglo-Catholicism, he acknowledged that "Catholicism without the element of humanism and criticism ... would be a Catholicism of despair."[76] This brings us to the question of why Eliot chose to embrace Anglo-Catholicism — a question with more than one answer.

In 1914, Eliot's studies of mysticism brought him to the conclusion that there is a universal human need for religion. By 1928, he had come to believe — like Josiah Royce — that religious salvation comes through loyalty to a community with a sturdy tradition. In 1951, after many years in the Church of England, he wrote that "no man has ever climbed to the higher stages of the spiritual life, who has not been a believer in a particular religion or at least a particular philosophy," adding that religious teaching "can only reveal its meaning to the reader who has his own religion of dogma and doctrine in which he believes."[77] This seems to be the rationale that prompted Eliot to choose a personal religion.

He apparently had some misgivings about *which* religion to embrace. His poetry reveals that he was particularly fascinated with Buddhism and Christianity — in symbolic terms, the Fire and the Rose. Eliot's response to I.A. Richards suggests that, for the sake of his poetry, he might just as easily have embraced Buddhism as Christianity, but his decision was not made for the sake of his poetry. His needs went much deeper than that; poetry was only a reflection of belief, or the lack thereof. What he needed from religion, on a personal level, was order and discipline. As a classicist, a philosopher and a public figure, he wanted a religion that could provide order and discipline for society — specifically for the society that he knew and belonged to. In his 1934 lecture *After Strange Gods*, Eliot reflects on his study of Hinduism and Buddhism, saying that he eventually reached the conclusion that "my only hope of really penetrating to the heart of that mystery would lie in forgetting how to think and feel as an American or a European: which, for practical as well as sentimental reasons, I did not wish to do."[78] In the aftermath of World War I, what Eliot wanted was a religion that could strengthen him as a person and strengthen the culture to which he belonged.

Belief and Politics

Prior to 1925, T.S. Eliot rarely weighed in on politics. A rare exception is a 1919 letter to publisher John Quinn, written on the eve of a major railway strike in London, in which he characterizes himself as a Liberal who is strongly opposed to the government.[79] A few months later, he wrote to British novelist Sydney Schiff about his aspirations as a literary critic: "I want to discuss 1) the modern public 2) the technique of poetry 3) the possible social employment of poetry."[80] This second letter suggests that, while he was developing a body of criticism on the first two topics, Eliot was quietly preparing his thoughts about politics and society, just as he had been refining his thoughts on religion since his days at Harvard.

F.O. Mathiessen notes that, between 1925 and 1928, Eliot began to voice his opinions about contemporary politics in a series of commentaries in *The Criterion*. His focus was on "the problem in the huge modern state caused by the heavy apathy of all elements in society to the responsibilities of intelligent democratic government." Whatever his misgivings about the British government — and we can safely assume that he would no longer consider himself a "Liberal" — he apparently had less faith in the masses to "believe in anything very strongly or to understand any situation very well."[81] This lack of faith in the common man led him to distrust democracy and take a political stance more comparable to that of Irving Babbitt and T.E. Hulme, both of whom were outspoken supporters of an anti-revolutionary movement in France known as Action Française.

Action Française was spearheaded by an ideologue named Charles Maurras (1868–1952), who had come to his own political beliefs by way of literary criticism. For years, he regarded himself as an "intellectual nationalist," but in the first decade of the 20th century, he began to turn his nationalist beliefs into political action. Maurras, like Eliot, was obsessed with reasoned order in art and in life. He blamed the social chaos of modern-day France on the French Revolution, which he regarded as the social counterpart of romanticism in literature.[82] Citing the German and British monarchies as examples of strong cultures, he argued that France should restore its own monarchy. His advocacy of royalism was as a means to unify the country under a strong leader, who could preserve the unique culture of France from divisive influences of Germans and Jews, Huguenots (French Protestants) and Freemasons. In a sense, Maurras and the Action Française wanted to turn back the clock, to recover the "purity" of France. They perceived the outcome of the First World War as an opportunity to mitigate German influence and campaigned for the recovery of land that had been lost decades earlier in the Franco-Prussian War.

While Eliot may have recognized the potential dangers of this postwar treatment of Germany, he admired Maurras's ideology — particularly his embrace of the Roman Catholic Church. Maurras was a professed agnostic, but because he associated the Church with the origins of French culture, he argued (after 1905) that Roman Catholicism should be reinstated as the official religion. It was, he said, beneficent to social order and the preservation of the classical tradition. In the wake of the Great War, Eliot must have considered the same theory in relation to the Church of England and the British government. Certainly he believed, as Lancelot Andrewes believed, that the Church was vitally connected to the cultural identity of the country and that without it England would face the threat of social chaos. In the interval between two world wars, with the whole of eastern Europe in chaos, the collapse of England was a terrifying possibility. For the sake of England and the sake of Europe, Eliot believed that it was extremely important to preserve England's monarch and its established state religion. Years later, Eliot writes of the influence that Maurras had on him:

> For some of us, Maurras was a kind of Virgil who led us to the doors of the temple. [...] Among those positive forces which oblige the reason to respond to the call of Faith — forces which one must distinguish from those which are merely seductive — one discerns the influences of other men who themselves have escaped neither from servitude nor unbelief.[83]

In June 1927, Eliot was baptized in the Church of England. In November, he became a British citizen. In the years that followed, he made a focused effort to share his beliefs as an Anglo-Catholic, a royalist and a classicist — culminating with his work *The Idea of a Christian Society* (1939). His early prescriptions for the Church of England were largely based on his own personal experience of conversion: he argued that what the modern world needed was humility and discipline. The only way forward, he believed, was to go back — a return to unifying traditions of the Church. The various alternatives roads would only lead to further chaos. In 1931, he wrote:

> The World is trying the experiment of attempting to form a civilized but non–Christian mentality. The experiment will fail; but we must be very patient in awaiting its collapse; meanwhile redeeming the time: so that the Faith may be preserved alive through the dark ages before us; to renew and rebuild civilization, to save the World from suicide.[84]

What is perhaps most interesting about Eliot's conclusion is his pessimistic tone. It is difficult to imagine such words coming from Josiah Royce, who said "Look forward to the human and visible triumph of no form of the Christian church." Both men propose that their readers wait without hope, but the difference between their messages is as different as Puritan New England, where the Eliot family had several generations of roots in America, and the wild California frontier, where Royce grew up.

The Wine of the Puritans

In 1948, T.S. Eliot wrote that "no man wholly escapes from the kind or wholly surpasses the degree of culture which he acquired from his early environment."[85] In his case, it wasn't for a lack of trying. By joining the Church of England and becoming a British citizen, he was carving a path back to his own family's English ancestry, as if he intended to erase his identity as an American. In the years to come, however, he acknowledged that it was his early life in America and the religious instruction of his family that had fundamentally shaped the way he thought.

At Harvard, Eliot had begun his study of religions outside the American tradition. His interest was perhaps initially a form of rebellion, but it quickly morphed into a deep dissatisfaction with the culture of his native country — not without a little help from one of his peers. Eliot's first piece of published prose is a 1909 review of *The Wine of the Puritans* by Van Wyck Brooks (1886–1963), who had recently graduated from Harvard. He writes that the book is a "definition of discontent" for those Americans of divided allegiance who "retained to their native country by relations or socialities or by a sense of duty — the last reason implying a real sacrifice — while their hearts are always in Europe." No doubt Eliot counted himself among those "double-dealers with themselves," seeing his own divided allegiance "surgically exposed" — like a patient etherized on a table.[86]

Brooks's book was a work of social criticism that described the alleged shortcomings of modern American culture as a result of a deeply imbedded strain of Puritanism in its people. He writes that the Puritans founded American civilization on the belief that economic necessity was more important than art, ritual and gaiety — in short, "all those things which an established civilization can support."[87] For pioneer life in an untamed wilderness, he concedes, this belief may well have been necessary for day-to-day survival, but a problem arises when this limited view of life is applied to a more civilized existence in subsequent generations. In the modern age, the worldview stunts intellectual growth. Puritan values, Brooks argues, "do not train the perception to large and universal truths. They do not widen the mind. They do not prepare the mind for the general questions of modern, cosmopolitan life."[88] Furthermore, he says that the religion, politics and art of modern America fail to form a coherent worldview or a sense of tradition and community. He concludes — like Henry Adams before him — that an American education is more confusing than enlightening and leaves many of its students feeling intellectually and emotionally disconnected from their own home. A few years later, Brooks writes:

> We are like explorers who, in the morning of their lives, have deserted the hearthstone of the human tradition and have set out for a distant treasure that has turned to dust in their hands; but having on their way neglected to mark their track they no longer know in which direction their home lies, nor how to reach it, and so they wander in the wilderness, consumed with a double consciousness of waste and impotence.[89]

For some — Adams and Eliot among them — Europe seemed like a natural refuge. There they hoped to find a culture in which the intermingling of religion, politics and art provided more vitality. Brooks refused that route and instead spent his life charting the progress of American literature through the centuries, critically analyzing its successes and failures. His hope was that he could help a new generation of native writers expand the boundaries of their admittedly limited tradition. "We must act," he says, "in such a way that this generation will have its romance and its tradition for those who come after."[90] Beginning with his 1915 essay "America's Coming of Age," Brooks applied his critical eye to the writings of New England's most formidable writers, including Ralph Waldo Emerson, Nathaniel Hawthorne and Henry James.

Ralph Waldo Emerson: The Web of God

Ralph Waldo Emerson (1803–1882) was the son of a Unitarian minister, and was himself ordained as a junior pastor in Boston at a young age, only to resign his position in 1832 due to a growing skepticism about the Unitarian position on the nature of God. Four years later, after much traveling, he wrote his first book, *Nature*. The work, like Unitarianism, was a revolt again religious tradition (especially Puritanism), and it was embraced by many Unitarians, including T.S. Eliot's mother, Charlotte, as an expression of American independence and optimism. It begins:

> Our age is retrospective. It builds the sepulchers of the fathers. It writes biographies, histories, and criticism. The foregoing generations beheld God and nature face to face; we, through their eyes. Why should we not also enjoy an original relation to the universe? Why should not we have

a poetry and philosophy of insight and not of tradition, and a religion by revelation to us, and not the history of theirs?[91]

Emerson goes on to explain how the individual can discover God. The universe, he says, is made up of Soul (the individual self) and Nature, "which Philosophy distinguishes as the NOT ME."[92] Beatitude results from the recognition that these two aspects may exist in harmony. Such recognition creates that harmony, giving Unity to the universe and making the individual, to some degree, divine. In what is perhaps the most famous passage in the book, Emerson tries to explain the effect of his own communion with Nature: "I become a transparent eye-ball. I am nothing. I see all. The currents of the Universal Being circulate through me; I am part or particle of God."[93]

Emerson believed that philosophy and poetry are one, each having beauty and truth (which he says are interchangeable) as their goal. He also believed that the personal experience out of which poetry and philosophy arise can come nearer to the truth than can history, and for that reason he issued a bold proclamation to American scholars in 1841: "Books are for the scholar's idle times. When he can read God directly, the hour is too precious to be wasted in other men's transcripts of their readings."[94] He reasons that the Age of Reflection must become an Age of Introspection, embracing a new American philosophy that he calls transcendentalism. Emerson defines the Transcendentalist view of the universe as follows:

> There is never a beginning, there is never an end to the inexplicable continuity of this web of God, but always circular power returning to itself. Therein it resembles his own spirit, whose beginning, whose ending, he can never find — so entire, so boundless. Far, too, as her splendors shine, system on system shooting like rays, upward, downward, without centre, without circumference, — in the mass and in the particle nature hastens to render account of herself to the mind. Classification begins.... But what is classification but the perceiving that those objects are not chaotic, and are not foreign, but have a law which is also a law of the human mind?[95]

Emerson argues that we must learn to trust our intuition. Through the innate ability of the human mind to perceive the divine nature, we become aware of our union with everything that exists.

As a classicist, T.S. Eliot was understandably wary of Emerson's teachings, which deny the "epical integrity" of the world's great religious texts.[96] He was also critical of the poet's lack of precision, as Irving Babbitt and Van Wyck Brooks had been before him. Babbitt called Emerson as "an important witness to certain truths of the spirit in an age of scientific materialism," but suggested that a lack of philosophical discipline undermines Emerson's philosophy:

> He is too satisfied with saying about half the time that everything is like everything else, and the rest of the time that everything is different from everything else. And so his genius has elevation and serenity, indeed, but at the same time a disquieting vagueness and a lack of grip in dealing with particulars.[97]

Brooks makes a similar criticism in a more dismissive tone: "Emerson is abstract at the wrong times and concrete at the wrong times, because he has so little natural sense of the relation between the abstract and the concrete."[98] In 1917, Eliot wrote to his mother that her favorite poet strikes him as too "wordy."[99] He may have been emotionally intrigued by Emerson's quasi-mystical "truths of the spirit," but he would have to look elsewhere for a sturdier American tradition that combined intellect with emotion.

The Hawthorne Aspect of Henry James

Nathaniel Hawthorne (1804–1864) was a contemporary and a friend of Emerson, but he did not subscribe to Emerson's philosophy of transcendentalism; his preoccupation was with the old tradition of Puritanism — but as material for art, rather than as a personal religion. In his book *A Literary History of America* (1900), Wendell Barrett explains:

> With the Puritans, of course, this sense of sin was a conviction of fact; they believed in the Devil, whose essential wickedness, lurking within every human heart, is bound if we lack divine help to sweep us into deserved and lasting torment. Hawthorne, on the other hand, felt all this only as a matter of emotional experience. To him Puritanism was no longer a motive of life; in final ripeness it had become a motive of art.[100]

Van Wyck Brooks, an advocate of art for art's sake, compares Hawthorne to Edgar Allan Poe, saying that the two men became the "principal artists in American literature"[101] by rejecting the popular American philosophy of their day, and withdrawing into "diaphanous private worlds of mist and twilight."[102] While the emotional effect of their writing is comparable, Hawthorne's strain of the Gothic is more distinctly American, rooted in the soil of New England's troubled past. For this reason, Hawthorne's work had a greater appeal for T.S. Eliot.

Hawthorne grew up in the town of Salem, Massachusetts, where his ancestor John Hawthorne had participated in the infamous Salem Witch Trials of 1692 — one of the darkest hours in colonial American history. Brooks therefore supposes that the author had the "Puritan conscience" in his blood and could not help conveying it through his writing. Hawthorne's stories prove, however, that he is as critical of Puritanism as he is of transcendentalism. In one of Hawthorne's earliest stories, "My Kinsman, Major Molineux" (1832), the author offers a symbolic representation of guilt over his own ancestry: the narrator of the story sees his kinsman tarred and feathered by his fellow citizens. A later story, "The Minister's Black Veil" (1836), is more directly concerned with the religion of his ancestors. In the story, a preacher emotionally isolates himself from his fellow man by concealing his face, with the result that he becomes ghost-like long before his death. The narrator/author is horrified by the preacher's behavior. The author seems equally horrified by the behavior of the modern scientists in "The Birth-Mark" (1843) and "Rappaccini's Daughter" (1844), who fail to show either humility or humanity in their intellectual experiments. For Hawthorne, the Puritan conscience seems to have so separated these individuals from their fellow man that they can regard them only as objects and subjects of experiment. In "Ethan Brand" (1850), the author makes his main criticism of the Puritan strain of American life explicit. In the story, a Faust-like character defines the Unpardonable Sin as "the sin of an intellect that triumphed over the sense of brotherhood with man, and reverence for God, and sacrificed everything to its own mighty claims!"[103] Like Mr. Hooper in "The Minister's Black Veil" and the scientists in "The Birth-Mark" and "Rappaccini's Daughter," Ethan Brand has become "a cold observer, looking on mankind as the subject of his own experiment."[104] What Hawthorne finds lacking in this way of life are the basic tenets of Christ's message — love for one's God and love for one's neighbor. He exposes a deeply flawed form of Christianity — too much head and not enough heart — at the core of American life.

In the introduction to his 1879 critical biography *Hawthorne*, Henry James writes that Hawthorne's body of work illustrates "that the flower of art blooms only where the soil is deep, that it takes a great deal of history to produce a little literature, that it needs a complex social machinery to set a writer in motion."[105] He regards Hawthorne's profound criticism of American culture — or rather, the culture of New England — as a rare example of genuine American art. T.S. Eliot, in turn, asserts that Henry James is a "continuator" of this "New England genius," arguing that James's "native taste" derives from Hawthorne.[106] What Hawthorne and James shared, according to Eliot, was a "deeper psychology," and a sense of "the past which is peculiarly American" — and perhaps also an understanding of its religious failures. In Hawthorne, that sense manifests itself in specific historical references. In James, it is rather "a sense of the sense" of the past.[107] Eliot regards Hawthorne's allegorical approach to history as proof of his limitations as a writer — limitations which Eliot theorizes were a product of environment. Because he lived in New England, he could not be objective about his sense of New England. On the other hand, James was able to transmute Hawthorne's "ghost-sense" into a substantial moral observation of the "social entity" of modern American and European life.[108] Eliot opined that it was James's physical abandonment of America that allowed him this success.

In a way, of course, Eliot is attempting to justify his own abandonment of America — for which Van Wyck Brooks would later rebuke him (and James). To this end, he was most fond of James's early fiction — *The American* (1877), *Daisy Miller* (1878), *The Europeans* (1879), *Washington Square* (1880) — which focus on the clash of American and European cultures. It is interesting that, in a 1918 essay on James, Eliot says not a word about Christopher Newman, the titular wandering hero of *The American* who fails to adapt to European society because of his distinctly American independence and kind nature. Instead, he comments on a minor character in the novel named Tom Tristram, an expatriate who has lived in Paris long enough to lose those qualities. James describes Tom Tristram as "shamefully idle, spiritless, sensual, snobbish."[109] Eliot, reflecting on the character, offers the following analysis: "It is the final perfection, the consummation of an American to become, not an Englishman, but a European — something which no born European, no person of an European nationality, can become."[110] This was Eliot's own personal goal — not to deny his native culture, but to fuse his American-ness with a more developed culture, which had itself already fused religion, philosophy and politics. What Eliot wanted was a ripe environment for education, a place where he could perfect his art.

In his 1941 book *American Renaissance,* literary critic F.O. Mathiessen argues that the "provincial American mind" — the haunted mind of Hawthorne and his literary successors — is ideally suited to moral observation. He offers the example of Eliot, "in whose own work the dark strain of Hawthorne is more visible than in the work of any other writer of the present."[111] After *The Waste Land*, Mathiessen says, Eliot realized that Hawthorne's moral resistance to the Puritan strain of American life was also in his own blood: "He came to believe that the choice lay between further disintegration of the sort that Hawthorne already foresaw, and a return to dogma upon which to base more adequate values than those of James."[112]

Ash Wednesday and the Ariel Poems: A Long Journey

In a 1953 interview, T.S. Eliot said, "I thought my poetry was over after 'The Hollow Men'... writing the Ariel poems released the stream and led directly to 'Ash Wednesday.'"[113] The first of the so-called Ariel poems, also the first poem following his religious conversion, was *Journey of the Magi*, published in August 1927. The poem begins with, then expands upon, a direct quote from Lancelot Andrewes's 1622 sermon on the Nativity, which itself expands on a Bible verse recounting the arrival of three wise men from the Orient to Jerusalem. When the three Magi arrive in Jerusalem, they inquire about the newborn baby Jesus, saying "Where is he that is born King of the Jews? For we have seen his star in the east, and are come to worship him" (Matthew 2: 2). Andrewes mines this brief verse to illustrate multiple steps in a profound spiritual journey. The first step, he says, is faith, which is the reason for their starting out: "*Faith*; in that they never aske, *Whither* He be; but *Where* He is *borne*: For, that *Borne He is*, that, they stedfastly beleeve." The next step is the physical journey itself, followed by a justification of their journey, which Andrewes paraphrases as follows: "*For*, they had *seen His starr*: And, *His starr* being *risen*, by it they knew, He must be *risen too*." The justification is followed by diligent inquiry about the child's whereabouts, which leads to the ultimate purpose of their journey: "And last, when they had found Him, the *End* of their *seeing, comming, seeking*; and all, for no other end, but to *Worship Him*."[114]

This particular sermon might have appealed to Eliot for several reasons. First, it illustrates the precision that Eliot so admired in Andrewes, who squeezes every individual word for any meaning it might yield. Second, the subject of the sermon is the Incarnation of God in the infant Christ, belief in which was a major stumbling block for Eliot, who had not been brought up to believe in the Incarnation. Third, the imagery used in the verse echoes the symbolism of Dante: a star represents the coming of Christ on earth and betokens a divine message to the hearts and minds of the faithful. Eliot saw himself, like Dante's pilgrim and the Magi, at the beginning of a hard journey of faith, faced with the symbolic hardships of desolate waste lands, rocky crags, thieves and murderers, and harsh weather: "the waies deep, the weather sharp, the daies short, the sunn farthest off *in solstitio brumali*, the very dead of Winter."[115] Andrewes praises the Magi for their strong faith. Those of us in the West, he says, are not often as willing and eager to endure such hardships:

> Our fashion is, to see and see againe, before we stirre a foot: Specially, if it be to the worship of Christ. Come such a Journey, at such a time? No: but fairely have put it off to the Spring of the yeare, till the dayes longer, and the waies fairer, and the weather warmer; till better travailing to Christ.[116]

In his poem *Journey of the Magi*, Eliot describes not only the journey of the Magi, but its aftermath — which is equally difficult. Being witness to the birth of Christ, the narrating Magus says, was like a death for the Magus himself. Afterwards, he had to return to the suffering of the mortal world, tormented by the knowledge that a world without suffering existed elsewhere. In Andrewes's sermon, the journey ends with worship at the cradle of the Christ child. In Eliot's poem, the journey has not ended, and will not end until death. His message is that faith is not the end, but only the beginning of another long, hard journey.

F.O. Mathiessen writes, "It would be glib to say that in *The Waste Land* and 'The Hollow Men' Eliot wrote his *Inferno*, and that since then his poems represent various stages of passing through a *Purgatorio*; still such a remark may possibly illuminate both his aims and achievement."[117] In *Journey of the Magi*, there are several descriptive passages reminiscent of *The Waste Land*: the Magus, like Marie Larisch, recalls memories of summer; the memories of both characters commingle with images of vegetation and rebirth, leading to distinctly religious imagery. In *The Waste Land*, we see the dead tree of the sacred wood, and the red rock of Isaiah's prophecy — images foreshadowing the arrival of Christ on earth. In *Journey of the Magi*, there are "three trees on the low sky" and an "old white horse."[118] The former is symbolic of the crucifixion, while the latter reminds us of apocalyptic revelations of John: "And

I saw, and behold a white horse: and he that sat on him had a bow; and a crown was given unto him: and he went forth conquering, and to conquer" (Revelation 6: 2). Whereas *The Waste Land* foreshadows the birth of Christ, *Journey of the Magi* foreshadows the death and the second coming of Christ. This is a clear reflection of the poet's new worldview, which was to be equally apparent in the longer poem *Ash Wednesday*, described by Eliot as "a first attempt at a sketchy application of the Vita Nuova to modern life."[119]

One part of *Ash Wednesday* (Part II) saw publication a few months after *Journey of the Magi* appeared in print, under the title "Salutation." At the beginning of "Salutation," the poet addresses his lady and proceeds to tell her his story:

> Lady, three white leopards sat under a juniper-tree
> In the cool of the day, having fed to satiety
> On my legs my heart my liver and that which had been contained
> In the hollow round of my skull....[120]

The description may initially seem startling — intended for shock value, like "a patient etherized upon a table" — but it is no more startling than Dante's first vision of his Lady Beatrice, wherein he finds her asleep in the arms of a frightening man. When Beatrice awakens, the man orders her to eat Dante's burning heart.[121] The poet surrenders his heart willingly, just as the poet in "Salutation" gives his entire body — and more — in worship to the Lady, who he recognizes as a representative of the Virgin Mary ("the single Rose") and of the one true God.

After this, Eliot's poetry moves more and more towards its fullest expression, which is the fusion of his newfound faith with all the things he has written and studied in the early part of his life. In Part I of *Ash Wednesday* (initially published as "Perch' Io Non Spero" in spring 1928), the poet meditates on the Bradleyan contrast between appearance and reality, and humbly begs God to teach him the stillness that unifies the two. *A Song for Simeon*, published in September 1928, seeks the same goal, using a biblical story for illustration: The Gospel of Luke says that Simeon saw the Christ child in a temple in a Jerusalem and, recognizing him as the instrument of God's salvation, prayed for the Lord to let him die soon in peace. In Eliot's poem, Simeon is still waiting for that peaceful death, and the poet echoes his prayer: "Grant us thy peace." Part III of *Ash Wednesday* (published as "Son de L'Escalina" in the autumn of 1929) returns to the imagery of Dante's *Purgatory*: the penitent pilgrim begins his ascent, gaining "strength beyond hope and despair."[122] Eliot too is trying to ascend, like Dante's pilgrim, using Andrewes as a spiritual guide.

Ash Wednesday and the Ariel Poems: The Turning Point

On February 10, 1619, Lancelot Andrewes delivered his fourth Ash Wednesday sermon, advising his congregation to embrace the day as an opportunity for "turning to the Lord." Andrewes preaches urgency: we are come from dust, he says, and will soon return to dust, so we cannot afford to wait for a "convenient time" to turn to God. *Now*, he emphasizes, is the time for the affirmation and reaffirmation of faith, when all of nature is preparing to be born and reborn:

> The *earth* and all her plants, after a *dead Winter*, returne to the first and best season of the yeare. The creatures, the Fowles of the *Aire*, the *Swallow* and the *Turtle*, the *Crane* and the *Storke know their seasons*, and make their just *returne* at this time, every yeare. Every thing now *turning*, that we also would make it our *time* to *turne* to *God* in.[123]

Eliot, who had in *The Waste Land* remarked that "April is the cruellest month," felt the urgency brought on by the sound of Time's winged chariot drawing near. In his earlier poem, he was tormented by "memory and desire," and found little consolation in stories of the Hanged God of James George Frazer's *The Golden Bough*. Eliot's third Ariel poem, *Animula*, finds the same tension in a struggle between "desire and control." In *Ash Wednesday*, Jesus Christ has replaced the Hanged God, and the poet finds himself willfully and eagerly acting out the motions of Andrewes's prescription for "turning to the Lord."

Andrewes bases his sermon on two verses from the book of Joel: "Therefore also now, saith the Lord, turn ye *even* unto me with all your heart, and with fasting, and with weeping, and with mourning: And rend your heart, and not your garments, and turn unto the Lord your God" (Joel 2: 12–13). The preacher deconstructs this passage to show that there are, in fact, *two* turnings toward God in a movement designed to prevent the pilgrim from ever turning back away. The first turn toward God, he says, is made with "all your heart." The second turn is made with a "*broken* and *rent*" heart, necessitating greater surrender. Andrewes describes the movement as follows:

> First, a *turne*, wherein we looke toward *God*, and with our *whole heart* resolve to *turne* to Him. Then, a *turne* again, wherein we looke backward to our *sinnes*, whereine we have *turned* from *God*; and with beholding them, our very *heart breaketh*. These two, are two distinct, both in *nature* and *names*: One, *Conversion from sinne*; the other, *Contrition for sinne*. One, resolving to amend that which is to come: the other, reflecting and sorrowing for that which is past. One, declining from evill to be done hereafter: the other, sentencing it selfe for evill done heretofore. These two between them make up a complete *repentance*, or (to keepe the word of the text) *a perfect revolution.*[124]

Part III of Eliot's *Ash Wednesday* describes the same movement: on the second stair, Eliot's pilgrim looks back and perceives his sins: "hope and despair." At that, he turns toward God for the first time, willfully shedding his petty attachment to human emotions. On the third stair, he turns back again and peers through a window into a spring pasture, where he has a more personal vision: a "broadbacked figure drest in blue and green," playing an antique flute, and "brown hair over the mouth blown, / Lilac and brown hair."[125] Exactly what these images represent only the poet can know for sure, but they seem to be his most vivid memories of hope and despair. In mourning, he turns his back on the past for the second and final time and proceeds toward God.

We may well ask where his resolve comes from. Andrewes says it must come from both mind and heart, thought and feeling: "And so requireth not only an alteration of the *mind*, but of the *will*: a change, not, of certaine *notions* only in the *head*, but of all the *affections* of the *heart* too."[126] The heart must turn with the rest of the body, Andrewes illustrates, or else the body will only make circles around the fixed heart, going nowhere. The heart must suffer, Andrewes says, because "*indignation* is the *essentiall passion* ... the principall and most proper *act* of a true *turning unto God*."[127] He refers to Paul's second letter to the Corinthians:

> For behold this selfsame thing, that ye sorrowed after a godly sort, what carefulness it wrought in you, yea, *what* clearing of yourselves, yea, *what* indignation, yea, *what* fear, yea, *what* vehement desire, yea, *what* zeal, yea, *what* revenge! In all *things* ye have approved yourselves to be clear in this matter [II Corinthians 7: 11].

With no attachments, the poet turns wholeheartedly toward God.

Ash Wednesday and the Ariel Poems: After the Turning

The second half of *Ash Wednesday* and the final Ariel poem offer glimpses of the newborn soul after the turning. In Part IV of *Ash Wednesday*, the Lady appears, as in the end of Dante's *Purgatorio*. Her message to the poet is the same message that Andrewes gave to his congregation on Ash Wednesday. The Lady says, "Redeem the time."[128] Andrewes says, "Our charge is to preach to men ... not, what for the present they would heare; but, what another day, they would wish they had heard."[129] *Now*, Andrewes emphasizes, is the time to start: "Now at this *time*, it is the time that all things *turne*; *Now*, is the onely sure part of our *time*. That which is *past*, is *come* and *gone*. That which is *to come*, may peradventure *never come*. Till to morrow, till this Evening, till an houre hence, we have no assurance. *Now therefore*."[130]

What follows, in Part V of *Ash Wednesday*, is the poet's return to the community of mankind on earth — similar to the return of the Magis to the East, but with more purpose. Eliot understands it as his personal goal to find the proper alchemy of words to share the Word with his community. For Eliot, who had conveyed the earliest impressions of his spiritual journey through landscape symbolism, it must have seemed natural to return to landscape symbolism. Having come full circle, the poet searches his mind for the right imagery — dismissing the desert and the rain; mainland, island and open sea. In this same section, Eliot quotes the Old Testament prophet Micah ("O my people, what have I done unto thee?"), who shared God's message with his community. When an anxious servant asked the prophet how he should come before the Lord, the prophet said: "He hath shewed thee, O man, what *is* good; and what doth the Lord require of thee, but to do justly, and to love mercy, and to walk humbly with thy God?" (Micah 6: 8). For Eliot, this *was* the Word: do justly, love mercy, walk humbly. How, he wondered, could landscape symbolism — desert or sea or garden — help to convey that?

In the sixth and final section of *Ash Wednesday*, the poet seems to find peace for the first time, and the imagery he uses here — of a "granite shore" and an open sea — has been chosen for very precise reasons. For years, the only place that Eliot and his wife had been able to find peace was by the sea. In 1916, he wrote to his father from the seaside village of Torquay, where he experienced "an atmosphere of perfect peace that nothing but the ocean has."[131] A few months later, he and Vivienne again escaped to the southern shores of England, where Eliot wrote an uncharacteristically lighthearted letter to his friend Conrad Aiken.[132] In 1921, on the shores of sea-sized Lake Lausanne in Switzerland, Eliot again found peace.

The sea obviously reminded Eliot of the summers that he had spent on the New England coast. Beginning with excised portions of *The Waste Land*, he returned there many times in his poetry, particularly after the 1929 death of his mother — a devastating reminder that he couldn't go home again. In the final section of *Ash Wednesday* and in the final Ariel poem, *Marina*, the poet presents very personal snapshots of the sea. For Eliot, the sea was also a universal symbol of the Eternal Feminine which had haunted Prufrock's imagination, swallowed Phlebas and now represented the ultimate end of the pilgrim's progress. Eliot had charted many variations of the poet's response to the Eternal Feminine in his studies — from Homer's use of the sea as a symbol of life's journey, to Ovid's symbol of tumultuous change, to the "open sea" of Nietzsche's existentialism, the "empty sea" of Wagner's romanticism, the damning sea of Poe's "Annabel Lee," the sea of surrender in Valéry and finally Dante's all-encompassing "sea / in which all things are drawn that it itself / creates or which the work of Nature makes."[133] At the end of *Ash Wednesday*, however, Eliot is not satisfied to conclude with this pervasive symbol; the poet still believes that he is hovering "between dying and birth."[134] In order to go all the way — beyond memory and desire — he calls on the Eternal Feminine to guide him:

> Sister, mother
> And spirit of the river, spirit of the sea,
> Suffer me not to be separated[135]

The invocation produces the symbolic image of a river journeying toward that great sea of change — an image used in Hinduism to represent the mortal life merging with the immortal life-force (and later used by Ovid, Wordsworth and Nietzsche to symbolize the same). This image too has personal connotations for Eliot, who as a child spent fall, winter and spring near the Mississippi River. In a 1928 preface to Edgar Ansel Mowrer's *This American World*, Eliot writes that when he was in Missouri he missed the "blue sea of Massachusetts" and when he was in New England he missed "the long dark river."[136] In 1930, he wrote to a St. Louis newspaper that "there is something in having passed one's childhood beside the big river, which is incommunicable to those who have not."[137] For Eliot, it was the best symbolic representation of his spiritual status: a river striving towards the sea.

At the end of *Ash Wednesday*, Eliot allows himself to wax nostalgic, but he is resolved not to live in the past. He is acutely aware of the fact that memory cannot reproduce the peaceful feelings of childhood. Memory can only produce the complex feelings of a man who has experienced much since then. As early as 1917, when Eliot decided to settle permanently in England, he was tormented by this realization of the "loss" of childhood. When his mother sent him an album of photographs from his childhood, he commented that "it gives one a strange feeling that Time is not before and after, but all at once, present and future and all the periods of the past."[138] He might as well have been quoting the observations of his thesis on F.H. Bradley: "The past lived over is not memory, and the past remembered was never lived." Henceforth, Eliot knew he could indulge only one point of view — that of a Christian and an American expatriate — if he was to maintain control over his thoughts and feelings. This willful control of his point of view was the intended effect of his "turning." The fragmented worldview of *The Waste Land* was behind him.

Ash Wednesday and the Ariel Poems: Life in Flux

In final analysis, it is important to recognize that although Eliot strictly advocated a Christian point of view in his future social criticism, he continued to use the imagery of ancient religion, mysticism and mythology in his poetry. In *Marina*, the poet's journey ends with allusions to *Pericles*, one of Shakespeare's final plays. *Pericles* is filled with pre–Christian ideas, as well as several of the ideas that Eliot found so inspiring in his own religion — that death is illusory, that the sea (and the life force it represents) is simultaneously destructive and creative, that those who wait without hope are ultimately rewarded. Eliot's name for the completed cycle (the Ariel poems) suggests that he may have thought of *Marina* as a counterpoint to his use of *The Tempest* in *The Waste Land*.

The play begins when Pericles, the prince of Tyre, flees from his homeland to escape the wrath of King Antiochus. At sea, a furious storm destroys his ship and tosses Pericles onto the shores of Greece. He becomes convinced that the gods are set against him and wishes to die in peace. Soon after, Pericles is greeted by three kind fishermen and welcomed by their king and his daughter Thaisa. She falls in love with the mysterious traveler and they wed. When word reaches Greece that Antiochus is dead, Pericles — who is heir to the throne — sets sail for his homeland, along with his pregnant wife. While at sea, Thaisa gives birth to their first daughter, whom they name Marina because of her birth at sea. The couple's happiness, however, does not last. Thaisa dies as a result of complications from childbirth, and a storm soon forces Pericles to bury his wife at sea and leave his newborn child in the care of a local islander. Later, when he returns for her, Marina's caretaker tells him that his daughter is dead. The king returns to the sea, only to become stranded again on the shores of a foreign land. This time, he simply begs to die, feeling as empty and desolate as Tristan felt on his death-bed, convinced that he had lost Isolde forever. It is then that Marina, having escaped her rumored death, finds her father on the island. When she sings to him, her music restores him. To Eliot, her song may have represented a counterpoint to the heart-rending song that Tristan heard on his deathbed, and which he had incorporated into *The Waste Land*.

The king also learns that his wife, too, is alive — revived by the goddess Diana. This detail, in combination with the epigraph that Eliot appended to his poem, was also very personal for the poet. Eliot prefaces *Marina* with an epigraph from Seneca's play *Hercules Furens*. Roughly translated, it reads: "What is this place, what country, what region of the world?" The words are spoken by Hercules when he regains his sanity, after murdering his wife in a mad frenzy. In a 1930 letter, Eliot explains that he intended "a crisscross between Pericles finding alive, and Hercules finding dead — the two extremes of the recognition scene."[139] He is reflecting on his recent religious conversion (the death of hope that leads to new life) as well as his own failed marriage.

In life, Eliot now had only one goal: to do justly, love mercy and walk humbly. In poetry, he was determined to reconcile the religious feelings of his youth with the resolve and understanding of his new point of view — uniting the Fire and the Rose, to create the Wisdom that he spoke of in his later years. Eliot acknowledged that his point of view, like the Church of England and the world itself, would never be static. In a 1924 letter to Sir Herbert Read, he writes:

> It seems to me that at the present time we need more dogma, and that one ought to have as precise and clear a creed as possible, when one thinks at all: but a creed is always in one sense smaller than the man, and in another sense larger; one's formulations never fully explain one, although it is necessary to formulate.[140]

Quite simply, Eliot was determined to exert greater control over his thoughts and feelings. He knew that he was still far from the end of his journey. In his 1928 preface to *This American World*, Eliot illuminates his own current point of view by praising the author's ability to look beyond the temporary afflictions of the world and of the self toward something more substantial: "He recognizes that if one looks hard enough ahead, none of these things that are happening seem either good or bad: they are merely change. Our task is simply to see what we are, and to know what we want in the immediate future, and to work towards that."[141]

Suggested Reading (1923–1930)

The Complete Poems and Plays, 1909–1950

"Eyes that last I saw in tears"
"The wind sprang up at four o'clock"

The Hollow Men
Sweeney Agonistes
Ariel Poems
Ash Wednesday

Selected Essays (1932)

The Varieties of Metaphysical Experience, ed. Ronald Schuchard

Lusts of an Old Man

In 1897, W.B. Yeats wrote his own variation on the biblical story of the journey of the Magi to Jerusalem. In "The Adoration of the Magi," the poet is visited by three old men at his home in the Irish countryside. The Magi are so cold that their beards are frozen, so the poet invites them in to warm themselves by the fire, and the Magi proceed to tell him their story. They say they are brothers who lived for many years on a remote island, caring only for the simple pleasures of classical literature. One day, a man named Michael Robartes came to them in a fishing boat and told them of "the coming again of the gods and the ancient things." Soon after, one of the brothers — while reading the Fifth Eclogue of Virgil — appeared to become possessed. A strange voice spoke through him, and bid the magi to go to Paris. They went, and found a woman in childbirth. There, the strange voice spoke again, identifying itself as Hermes the Shepherd of the Dead, and saying that the woman has given birth to a creature with the "likeness of a unicorn." The possessed man later told his brother that he had a dream of three old men low beside a manger, surrounded by livestock. Before the dream ended, one of the animals spoke, saying, "Foolish old men, you had once all the wisdom of the stars." The three brothers then employed a pagan ritual to decipher this dream, and concluded:

> When people are good the world likes them and takes possession of them, and so eternity comes through people who are not good and who have been forgotten. Perhaps Christianity was good and the world liked it, so now it is going away and the Immortals are beginning to awake.[1]

When the three old men leave, the narrator is afraid. Soon after, he tells us, he turned away from a magical cult with which he had become involved and embraced a simple life of humble prayer.

After the death of Yeats in 1939, T.S. Eliot gave a memorial lecture at the Abbey Theater in Dublin. Though Eliot had been somewhat dismissive of Yeats's early work — believing it to be an outdated form of romanticism with only regional appeal — he had gradually come to respect his peer's creative development. "It is my experience," Eliot wrote in a 1940 essay, "that towards middle age a man has three choices: to stop writing altogether, to repeat himself with perhaps an increasing skill of virtuosity, or by taking thought to adapt himself to middle age and find a different way of working."[2] Yeats had adapted brilliantly. A few years after Yeats wrote "The Adoration of the Magi," the poet underwent his own transformation: he renounced transcendentalism and began writing more realistic poetry. In 1916, at age 51, he reinvented himself again, this time as a playwright. Yeats won the Nobel Prize in 1923, then went on to write his best poetry. For his longevity and his unwillingness to repeat himself, Eliot saw Yeats as a role model.

Of course, Eliot also saw himself in Yeats. The form and content of his own poetry had changed significantly after religious conversion. Eliot's criticism also changed profoundly, its focus shifting from literature to religion and society. In the 1930s, Eliot all but abandoned poetry for lyrical drama, and attempted to establish himself as a playwright. This new practice eventually produced the first lines of *Burnt Norton* (1935). By the time he gave his lecture on Yeats, Eliot had begun to think of *Burnt Norton* as the first in a quartet of poems — his ultimate poetic statement. His essay on Yeats is a personal plan of action.

The first secret of Yeats's ability, he says, was "to remain always a contemporary." In 1925, Eliot left his job as a bank clerk and began work as an editor at Faber & Faber publishing house. The new job meant that he was constantly exposed to new writers and new ideas, thus remaining always a contemporary. The second secret was "continual development." Just as the world continually changes, Eliot says, so must the artist — lest he lapse into insincere self-mimicry.[3] He explains, with reference to Yeats:

> It is not that he became a different man, for, as I have hinted, one feels sure that the intense experience of youth had been lived through — and indeed, without this early experience, he could never have attained anything of the wisdom which appears in his later writing. But he had to wait for a later maturing to find expression of early experience; and this makes him, I think, a unique and especially interesting poet.[4]

Eliot marks Yeats's turning point in 1914, when the poet was 49 years old. In 1940, T.S. Eliot was 52, and hoped that he too could continue to develop with intellectual maturity and emotional sincerity. For true poets, he says, only death completes their growth. After the death of great artists — like Dante, Shakespeare, Goethe and Yeats — readers can chart a continual artistic development in the work by studying the later work in light of the former, and vice versa. In lesser artists, readers find evidence of a stunted development, where the later work offers no illumination of the earlier work. In 1940, Eliot had not yet reached the culmination of his own artistic development. He realized as much, while working on *Four Quartets*.

Afterword

I started this book in the spring of 2004. I began my research not with biographies or critical studies of T.S. Eliot but with an essay by W.B. Yeats called "The Autumn of the Body," in which the author expresses his belief that the arts will soon supplant religion. I was particularly intrigued by this idea because, by the time I was in high school, I was experiencing greater feelings of awe in my studies of literature than in the church of my childhood. I assumed that the same must have been true for T.S. Eliot when he was my age, since it seemed to me that he had felt his way toward God via his own reading and writing. With a personal stake in the subject, I started investigating his development as a philosopher-poet.

I began, as he began, with Poe, Fitzgerald, the Rhymers and the French Symbolists — all of whom appealed to my emotions, reminding me of the time when metaphysical dread had first drawn me to the literature of Edgar Allan Poe, Arthur Rimbaud, the English Romantic writers, T.S. Eliot and Stephen King. Next, I read Irving Babbitt and reread the Western classics that still dominate the American high school curriculum. Continuing to follow Eliot's lead, I turned my attention to various Eastern classics, of which I had been only vaguely aware. In the fall of 2004, I traveled to India, where I became particularly interested in the Vedanta school of Hinduism, thanks to the writings of A. Parsatharathy. After only a few months of reading, I already had quite a bit of material to sort out in my own mind, and I soon developed expectations about where Eliot must have gone from there.

It turned out that I was wrong. Eliot's worldview, like the world he grew up in and the world in which he chose to live his adult life, was very different from mine. His intellectual development followed from an artistic fusion of Romantic ideals and Classical ideas, and I believe that combination of influences reinforced an intuitive belief that the beginning of true wisdom is fear of God. With this I am in agreement, but unlike Eliot I have not found my way to any organized religion. I prefer Carl Jung's explanation of God to the explanation of any religious text: "What men have always named God is the unfathomable itself."[5] At times, I wonder if Eliot himself did not — after the Church of England had addressed his personal need for self-discipline — begin to question it as well. My thesis for a follow-up book, if there ever is one, would be that the second half of Eliot's career fuses the metaphysical dread of his youth with the careful resolve of his mature years, ultimately producing the complex artistic formulation of the Unknowable God in *Four Quartets*. Forthcoming editions of Eliot's complete prose and letters promise to make such a study possible for readers and students like myself.

While I wait, I have no doubt that my thoughts on Eliot will continue to change. Quite often, in casual reading, I encounter images, thoughts and feelings that inadvertently contribute

155

to a more complex and personal understanding of his development — but, as Eliot would have noted, this understanding ultimately says more about my point of view than about his. In the spring of 2006, I took several trips to learn more about my own ancestors — some of whom have been in North America almost as long as Eliot's ancestors. Not long after I discovered my roots, I moved from my home state of Virginia to Southern California. When Eliot left for England, he could not help thinking of St. Louis as "the southwest." California still had the mythical allure of the American frontier. I couldn't help wondering how Eliot would have responded to the sight of the desert wastes of the new southwest: would it have evoked the optimism of the American pioneer mentality, or would he have opined that it was destined to become the "heart of darkness" of modern Western civilization? For me, those first sightings of Monument Valley at dusk and the Grand Canyon at dawn conjured abstract thoughts of an Unknowable God. For the time being, this is where I break with Eliot — preferring the less precise, more individualistic (and arguably, more American) formulations of Jung or Emerson to the scriptures of the Church.

In 1898, a middle-aged art historian and critic named John C. Van Dyke wandered into the unsettled Colorado desert, searching for something he couldn't define. He returned with an amazing record of thoughts and observations about that untamed landscape, published in 1902 as *The Desert*. What amazed Van Dyke was the vastness, the desolation, the profound stillness and silence. In spite of these things, he also noticed persistent signs of new life — in the land and in himself. At one point, he is captivated by the image of the mud-red Colorado River flowing toward the sea. "The Silent River," he says, "moves on carrying desolation with it; and at every step the waters grow darker, darker with the stain of red — red the hue of decay."[6] All that decay silently disappears into the great ocean, where it becomes as blue as the endless sky. I myself cannot read this without comparing it to Eliot's short landscape poem "Virginia," written about the Rivanna River in my hometown of Charlottesville, which flows into the James River, where my ancestors settled in 1681. I also think of the sacred River Ganges in India, which the Hindus associate with the god Shiva, a creator and a destroyer. Eliot invoked this symbol in the climactic section of *The Waste Land*, to highlight his intellectual conflict with the dual aspects of Nature. In his journey through the desert, Van Dyke contemplates the same:

> With the same indifferent spirit that she planted in us an eye to see or an ear to hear, she afterward plants a microbe to breed and a cancer to eat. She in herself is both growth and decay. The virile and healthy things of the earth are hers; and so, too, are disease, dissolution, and death. The flower and the grass spring up, they fade, they wither; and Nature neither rejoices in the life nor sorrows in the death. She is neither good nor evil; she is only the great law of change that passeth understanding.[7]

Van Dyke's perspective seems to me much closer to that of Emerson (or, for that matter, Homer) than to the middle-aged Eliot. Still, these writers reach some of the same conclusions. Van Dyke writes that death is "the culmination of character," and life "but the process of its development."[8] Eliot writes that the purpose of art is continual development, up until the moment of death. Both statements convey the belief that the journey — in art, if not in life — is what makes us whole.

A Chronology of Eliot's Collected Poetry, Written Between 1905 and 1916

1905

"A Lyric: If time and space, as Sages say" — *Poems Written in Early Youth*
"A Fable for Feasters" — *Poems Written in Early Youth*
"At Graduation 1905" (recited) — *Poems Written in Early Youth*

1907

"Song: When we came home across the hill" — *Poems Written in Early Youth*
"Song: If time and space as Sages say" — *Poems Written in Early Youth*

1908

"Before Morning" — *Poems Written in Early Youth*
"Circe's Palace" — *Poems Written in Early Youth*

1909

"Song: The moonflower opens to the moth" — *Poems Written in Early Youth*
"On a Portrait" — *Poems Written in Early Youth*
"Nocturne" — *Poems Written in Early Youth*
"First Caprice in North Cambridge" — *Inventions of the March Hare*
"Second Caprice in North Cambridge" — *Inventions of the March Hare*
"Opera" — *Inventions of the March Hare*
"Humouresque (After J. Laforgue)" — *Poems Written in Early Youth*

"Conversation Galante" — *Prufrock and Other Observations*

1910

"Spleen" — *Poems Written in Early Youth*
"Convictions (Curtain Raiser)" — *Inventions of the March Hare*
"First Debate between the Body and Soul" — *Inventions of the March Hare*
"Easter: Sensations of April" — *Inventions of the March Hare*
"Ode" — *Poems Written in Early Youth*
"Silence" — *Inventions of the March Hare*
"Mandarins" — *Inventions of the March Hare*
"Goldfish (Essence of Summer Magazines)" — *Inventions of the March Hare*
"Suite Clownesque" — *Inventions of the March Hare*
"The Triumph of Bullshit" — *Inventions of the March Hare*
"Fourth Caprice in Montparnasse" — *Inventions of the March Hare*
"Portrait of a Lady [I, II]" — *Prufrock and Other Observations*
"Preludes [I, II]" — *Prufrock and Other Observations*

1911

"Entretien Dans un Parc" — *Inventions of the March Hare*
"Interlude: In a Bar" — *Inventions of the March Hare*

"Bacchus and Ariadne"—*Inventions of the March Hare*

"The Smoke that Gathers Blue and Sinks"—*Inventions of the March Hare*

"He Said: This Universe is Very Clever"—*Inventions of the March Hare*

"Inside the gloom"—*Inventions of the March Hare*

"Interlude in London"—*Inventions of the March Hare*

"Rhapsody on a Windy Night"—*Prufrock and Other Observations*

"The Love Song of J. Alfred Prufrock"—*Prufrock and Other Observations*

"Ballade Pour La Grosse Lulu"—*Inventions of the March Hare*

"Portrait of a Lady [III]"—*Prufrock and Other Observations*

"Preludes [III, IV]"—*Prufrock and Other Observations*

"La Figlia Che Piange"—*Prufrock and Other Observations*

1911 or 1912

"Do I know how I feel? Do I know what I think?"—*Inventions of the March Hare*

1911–1914

"The Little Passion: from 'An Agony in the Garret'"—*Inventions of the March Hare*

1912

"Prufrock's Pervigilium"—*Inventions of the March Hare*

1914

"The Burnt Dancer"—*Inventions of the March Hare*

"Now while Columbo and his men"—*Letters, Vol. I*

"Oh Little Voices of the Throats of Men"—*Inventions of the March Hare*

"Appearances appearances he said"—*Letters, Vol. I*

"The Love Song of St. Sebastian"—*Inventions of the March Hare*

"Morning at the Window"—*Prufrock and Other Observations*

"Paysage Triste"—*Inventions of the March Hare*

"Suppressed Complex"—*Inventions of the March Hare*

"Afternoon"—*Inventions of the March Hare*

"So through the evening"—*The Waste Land Facsimile*

"After the turning"—*The Waste Land Facsimile*

"I am the Resurrection"—*The Waste Land Facsimile*

1915

"The Death of Saint Narcissus"—*Poems Written in Early Youth*

"The 'Boston Evening Transcript'"—*Prufrock and Other Observations*

"Aunt Helen"—*Prufrock and Other Observations*

"Cousin Nancy"—*Prufrock and Other Observations*

"Hysteria"—*Prufrock and Other Observations*

"In the Department Store"—*Inventions of the March Hare*

"Mr. Apollinax"—*Prufrock and Other Observations*

Exact Date Unknown (before 1921)

"Introspection"—*Inventions of the March Hare*

"While you were absent in the lavatory"—*Inventions of the March Hare*

"O lord, have patience"—*Inventions of the March Hare*

"Hidden under the heron's wing"—*Inventions of the March Hare*

"The Engine"—*Inventions of the March Hare*

"In silent corridors of death"—*Inventions of the March Hare*

"Fragments: There was a Jolly tinker..."—*Inventions of the March Hare*

"Columbo and Bolo Verses"—*Inventions of the March Hare* (1910–?)

A Chronology of Eliot's Collected Poetry and Fiction, Published Between 1915 and 1930

1915

"The Love Song of J. Alfred Prufrock"—*Poetry* (June 1915)
"Preludes"—*Blast* (July 1915)
"Rhapsody of a Windy Night"—*Blast* (July 1915)
"Portrait of a Lady"—*Others* (September 1915)
"The Boston Evening Transcript"—*Poetry* (October 1915)
"Aunt Helen"—*Poetry* (October 1915)
"Cousin Nancy"—*Poetry* (October 1915)
"Hysteria"—*Catholic Anthology* (November 1915)

1916

"Conversation Galante"—*Poetry* (September 1916)
"La Figlia che Piange"—*Poetry* (September 1916)
"Mr. Apollinax"—*Poetry* (September 1916)
"Morning at the Window"—*Poetry* (September 1916)

1917

"Eeldrop and Appleplex, I"—*Little Review* (May 1917)
"La Directeur"—*Little Review* (July 1917)
"Mélange Adultère de Tout"—*Little Review* (July 1917)
"Lune de Miel"—*Little Review* (July 1917)
"The Hippopotamus"—*Little Review* (July 1917)
"Eeldrop and Appleplex, II"—*Little Review* (September 1917)

1918

"Sweeney among the Nightingales"—*Little Review* (September 1918)
"Whispers of Immortality"—*Little Review* (September 1918)
"Dans le Restaurant"—*Little Review* (September 1918)
"Mr. Eliot's Sunday Morning Service"—*Little Review* (September 1918)

1919

"A Cooking Egg"—*Coterie* (May 1919)
"Burbank with a Baedeker: Bleinstein with a Cigar"—*Arts and Letters* (Summer 1919)
"Sweeney Erect"—*Arts and Letters* (Summer 1919)

1920

"Gerontion"—*Ara Vos Prec* by T.S. Eliot
"Ode on Independence Day, July 4th 1918"—*Poems* by T.S. Eliot

1921

"Song to the Opherian"—*The Tyro* (April 1921)

1922

"The Waste Land"—*Criterion* (October 1922)

1924

"Eyes that last I saw in tears" (Part I of "Doris's Dream Songs," reprinted as Part II of "Three Poems") — *The Chapbook* (November 1924)

"The wind sprang up at four o'clock" (revision of "Song to the Opherian," Part II of "Doris's Dream Songs") — *The Chapbook* (November 1924)

"This is the dead land" (Part III of "Doris's Dream Songs," reprinted as Part III of "The Hollow Men") — *The Chapbook* (November 1924)

"Poème Inédit" (reprinted as Part I of "The Hollow Men") — *Commerce* (November 1924)

1925

"Eyes I dare not meet in dreams" (Part I of "Three Poems," reprinted with changes as Part II of "The Hollow Men") — *Criterion* (January 1925)

"The eyes are not here" (Part III of "Three Poems," reprinted with changes as Part IV of "The Hollow Men") — *Criterion* (January 1925)

"The Hollow Men, I – III" — *The Dial* (March 1925)

"The Hollow Men, I – V" — *Poems 1909–1925* by T.S. Eliot (November 1925)

1926

"Fragment of a Prologue" (reprinted as Part I of "Sweeney Agonistes") — *Criterion* (October 1926)

1927

"Fragment of an Agon" (reprinted as Part II of "Sweeney Agonistes") — *Criterion* (January 1927)

Journey of the Magi by T.S. Eliot (August 1927)

"Salutation" (reprinted as Part II of "Ash Wednesday") — *Saturday Review of Literature* (December 1927)

1928

"From 'Anabase'" (a translation) — *Criterion* (February 1928)

"Perch' Io Non Spero" (French translation of Part I of "Ash Wednesday") — *Commerce* (Spring 1928)

A Song for Simeon by T.S. Eliot (September 1928)

1929

"Son de L'Escalina" (French translation of Part III of "Ash Wednesday") — *Commerce* (Autumn 1929)

Animula by T.S. Eliot (October 1929)

1930

Ash Wednesday by T.S. Eliot (April 1930)

Anabasis by St.-John Perse (translation by T.S. Eliot) (May 1930)

Marina by T.S. Eliot (September 1930)

A Chronology of Eliot's Collected Criticism, 1916–1932

SW   = *The Sacred Wood and Major Early Essays*
SE   = *Selected Essays* (1950)
SP   = *Selected Prose of T.S. Eliot* (1975) edited by Frank Kermode
TCTC = *To Criticize the Critic and Other Writings*
AWL = *The Annotated Waste Land with Eliot's Contemporary Prose* (1995) edited by Lawrence Rainey

"A Note on the American Critic" (originally titled "An American Critic") (1916) — SW

Knowledge and Experience in the Philosophy of F.H. Bradley (1916)

Ezra Pound, His Metric and Poetry (1917) — TCTC

"Reflections on Vers Libre" (1917) — TCTC

"(In Memory of) Henry James" (1918) — SP

"A Romantic Aristocrat" (originally titled "A Romantic Patrician") (1919) — SW

"Rhetoric and Poetic Drama" (originally titled "Whether Rostand Had Something about Him") (1919) — SW / SE

"(Some Notes on the Blank Verse of) Christopher Marlowe" (1918) — SW / SE

"Tradition and the Individual Talent" (1919) — SW / SE

"Swinburne as Critic" (originally titled "Swinburne and the Elizabethans") (1919) — SW

"Hamlet and His Problems" (1919) — SW / SE

"Ben Jonson" (1919) — SW / SE

"The Local Flavour" (1919) — SW

"Swinburne As Poet" (1920) — SW / SE

"Blake" (originally titled "The Naked Man") (1920) — SE

"Euripides and Professor Murray" (1920) — SE

"Dante (as a 'Spiritual Leader')" (1920) — SW

"Philip Massinger" (1920) — SE

"The Perfect Critic" (1920) — SP

"The French Intelligence" (1920) — SW

"The Possibility of a Poetic Drama" (1920) — SW

"London Letter, March 1921" — AWL

"The Romantic Englishman, the Comic Spirit and the Function of Criticism" (1921) — AWL

"The Lesson of Baudelaire" (1921) — AWL

"Andrew Marvell" (1921) — SE / SP / AWL

"Prose and Verse" (1921) — AWL

"London Letter, May 1921" — AWL

"London Letter, September 1921" — AWL

"The Metaphysical Poets" (1921) — SE / AWL

"John Dryden" (1922) — SE

"(In Memoriam) Marie Lloyd" (1923) — SE / SP

"The Function of Criticism" (1923) — SE / SP

"Ulysses, Order and Myth" (1923) — SP

"Four Elizabethan Dramatists: A Preface" (1924) — SE

"Lancelot Andrewes" (1926) — SE / SP

The Clark Lectures (1926) — *The Varieties of Metaphysical Experience*

"Baudelaire (in Our Time)" (originally titled "Poet and Saint...") (1927) — SE

"Thomas Middleton" (1927) — SE

"John Bramhall" (originally titled "Archbishop Bramhall") (1927) — SE

"Wilkie Collins and Dickens" (1927) — SE

"Francis Herbert Bradley" (originally titled "Bradley's 'Ethical Studies'") (1927) — SE / SP

"Seneca in Elizabethan Translation" (1927) — SE

Shakespeare and the Stoicism of Seneca (1927) — SE

"The Humanism of Irving Babbitt" (1928) — SE / SP

"Second Thoughts on Humanism" (1929) — SE

"A Dialogue on Dramatic Poetry" (originally titled *A Dialogue on Poetic Drama*) (1928) — SE

Dante (1929) — SE / SP

"Baudelaire" (Introduction) (1930) — SE

"Preface to *From Anabasis* by St. John Perse" (1930) — SP

"Arnold and Pater" (originally titled "The Place of Pater") (1930) — SE

"Cyril Tourneur" (1930) — SE

"Pascal's Pensées" (originally an Introduction to *The Pensées of Pascal*) (1931) — SP

Thoughts after Lambeth (1931) — SE

"Thomas Heywood" (1931) — SE

"John Ford" (1932) — SE

Charles Whibley: A Memoir (1932) — SE

Notes

Preface

1. T.S. Eliot, "The Frontiers of Criticism," from *On Poetry and Poets* (London: Faber, 1957), 106.
2. Howarth 74.
3. Eliot directly stated his preference for the King James Version over the "New English Bible" in a December 16, 1962, letter to the *Sunday Telegraph*.
4. Huxley, *Doors*, 78.
5. T.S. Eliot, *George Herbert*, 28.
6. T.S. Eliot, "Tradition and the Individual Talent," from *Selected Prose of T.S. Eliot*, ed. Frank Kermode (New York: Harcourt, 1975), 30.

Part I

1. Howarth 10.
2. T.S. Eliot, "American Literature and the American Language," in *To Criticize the Critic* (Lincoln: University of Nebraska Press, 1965), 44.
3. Wendell 278.
4. Ackroyd 17.
5. In his book *T.S. Eliot: The Making of an American Poet*, James E. Miller refers to a conversation between Eliot and William Turner Leavy, in which Eliot used this phrase to describe his Unitarian upbringing — see p. 18.
6. T.S. Eliot, *Nightwood*, xiii.
7. T.S. Eliot, *Letters*, xix.
8. Ackroyd 27.
9. Poe 996.
10. T.S. Eliot, "From Poe to Valéry," from *To Criticize*, 29–30.
11. Poe 1010–1011.
12. T.S. Eliot, "From Poe to Valéry," from *To Criticize*, 35.
13. T.S. Eliot, *Use*, 24.
14. Fitzgerald 72.
15. T.S. Eliot, *Poems*, 10.
16. T.S. Eliot, *Use*, 24.
17. T.S. Eliot, *Inventions*, 388.
18. Symons, "Memoir."
19. Dowson 36.
20. Symons, "Memoir."
21. Dowson 48.
21. See the poem "Carthusians."
23. Dowson, "A Requiem," from *The Poetry of Ernest Dowson*, ed. Desmond Flower (Cranbury, N.J.: Associated University Presses, 1970), 64.
24. Dowson, "Cease smiling, Dear! A little while be sad," from *The Poetry of Ernest Dowson*, 84.
25. Dowson 127.
26. Symons, "Memoir."

27. Yeats, "The Autumn of the Body," from *Essays and Introductions* (New York: Collier, 1986), 192.
28. Ibid., 193.
29. Symons, *Symbolist*, 94.
30. Babbitt, *Literature*, 81.
31. Baudelaire, "Au Lecteur," from *Echoes of Baudelaire*, ed. Kendall Lappin (Santa Maria, Calif.: Asylum Arts, 1992), 13.
32. Laforgue 211.
33. T.S. Eliot, "What Dante Means to Me," from *To Criticize*, 126.
34. T.S. Eliot, *Inventions*, 398.
35. Davidson.
36. Thomson.
37. Baudelaire, "Travel," from *Echoes of Baudelaire*, 165.
38. Rimbaud 12.
39. Ibid., 13.
40. Rimbaud, "The Righteous Man…," from *Rimbaud Complete*, ed. Wyatt Mason (New York: Modern Library, 2002), 90.
41. Ibid., 90.
42. Rimbaud, "Deliria II: Alchemy of the Word," from *Rimbaud Complete*, 208.
43. Rimbaud 213.
44. Rimbaud, "The Impossible," from *Rimbaud Complete*, 215.
45. Symons, *Symbolist*, 36.
46. Rimbaud, "Farewell," from *Rimbaud Complete*, 220.
47. Symons, *Symbolist*, 53.
48. Laforgue 242.
49. William Jay Smith 21.
50. Laforgue, "Parisian Landscapes," from *Selected Writings of Jules Laforgue*, ed. William Jay Smith (New York: Grove, 1956), 201–202.
51. Laforgue 90.
52. Ibid., 133.
53. Ibid., 106.
54. Ibid., 113.
55. Ibid., 123.
56. Ibid., 124.
57. Ibid., 125.
58. Ibid., 108.
59. Ibid., 135.
60. T.S. Eliot, "Reflections on Contemporary Poetry," from *Inventions of the March Hare, Poems 1909–1917*, ed. Christopher Ricks (New York: Harcourt, 1996), 400.
61. T.S. Eliot, "Circe's Palace," from *Poems Written in Early Youth*, ed. John Hayward (New York: Farrar, Straus, 1967), 20.
62. T.S. Eliot, "Song (The moonflower opens to the moth)," from *Poems*, 22.

63. T.S. Eliot, *Poems,* 23.
64. T.S. Eliot, "First Caprice in North Cambridge," from *Inventions,* 13.
65. T.S. Eliot, *Inventions,* 17.
66. See "Spleen," "Convictions (Curtain Raiser)," "First Debate between the Body and Soul," "Mandarins," "Fourth Caprice in Montparnasse."
67. T.S. Eliot, *Inventions,* 35.
68. T.S. Eliot, "Goldfish (Essence of Summer Magazines)," from *Inventions,* 26.

Part II

1. Watson 74.
2. T.S. Eliot, *Letters,* xix–xx.
3. Babbitt, *Literature,* 160–161.
4. Ibid., 125.
5. T.S. Eliot, "Tradition and the Individual Talent," from *Selected Prose,* 27.
6. See "Faith That Illuminates" (1934).
7. Babbitt, *Literature,* 102–103.
8. T.S. Eliot, *Varieties,* 95.
9. Harris 424.
10. Hamilton 61.
11. Aeschylus, *Agamemnon,* from *The Complete Greek Tragedies, Volume I,* ed. David Grene and Richard Lattimore (Chicago: University of Chicago Press, 1953), lines 1560–1566.
12. Ibid., lines 517–525.
13. Plato, *Republic,* from *Five Dialogues,* ed. G.M.A. Grube (Indianapolis: Hackett, 1981), III.401.
14. Santayana 35.
15. Plato, *Meno,* from *Five Dialogues,* 1.81.
16. Plato, *Phaedo,* from *Great Dialogues of Plato,* ed. Eric H. Warmington and Philip G. Rouse (New York: Signet, 1999), I.99.
17. Ibid., I.82.
18. Plato, *Republic,* from *The Collected Dialogues of Plato,* ed. Edith Hamilton and Huntington Cairns (Princeton: Princeton University Press, 1961), X.614–621.
19. Plato, *Republic,* from *Five Dialogues,* VII.518.
20. Howarth 30.
21. Ibid., 85.
22. Plato, *Republic,* from *Five Dialogues,* V.476.
23. Aristotle, *Physics,* from *A New Aristotle Reader,* ed. J.L. Akrill (Princeton: Princeton University Press, 1987), I.vii.191a.18.
24. Ibid., II.i.193a.29.
25. Aristotle, *On the Soul,* from *A New Aristotle Reader,* II.iv.415b.8.
26. Ibid., II.v.417b.23–24.
27. Ibid., III.viii.432.20.
28. Aristotle, *Metaphysics,* from *A New Aristotle Reader,* VII.vi.1031b.12–15.
29. Ibid., I(A).i.981a.15.
30. Ibid., XII.viii.1074b.
31. T.S. Eliot, "The Perfect Critic," from *The Sacred Wood and Major Early Essays* (Mineola, N.Y.: Dover, 1998), 6.
32. Santayana 63.
33. Ibid., 54.
34. Ibid., 148.
35. Ibid., 152.
36. Ibid., 99–100.
37. Ibid., 139.
38. See Eliot's 1929 preface to *Dante.*
39. T.S. Eliot, "Virgil and the Christian World," from *On Poetry,* 124.
40. T.S. Eliot, "What is a Classic?," from *Selected Prose,* 123.
41. Virgil VI.860–890.

42. Ovid I.26.
43. Ibid., XV: 222–234.
44. T.S. Eliot, "Virgil and the Christian World," from *On Poetry,* 123.
45. Augustine I.vi.
46. Ibid I.xvi.
47. Ibid., II.x.
48. Ibid., VIII.vii.
49. Ibid., VII.v.
50. Ibid., VII.xii.
51. Ibid., III.vii.
52. Ibid., VIII.v.
53. Ibid., VII.xviii.
54. Ibid., IV.ii.
55. Dante, *Inferno,* from *The Portable Dante,* ed. Mark Musa (New York: Penguin, 1995), III.23.
56. Dante, *Purgatory,* from *The Portable Dante,* XXV.106.
57. Aquinas 201.
58. Dante, *Inferno,* from *The Portable Dante,* III.38.
59. Ibid., III.56–57.
60. Dante, *Purgatory,* from *The Portable Dante,* XVIII.28–33.
61. Howarth 73.
62. Egendorf 41–42.
63. See his essay "Seneca in Elizabethan Translation."
64. Yeats, "At Stratford-on-Avon," from *Essays and Introductions* (New York: Collier, 1986), 110.
65. Kaufmann 5.
66. Halliday 112.
67. T.S. Eliot, *Use,* 24.
68. T.S. Eliot, "Seneca in Elizabethan Translation," from *Selected Essays* (New York: Harcourt, 1950), 69.
69. T.S. Eliot, "Some Notes on the Blank Verse of Christopher Marlowe," from *Sacred,* 50.
70. T.S. Eliot, "Hamlet and His Problems," from *Sacred,* 58.
71. Ibid., 59.
72. T.S. Eliot, "Shakespeare and the Stoicism of Seneca," from *Selected Essays,* 108.
73. T.S. Eliot, *Complete,* 10.
74. Ibid., 10.
75. T.S. Eliot, "First Debate between the Body and Soul," from *Inventions,* 65.
76. T.S. Eliot, *Complete,* 8.
77. Ibid., 9.
78. T.S. Eliot, *Inventions,* 307.
79. Bergson 325.
80. Ibid., 155.
81. Ibid., 176.
82. Ibid., 177.
83. Ibid., 192.
84. Ibid., 188.
85. Ibid., 342.
86. Whitman, Introduction to the 1855 edition of "Leaves of Grass," from *The Norton Anthology of American Literature* (New York: Norton, 1989), 1972.
87. Whitman, "Song of Myself," from *Norton,* 1975.
88. Ibid., 2016.
89. T.S. Eliot, *Inventions,* 51.
90. See T.S. Eliot, *Letters,* 24.
91. T.S. Eliot, *Poems,* 26.
92. Poe 958.

Part III

1. T.S. Eliot, *Collected,* 20.
2. Gordon 85.
3. Thoreau 86.
4. Williams 4.

5. Ibid., xxxiii.
6. Williams 9.
7. Muller (II) ix.
8. Ibid., 112.
9. Dalrymple 281.
10. Easwaran, *Upanishads*, 46.
11. Muller (II) 189–190.
12. Easwaran, *Bhagavad*, 114.
13. Ibid., 134–135.
14. Parsatharathy 17.
15. Thomas 43.
16. Reat 16.
17. Ackroyd 27.
18. T.S. Eliot, "What Is Minor Poetry?" from *On Poetry*, 42.
19. Edwin Arnold 82.
20. Anesaki 66.
21. Babbitt, *Dhammapada*, 99.
22. Matsunami 38.
23. Ibid., 41.
24. Warren 352.
25. Edwards 336.
26. Royce 62.
27. Ibid., 199.
28. Ibid., 90.
29. Ibid., 95.
30. Ibid., 83.
31. Ibid., 98.
32. Ibid., 104.
33. Ibid., 148.
34. Ibid., 218.
35. Ibid., 191.
36. Underhill 104.
37. Wolters 63.
38. Underhill 48.
39. Ibid., 333.
40. Barnstone 40.
41. Plotinus I.6[1].8.
42. Ibid., VI.9[9].4.
43. Ibid., IV.8[6].1.
44. Ibid., VI.9[9].8.
45. Underhill 104.
46. Ibid., 118.
47. Julian of Norwich 294.
48. Hilton 378.
49. John of the Cross I.viii.4.
50. Ibid., II.ix.4.
51. Ibid., II.x.1.
52. See T.S. Eliot, *Letters*, 21.
53. Russell, "Mysticism," 25.
54. Ibid., 21.
55. Ibid., 31.
56. Ibid., 35.
57. Ibid., 48.
58. Ibid., 47.
59. Gordon 87.
60. Ibid., 92.
61. Eliot to Conrad Aiken, 19 July 1914, in T.S. Eliot, *Letters*, 42.
62. T.S. Eliot, "Afternoons," from *Inventions*, 53.
63. T.S. Eliot, *Letters*, 58–59.
64. Ibid., 69.
65. T.S. Eliot, *Knowledge*, 18.
66. Ibid., 21–22.
67. Ibid., 31.
68. Ibid., 118.
69. Aristotle, *On the Soul*, from *A New Aristotle Reader*, III.viii.432.
70. T.S. Eliot, *Letters*, 80.
71. Bradley 552.
72. Ibid., xiv.
73. Ibid., 3–4.
74. Ibid., 5.
75. Ibid., 6.
76. Ibid., xiii.
77. T.S. Eliot, *Knowledge*, 46.
78. Ibid., 44.
79. Ibid., 39.
80. Freud 376.
81. T.S. Eliot, *Knowledge*, 48.
82. Ibid., 51.
83. Ibid., 55–56.
84. Ibid., 76.
85. Ibid., 79.
86. Ibid., 104.
87. Ibid., 82.
88. Ibid., 162.
89. Ibid., 163.
90. Ibid., 169.
91. Hulme, "A Lecture on Modern Poetry," from *Selected Writings*, ed. Patrick McGuinness (Manchester, U.K.: Carcanet, 1998), 66.
92. Hulme, "Cinders," from *Selected Writings*, 19–20.
93. Ibid., 33.
94. Hulme, "A Lecture on Modern Poetry," from *Selected Writings*, 63.
95. Hulme, "Notes on Language and Style," from *Selected Writings*, 46–47.
96. Ibid., 46.
97. Ibid., 49.
98. Ibid.
99. T.S. Eliot, *The Waste Land*, 93.
100. T.S. Eliot, *Poems*, 28.
101. Hulme, "Cinders," from *Selected Writings*, 25.
102. Ibid., 33–34.

Part IV

1. T.S. Eliot, *Letters*, 88.
2. Seymour-Jones 78.
3. Ibid., 83.
4. T.S. Eliot, *Letters*, 110–111.
5. Russell, *Autobiography*, 54.
6. Seymour-Jones 6.
7. Ibid., 116.
8. Ibid., 126.
9. T.S. Eliot, *Waste*, xvii.
10. See T.S. Eliot, *Letters*, 217.
11. Adams 3.
12. Ibid., 65.
13. Ibid., 73.
14. Ibid., 34.
15. Seymour-Jones 200.
16. T.S. Eliot, *Complete*, 18.
17. Matthews 50.
18. Schuchard 27–28.
19. See Eliot's essay "For Lancelot Andrewes" (1928).
20. Schuchard 28.
21. Matthew Arnold, "The Scholar Gypsy," *The Norton Anthology of American Literature*, ed. Nina Baym, et al. (New York: Norton, 1989), 1353.
22. Matthew Arnold, "On Translating Homer," from *Selections from the Prose Writings of Matthew Arnold* (New York: Henry Holt, 1898), 41.
23. Matthew Arnold, "The Grand Style," from *Selections*, 85–87.
24. Matthew Arnold, "On Translating Homer," from *Selections*, 60.
25. Matthew Arnold, "The Function of Criticism at the Present Time," from *Selections*, 8.

26. Ibid., 7.
27. Ibid., 5.
28. T.S. Eliot, *Use*, 97–98.
29. Matthew Arnold, "Sweetness and Light," from *Selections*, 178.
30. See, in particular, "Literature and Science" (1882).
31. See, in particular, "Sweetness and Light" (1867).
32. Matthew Arnold, "The Study of Poetry," from *Norton*, 1424.
33. T.S. Eliot, "The Second Order Mind."
34. T.S. Eliot, *Use*, 100.
35. T.S. Eliot, "Modern Education and the Classics," from *Selected Essays* (New York: Harcourt, 1950), 180.
36. T.S. Eliot, "Cyril Tourneur," from *Selected Essays*, 169.
37. T.S. Eliot, "Hamlet and His Problems," from *Sacred Wood*, 57.
38. T.S. Eliot, "Cyril Tourneur," from *Selected Essays*, 161.
39. T.S. Eliot, "Thomas Middleton," from *Selected Essays*, 144.
40. Ibid., 146.
41. T.S. Eliot, "Four Elizabethan Dramatists," from *Selected Essays*, 93.
42. Ibid., 98.
43. Ibid., 96.
44. Valerie Eliot, *Letters*, 173.
45. T.S. Eliot, "Eeldrop and Appleplex."
46. T.S. Eliot, *Letters*, 199.
47. Ibid., 214.
48. Gordon 137.
49. T.S. Eliot, *Complete*, 35.
50. Schuchard 96.
51. Ibid., 96.
52. Drew 39.
53. T.S. Eliot, *Complete*, 25.
54. Ibid., 43.
55. Ibid., 43.
56. Ibid., 80.
57. Ibid., 83.
58. T.S. Eliot, *Letters*, 608.
59. Vivienne Eliot to Charlotte C. Eliot, 15 December 1918, in T.S. Eliot, *Letters*, 261.
60. T.S. Eliot, "Whispers of Immortality, draft A-B," from *Inventions*, 365.
61. See T.S. Eliot, *Inventions*, 368.
62. T.S. Eliot, *Collected*, 32.
63. T.S. Eliot, "Whispers of Immortality, draft D-E," from *Inventions*, 370.
64. T.S. Eliot, "Imperfect Critics," from *Sacred*, 13.
65. T.S. Eliot, "The Metaphysical Poets," from *Selected Prose*, 117.
66. "The Bait."
67. "A Valediction: Forbidding Mourning."
68. "To His Mistress, Going to Bed."
69. "The Flea."
70. Donne, "The Canonization," from *The Essential Donne*, ed. Amy Clampitt (Hopewell, N.J.: Ecco, 1988), 68.
71. He refers to this image in his 1917 essay "Reflections on Contemporary Poetry," his 1920 essay "The Metaphysical Poets," and in the fourth of his lectures on metaphysical poetry delivered in 1926 at Trinity College, Cambridge.
72. "Mundus Mare," as it appears in *Donne's Sermons: Selected Passages*, with an essay by Logan Pearsall Smith.
73. T.S. Eliot, "The Preacher As Artist."
74. Donne 92.
75. T.S. Eliot, *Varieties*, 133.
76. T.S. Eliot, "Shakespeare and the Stoicism of Seneca," from *Selected Essays*, 118.
77. T.S. Eliot, "The Metaphysical Poets," from *Selected Prose*, 119.
78. Ibid., 117.
79. Ibid., 117.
80. T.S. Eliot, "Andrew Marvell," from *Sacred*, 107.
81. Ibid., 120.
82. T.S. Eliot, *Varieties*, 198.
83. Wordsworth, *The Two-Part Prelude* (1799), from *Norton*, 245.
84. Wordsworth, "Composed upon Westminster Bridge, September 3, 1802" from *Norton*, 186.
85. Wordsworth, *The Two-Part Prelude* (1799), from *Norton*, 249.
86. Wordsworth, *Preface to Lyrical Ballads* (1802), from *Norton*, 138.
87. Wordsworth, "Lines Composed a Few Miles above Tintern Abbey," from *Norton*, 122.
88. Wordsworth, *The Two-Part Prelude* (1799), from *Norton*, 199.
89. Coleridge, *Biographia Literaria* (1812), from *Norton*, 352–353.
90. Coleridge, "The Rime of the Ancyent Marinere," from *Norton*, 295.
91. Ibid., 306.
92. Hazlitt 782.
93. Coleridge, *Biographia* (1812), from *Norton*, 351.
94. Ibid., 357.
95. Coleridge, *Aids*, 1.
96. Ibid., 17.
97. Lovecraft.
98. Shelley, "Alastor, or The Spirit of Solitude," from *Norton*, 515.
99. Ibid., 520.
100. Ibid., 512.
101. Browning, "Childe Rolande to the Dark Tower Came," from *Norton*, 1153.
102. Ibid., 1156.
103. Yeats, "William Blake and the Imagination," from *Essays and Introductions* (New York: Collier, 1986), 111.
104. Blake, "Auguries of Innocence," from *The Complete Poetry & Prose of William Blake*, ed. David V. Erdman (New York: Anchor, 1988), 490.
105. Blake, "There Is No Natural Religion," from *Complete*, 3.
106. Blake, "London," from *Complete*, 26.
107. Blake 13.
108. Blake, "The Marriage of Heaven and Hell," from *Complete*, 34.
109. Blake 38.
110. Ibid., 39.
111. Blake, "The Marriage of Heaven and Hell," from *Complete*, 39.
112. T.S. Eliot, "William Blake," from *Sacred*, 88.
113. Ibid., 88.
114. Ibid., 92.
115. Ibid., 90.
116. Ibid., 91.
117. Valerie Eliot, *Letters*, 266.
118. Eliot to His Mother, 19 January 1919, in T.S. Eliot, *Letters*, 268.
119. Mathiessen, *Achievement*, 73–74.
120. Eliot to Mary Hutchinson, 11 July 1919, in T.S. Eliot, *Letters*, 318.
121. T.S. Eliot, *Sacred*, 33.
122. Ibid., 30–31.
123. Ibid., 33.
124. Eliot to Brigit Patmore, 27 May 1919, in T.S. Eliot, *Letters*, 297.
125. T.S. Eliot, *Sacred*, 58.
126. T.S. Eliot, *Letters*, 351.

127. Ibid., 414.
128. T.S. Eliot, *Sacred,* 98–100.
129. T.S. Eliot, *Letters,* 375.
130. Eliot to Sydney Schiff, 10 September 1920, in T.S. Eliot, *Letters,* 406.
131. Eliot to Richard Aldington, 6 July 1921, in T.S. Eliot, *Letters,* 460.
132. T.S. Eliot, "The Perfect Critic," from *Sacred,* 6.
133. T.S. Eliot, "The Possibility of Poetic Drama," from *Sacred,* 37.
134. Eliot to His Mother, 20 September 1920, from *Letters of T.S. Eliot,* 408.
135. T.S. Eliot, *Letters,* 441.
136. Ibid., 462.
137. Ibid., 465.
138. Eliot to Henry Eliot, 3 October 1921, in T.S. Eliot, *Letters,* 471.
139. William James 195.

Part V

1. Spengler 14.
2. Ibid., 18.
3. Ibid., 19.
4. Ibid., 22.
5. Ibid., 41.
6. Ibid., 21.
7. Durant, *Mansions,* 130–131.
8. Goethe, *Faust* Part I, lines 364–365.
9. Ibid., lines 1224–1237.
10. Ibid., lines 713–719.
11. Ibid., lines 1620–1626.
12. Ibid., line 113.
13. Ibid., lines 3454–3458.
14. Ibid., lines 3462–3465.
15. Goethe: *Faust* Part II, lines 11936–11937.
16. Ibid., lines 11807–11808.
17. Kaufmann 56.
18. Mann 22.
19. Nietzsche, *Basic,* 111.
20. Ibid., 135.
21. Ibid., 128.
22. Ibid., 127.
23. Ibid., 127.
24. Jean Verdenal to Eliot, 5 February 1912, in T.S. Eliot, *Letters,* 31.
25. Nietzsche, "Ecce Homo," from *Basic Writings of Nietzsche,* ed. Walter Kaufmann (New York: Modern Library, 2000), 756.
26. Nietzsche, *Portable,* 125.
27. Ibid., 232.
28. Ibid.
29. Ibid., 200.
30. Ibid., 137.
31. Ibid., 233.
32. Ibid., 125.
33. Ibid., 101.
34. Ibid., 258.
35. Ibid., 266.
36. Ibid., 270.
37. Ibid., 251.
38. Ibid., 342.
39. Ibid., 69.
40. Ibid., 185.
41. Nietzsche, "Mixed Opinions and Maxims," from *Portable,* 66.
42. Nietzsche, *Portable,* 307.
43. Ibid., 251.
44. T.S. Eliot, "John Bramhall," from *Selected Essays* (New York: Harcourt, 1950), 317.
45. See Eliot's review of *The Philosophy of Nietzsche* by A. Wolf, published in the *International Journal of Ethics,* April 1916.
46. William James 48.
47. Nietzsche, *Portable,* 159.
48. Ibid., 549.
49. Bergonzi 102 (quoted from the *Athaenaeum,* May 30, 1919).
50. Ibid., 102 (quoted from *The Dial,* September 1922).
51. Dostoyevsky, *Notes,* 203.
52. Dostoevsky, "The Grand Inquisitor."
53. Ibid.
54. Ibid.
55. Hesse, "*The Brothers Karamazov,* or The Downfall of Europe."
56. Ibid.
57. Ibid.
58. Hesse, *Soul,* 74.
59. Ibid., 81.
60. Ibid., 89.
61. Hesse, *If the War,* 59–60.
62. Hesse, *Demian,* 24–25.
63. Ibid., 52.
64. Ibid., 119.
65. Ibid., 128.
66. Ibid., 139.
67. Hesse, "On Recent German Poetry."
68. Valerie Eliot, *Letters,* 509–510.
69. Frazer 417.
70. Jung, *Psychology,* 85.
71. Ibid., 80.
72. Ibid., 85.
73. Ibid., 343.
74. Ibid., 263.
75. Ibid., 479.
76. Jung, *Modern,* 165.
77. T.S. Eliot, "Ulysses, Order and Myth," from *Selected Prose,* 177.
78. Ashe 215–217.
79. Malory 608.
80. Ibid., 665.
81. Ibid., 666.
82. Ibid., 705.
83. Tennyson 214.
84. Ibid., 216.
85. Ibid., 218.
86. Ibid., 230.
87. Frazer 11.
88. Jung, *Psychology,* 236.
89. Frazer 104.
90. Weston 88.
91. Ibid., 126.
92. Ibid., 80.
93. Gardner, *Art* 87.
94. Ibid., 87.
95. Vittoz 13.
96. Ibid., 13.
97. See T.S. Eliot, *Letters,* 495.
98. Gordon 183.
99. Seymour-Jones 296.
100. Vittoz 28.
101. Eliot to Henry Eliot, 15 December 1921, in T.S. Eliot, *Letters,* 493.
102. Eliot to Sydney Waterlow, 19 December 1921, in T.S. Eliot, 495.
103. Morris 86–88.
104. T.S. Eliot, *Early Youth,* 30.
105. Jung, *Psychology,* 323.
106. T.S. Eliot, *Complete,* 38.
107. Ibid.

108. Jung, *Psychology,* 117.
109. Ibid., 41.
110. T.S. Eliot, *Complete,* 38.
111. Huxley, *Crome,* 93.
112. Ibid., 34.
113. Ibid., 36.
114. Gordon 178.
115. Weston 79.
116. T.S. Eliot, *Complete,* 51.
117. Dwivedi 49.
118. T.S. Eliot, *Complete,* 39.
119. Ibid., 39.
120. Jung, *Psychology,* 50.
121. Vittoz 25.
122. T.S. Eliot, *Complete,* 52.
123. Ibid., 40.
124. Valerie Eliot, *Letters,* 584.
125. T.S. Eliot, *Complete,* 41.
126. Edwin Arnold 70.
127. Ibid., 71.
128. Ibid., 77.
129. Spender 46.
130. T.S. Eliot, *Waste,* 31.
131. T.S. Eliot, *Complete,* 42.
132. Ibid., 42–43.
133. Ibid., 43.
134. Grover Smith 84.
135. T.S. Eliot, *Complete,* 43.
136. Grover Smith 87.
137. T.S. Eliot, *Complete,* 52.
138. Ibid., 52.
139. Hargrove 77.
140. T.S. Eliot, *Complete,* 47.
141. Eliot, T.S., "London Letter, May 1921," from *The Annotated Waste Land and Eliot's Contemporary Prose,* ed. Lawrence Rainey (New Haven: Yale University Press, 1995), 170.
142. Eliot, T.S., "London Letter, July 1921," from *The Annotated Waste Land,* 183.
143. T.S. Eliot, *Complete,* 46.
144. Ibid., 46.
145. T.S. Eliot, *Waste,* 67.
146. T.S. Eliot, *Complete,* 47.
147. Ibid., 53.
148. Ibid., 38.
149. Ibid., 48.
150. Ibid., 48.
151. Hargrove 84–85.
152. Tennyson 74.
153. Ibid., 175.
154. T.S. Eliot, *Complete,* 49.
155. Ibid., 55.
156. Dwivedi 151.
157. Vittoz 41.
158. Ibid., 45.
159. T.S. Eliot, *Complete,* 49–50.
160. T.S. Eliot, *Letters,* 490.
161. Dwivedi 151.
162. T.S. Eliot, *Complete,* 53.
163. T.S. Eliot, *Waste,* 129.

Part VI

1. Eliot to Richard Aldington, 15 November 1922, in T.S. Eliot, *Letters,* 596.
2. Eliot to Henry Eliot, 11 October 1922, in T.S. Eliot, *Letters,* 580.
3. Seymour-Jones 329.
4. Ibid., 356–366.

5. Gordon 188.
6. Dante, "Vita Nuova," from *The Portable Dante,* II.
7. Ibid., XII.
8. Ibid., XXXI.
9. Aquinas 120.
10. Dante, "Purgatory," from *The Portable Dante,* XVIII. 34–39.
11. Dante, "Paradise," from *The Portable Dante,* XXXIII. 133–145.
12. T.S. Eliot, "Dante," from *Sacred,* 100.
13. Ibid., 99.
14. T.S. Eliot, *Varieties,* 220.
15. Ibid., 53.
16. T.S. Eliot, "Shakespeare and the Stoicism of Seneca," from *Selected Essays,* 116.
17. T.S. Eliot, "Dante," from *Selected Essays,* 214.
18. T.S. Eliot, *Varieties,* 115.
19. Ibid., 54.
20. Ibid., 115.
21. See T.S. Eliot, *Varieties,* 125, 222.
22. T.S. Eliot, "Baudelaire," from *Selected Essays,* 378–379.
23. T.S. Eliot, *Varieties,* 212–213.
24. Ibid., 216.
25. Andrewes, *Sermons* (1635), 890.
26. Welsby 148.
27. Ibid., 149.
28. T.S. Eliot, "Lancelot Andrewes," from *Selected Essays,* 301.
29. T.S. Eliot, *Selected Prose,* 70.
30. Ibid., 71.
31. T.S. Eliot, "Lancelot Andrewes," *Selected Essays,* 301.
32. T.S. Eliot, *Complete,* 77.
33. Ibid., 90.
34. Ibid., 90.
35. Ibid., 57.
36. Ibid., 57.
37. Ibid., 58.
38. Dante, "Purgatory," from *The Portable Dante,* XXXI. 5, 10–11.
39. T.S. Eliot, *Complete,* 40.
40. Grover Smith, 102.
41. T.S. Eliot, *Letters,* 25.
42. Conrad, *Great,* 203.
43. Conrad, *Heart,* 1855.
44. Ibid., 1861.
45. Ibid., 1841, 1844.
46. Ibid., 1850.
47. Ibid., 1877.
48. Ibid., 1885.
49. Ibid., 1897.
50. T.S. Eliot, *Letters,* 497.
51. Frazer 705–706.
52. T.S. Eliot, *Use,* 148.
53. Ibid., 111.
54. Valéry, "Poetry and Abstract Thought," from *Paul Valéry: An Anthology,* ed. James R. Lawler (Princeton: Princeton University Press, 1977), 158–159.
55. T.S. Eliot, "A Brief Introduction to the Method of Paul Valéry," from *Le Serpent* (London: The Criterion, 1924), 8.
56. Valéry, "Man and the Sea Shell," from *Paul Valéry: An Anthology,* 132.
57. Ibid., 132.
58. Valéry, "The Graveyard by the Sea," from *Paul Valéry: An Anthology,* 164.
59. Valéry, "Poetry and Abstract Thought," from *Paul Valéry: An Anthology,* 156–157.
60. T.S. Eliot, "A Brief Introduction," from *Le Serpent,* 10.

61. Swinburne, "By the North Sea."
62. Valéry, *Le Serpent,* 271.
63. Ibid., 271.
64. Ibid., 273.
65. Ibid., 277.
66. T.S. Eliot, "A Brief Introduction," from *Le Serpent,* 12.
67. Bergonzi 111 (from "A Note on Poetry and Belief," *The Enemy,* January 1927).
68. Royce 404.
69. Ibid., 404.
70. Ibid., 197.
71. Ibid., 404.
72. Babbitt, *Literature,* 75.
73. Royce 213.
74. T.S. Eliot, "The Humanism of Irving Babbitt," from *Selected Essays,* 423.
75. T.S. Eliot, "A Dialogue on Dramatic Poetry," from *Selected Essays,* 36.
76. T.S. Eliot, "The Humanism of Irving Babbitt," from *Selected Essays* 426.
77. T.S. Eliot, Preface, from *Thoughts for Meditation: A Way to Recovery from Within* (London: Faber, 1951), 13.
78. T.S. Eliot, *After,* 40–41.
79. Valerie Eliot, *Letters,* 336.
80. Eliot to Sydney Schiff, 12 January 1920, in T.S. Eliot, *Letters,* 355.
81. Mathiessen, *Achievement,* 142.
82. Buthman 157.
83. Margolis 95 (quoted from "Hommage à Charles Maurras," 1948).
84. T.S. Eliot, "Thoughts after Lambeth," from *Selected Essays,* 342.
85. T.S. Eliot, *Notes,* 115.
86. Sigg 149.
87. Brooks 4.
88. Ibid., 38.
89. Brooks, "The Seven-Arts Essays," from *Van Wyck Brooks: The Early Years, A Selection from His Works 1908–1925,* ed. Claire Sprague (Boston: Northeastern University Press, 1993), 187.
90. Brooks 56.
91. Emerson, "Nature," from *Norton,* 903.
92. Ibid., 904.
93. Ibid., 905.
94. Emerson, "The American Scholar," from *Norton,* 935.
95. Ibid., 933.
96. Emerson, "The Divinity School Address," from *Norton,* 949.

97. Babbitt 86.
98. Brooks 113.
99. Eliot to his Mother, 19 September 1917, in T.S. Eliot, *Letters,* 196.
100. Barrett 433.
101. Brooks 99.
102. Ibid., 110.
103. Hawthorne 1057.
104. Ibid., 1064.
105. Henry James, *Hawthorne.*
106. T.S. Eliot, "Hawthorne," 33.
107. Ibid., 35.
108. Ibid., 31.
109. Henry James, *The American,* 543.
110. T.S. Eliot, "Hawthorne," 30.
111. Mathiessen, *American,* 193.
112. Ibid., 368.
113. Southam 137.
114. Andrewes, *Sermons* (1967), 100–101.
115. Ibid., 109.
116. Ibid., 110.
117. Mathiessen, *Achievement,* 11.
118. T.S. Eliot, *Collected,* 68.
119. Southam 129.
120. T.S. Eliot, *Collected,* 61.
121. Dante, "Vita Nuova," from *The Portable Dante,* III.
122. T.S. Eliot, *Complete,* 63.
123. Andrewes, *Sermons* (1967), 120.
124. Ibid., 122–123.
125. T.S. Eliot, *Complete,* 63.
126. Andrewes, *Sermons* (1967), 129.
127. Ibid., 140.
128. T.S. Eliot, *Complete,* 64.
129. Andrewes, *Sermons* (1967), 122.
130. Ibid., 141.
131. Eliot to his Father, 14 January 1916, in T.S. Eliot, *Letters,* 127.
132. T.S. Eliot, *Letters,* 145.
133. Dante, "Paradise," from *The Portable Dante,* III. 85–87.
134. T.S. Eliot, *Complete,* 66.
135. Ibid., 67.
136. T.S. Eliot, Preface, from *This American World* (London: Faber, 1928), xiv.
137. Mathiessen, *Achievement,* 186.
138. Eliot to his Mother, 30 December 1917, *Letters of T.S. Eliot,* 215.
139. Southam 146.
140. Read 26.
141. T.S. Eliot, Preface, from *This American World.*

Bibliography

Ackroyd, Peter. *T.S. Eliot: A Life*. New York: Simon and Schuster, 1984.

Adams, Henry. *The Education of Henry Adams: An Autobiography*. Cambridge: Riverside, 1918.

Aeschylus. *Agamemnon. The Complete Greek Tragedies, Volume 1*. Ed. David Grene and Richmond Lattimore. Chicago: University of Chicago Press, 1953.

_____. *The Eumenides. The Complete Greek Tragedies, Volume 1*. Ed. David Gerene and Richmond Lattimore. Chicago: University of Chicago Press, 1953.

Andrewes, Lancelot. *Sermons*. 4th Edition. : London: Richard Badger, 1635.

_____. *Sermons*. Ed. G.M. Story. Oxford: Oxford University Press, 1967.

Anesaki, Masaharu. *History of Japanese Religion, with Special Reference to the Social and Moral Life of the Nation*. Rutland, Vt.: Charles E. Tuttle, 1963.

Aquinas, Thomas. *Aquinas's Shorter Summa: Saint Thomas's Own Concise Version of His Summa Theologica*. Trans. Cyril Vollert. Manchester, N.H.: Sophia Institute Press, 2002.

Aristotle. *A New Aristotle Reader*. Ed. J.L. Akrill. Princeton: Princeton University Press, 1987.

Arnold, Edwin. *The Light of Asia; or, The Great Renunciation: Being the Life and Teaching of Gautama, Prince of India and Founder of Buddhism*. Philadelphia: David McKay, 1932.

Arnold, Matthew. "The Buried Life." *The Norton Anthology of American Literature*. Third Edition, Volume 1. Ed. Nina Baym, et al. New York: Norton, 1989.

_____. "Dover Beach." *The Norton Anthology of American Literature*. Third Edition, Volume 1. Ed. Nina Baym, et al. New York: Norton, 1989.

_____. "The Scholar Gypsy." *The Norton Anthology of American Literature*. Third Edition, Volume 1. Ed. Nina Baym, et al. New York: Norton, 1989.

_____. "The Study of Poetry." *The Norton Anthology of American Literature*. Third Edition, Volume 1. Ed. Nina Baym, et al. New York: Norton, 1989.

Arnold, Matthew, and Lewis E. Gates. *Selections from the Prose Writings of Matthew Arnold*. New York: Henry Holt, 1898.

Ashe, Geoffrey. *Mythology of the British Isles*. North Pomfret, Vt.: Trafalgar Square, 1990.

Augustine. *Confessions*. Trans. R.S. Pine-Coffin. New York: Penguin, 1961.

Babbitt, Irving. *The Dhammapada: Translated from the Pali with an Essay on Buddha and the Occident*. New York: Oxford University Press, 1936.

_____. *Literature and the American College: Essays in Defense of the Humanities*. Washington D.C.: National Humanities Institute, 1986.

Barnstone, Willis. "Manichean Creation Myths." *The Other Bible*. San Francisco: HarperSanFrancisco, 2005.

Baudelaire, Charles. *Echoes of Baudelaire: Selected Poems*. Trans. and ed. Kendall Lappin. Santa Maria, Calif.: Asylum Arts, 1992.

Bentley, Eric, ed. *John Webster and Cyril Tourneur: Four Plays*. New York: Hill and Wang, 1956.

Bergonzi, Bernard. *T.S. Eliot (Masters of World Literature)*. New York: Macmillan, 1972.

Bergson, Henri. *Creative Evolution*. Trans. Arthur Mitchell. New York: Henry Holt, 1913.

Blake, William. *The Complete Poetry and Prose of William Blake*. Ed. David V. Erdman. New York: Anchor, 1988.

Bradley, F.H. *Appearance and Reality: A Metaphysical Essay*. Sixth Impression (Corrected). London: George Allen & Unwin, 1916.

Brooks, Van Wyck. *Van Wyck Brooks: The Early Years, A Selection from His Works 1908–1925*. Revised Edition. Ed. Claire Sprague. Boston: Northeastern University Press, 1993.

Browning, Robert. "Childe Roland to the Dark Tower Came." *The Norton Anthology of American Literature*. Third Edition, Volume 1. Ed. Nina Baym, et al. New York: Norton, 1989.

Bush, Ronald. *T.S. Eliot: A Study in Character and Style*. New York: Oxford University Press, 1983.

Buthman, William Curt. *The Rise of Integral Nationalism in France, with Special Reference to the Ideas and Activities of Charles Maurras*. New York: Columbia University Press, 1939.

Coleridge, Samuel Taylor. *Aids to Reflection, to which are added His Essays on Faith and the Book of Common Prayer, etc.* New Edition, Revised. Eugene, Ore.: Wipf & Stock, 2006.

_____. "Biographia Literaria." *The Norton Anthology of American Literature.* Third Edition, Volume 1. Ed. Nina Baym, et al. New York: Norton, 1989.

_____. "The Rime of the Ancyent Marinere." *The Norton Anthology of American Literature.* Third Edition, Volume 1. Ed. Nina Baym, et al. New York: Norton, 1989.

Conrad, Joseph. *Great Works of Joseph Conrad.* New York: Perennial, 1966.

_____. "Heart of Darkness." *The Norton Anthology of American Literature.* Third Edition, Volume 1. Ed. Nina Baym, et al. New York: Norton, 1989.

Dalrymple, William. *City of Djinns: A Year in Delhi.* New York: Penguin, 1993.

Dante Alighieri. *The Portable Dante.* Trans. Mark Musa. New York: Penguin, 1995.

Davidson, John. "Thirty Bob a Week." Representative Poetry Online. Ed. Ian Lancashire. 1998. Department of English, University of Toronto. 8 August 2007. http://rpo.library.utoronto.ca/poem/626.html.

Donne, John. *The Essential Donne.* Ed. Amy Clampitt. Hopewell, N.J.: Ecco, 1988.

Dostoevsky, Fyodor. "The Grand Inquisitor." Trans. Constance Garnett. 1879. Comp. Ben Corbett. Webster University. 30 April 2007. http://www.webster.edu/~corbetre/philosophy/existentialism/dostoevsky/grand.html.

_____. *Notes from Underground, White Nights, The Dream of a Ridiculous Man, and Selections from The House of the Dead.* Trans. Andrew R. MacAndrew. New York: Signet, 1961.

Dowson, Ernest. *The Poetry of Ernest Dowson.* Ed. Desmond Flower. Cranbury, N.J.: Associated University Presses, 1970.

Drew, Elizabeth. *T.S. Eliot: The Design of His Poetry.* New York: Scribner, 1949.

Durant, Will. *The Mansions of Philosophy.* New York: Simon and Schuster, 1929.

Dwivedi, A.N. *T.S. Eliot: A Critical Study.* New Delhi, India: Atlantic, 2002.

Easwaran, Eknath, trans. *The Bhavagad Gita.* Berkeley, Calif.: Blue Mountain, 1985.

_____, trans. *The Upanishads.* Berkeley, Calif.: Blue Mountain, 1987.

Edwards, Jonathan. "Sinners in the Hands of an Angry God." *The Norton Anthology of American Literature.* Third Edition, Volume 1. Ed. Nina Baym, et al. New York: Norton, 1989.

Egendorf, Lauren K., ed. "The Characteristics of Elizabethan Drama." *Elizabethan Drama: The Greenhaven Press Companion to Literary Movements and Genres.* San Diego: Greenhaven, 2000.

Eliot, T.S. *After Strange Gods: A Primer of Modern Heresy: The Page-Barbour Lectures at the University of Virginia, 1933.* London: Faber, 1934.

_____. *The Annotated Waste Land with Eliot's Contemporary Prose.* Ed. Lawrence Rainey. New Haven: Yale University Press, 1995.

_____. "A Brief Introduction to the Method of Paul Valéry." *Le Serpent.* London: The Criterion, 1924.

_____. *The Complete Poems and Plays, 1909–1950.* New York: Harcourt, 1967.

_____. "Eeldrop and Appleplex." Project Gutenberg. 8 August 2007. http://www.gutenberg.org/etext/5982.

_____. *George Herbert (Writers and Their Work).* Plymouth, UK: Northcote House, 1994.

_____. "The Hawthorne Aspect." *Critics on Henry James.* Ed. J. Don Vann. Coral Gables: University of Miami Press, 1972.

_____. *Inventions of the March Hare, Poems 1909–1917.* Ed. Christopher Ricks. New York: Harcourt, 1996.

_____. *Knowledge and Experience in the Philosophy of F.H. Bradley.* New York: Farrar, Straus, 1964.

_____. *The Letters of T.S. Eliot, Volume I: 1898–1922.* Ed. Valerie Eliot. New York: Harcourt, 1988.

_____. *Notes towards the Definition of Culture. Christianity and Culture.* New York: Harcourt, 1949.

_____. *On Poetry and Poets.* London: Faber, 1957.

_____. *Poems Written in Early Youth.* Ed. John Hayward. New York: Farrar, Straus, 1967.

_____. "The Preacher As Artist." 1919. Ed. Richard A. Parker. Exploring Online Books. March 17, 2007. http://world.std.com/~raparker/exploring/books/the_preacher_as_artist.html.

_____. Preface. *Nightwood.* London: Faber, 1936.

_____. Preface. *This American World.* London: Faber, 1928.

_____. Preface. *Thoughts for Meditation: A Way to Recovery from Within.* London: Faber, 1951.

_____. *The Sacred Wood and Major Early Essays.* Mineola, N.Y.: Dover, 1998.

_____. "The Second Order Mind." 1920. Ed. Judy Boss. Electronic Text Center, University of Virginia Library. 19 February 2007. http://etext.lib.virginia.edu/etcbin/browse-mixednew?tag=public&images=images/modeng&data=/texts/english/modeng/parsed&part=0&id=EliMind.

_____. *Selected Essays (New Edition).* New York: Harcourt, 1950.

_____. *Selected Prose of T.S. Eliot.* Ed. Frank Kermode. New York: Harcourt, 1975.

_____. *To Criticize the Critic and Other Writings.* Lincoln: University of Nebraska Press, 1965.

_____. *The Use of Poetry and the Use of Criticism: The Charles Eliot Norton Lectures for 1932–33.* Cambridge: Harvard University Press, 1933.

_____. *The Varieties of Metaphysical Poetry: The Clark Lectures at Trinity College, Cambridge, 1926, and The Turnbull Lectures at The Johns Hopkins University, 1933.* Ed. Ronald Schuchard. New York: Harcourt, 1993.

_____. *The Waste Land: A Facsimile and Transcript of the Original Drafts Including the Annotations of Ezra Pound.* Ed. Valerie Eliot. New York: Harvest, 1971.

Emerson, Ralph Waldo. "The American Scholar." *The Norton Anthology of American Literature.* Third Edition, Volume 1. Ed. Nina Baym, et al. New York: Norton, 1989.

_____. "The Divinity School Address." *The Norton Anthology of American Literature.* Third Edition, Volume 1. Ed. Nina Baym, et al. New York: Norton, 1989.

_____. "Nature." *The Norton Anthology of American Literature.* Third Edition, Volume 1. Ed. Nina Baym, et al. New York: Norton, 1989.

Fitzgerald, Edward. *The Rubaiyat of Omar Khayyam.* New York: Arden, 1967.

Frazer, James George. *The Golden Bough: A Study in Magic and Religion (Abridged).* New York: Macmillan, 1963.

Freud, Sigmund. *The Interpretation of Dreams.* Trans. James Strachey. New York: Avon, 1965.

Gallup, Donald. *T.S. Eliot: A Bibliography.* New York: Harcourt, 1953.

Gardner, Helen. *The Art of T.S. Eliot.* New York: E.P. Dutton, 1949.

Goethe, Johann Wolfgang. *Faust: Part One and Sections from Part Two.* Trans. Walter Kaufmann. New York: Anchor, 1990.

Gordon, Lyndall. *T.S. Eliot: An Imperfect Life.* New York: Norton, 1998.

Halliday, F.E. *The Life of Shakespeare.* Baltimore: Penguin, 1961.

Hamilton, Edith. *Mythology: Timeless Tales of Gods and Heroes.* Boston: Little, Brown, 1940.

Hargrove, Nancy Duvall. *Landscape as Symbol in the Poetry of T.S. Eliot.* Jackson: University of Mississippi Press, 1978.

Harris, Stephen L., and Gloria Platzner. *Classical Mythology: Images and Insights.* Second Edition. Mountain View, Calif.: Mayfield, 1998.

Hawthorne, Nathaniel. *Tales and Sketches: Including Twice-told Tales, Mosses from an Old Manse, and The Snow-Image.* New York: Penguin, 1996.

Hazlitt, William. "My First Acquaintance with Poets." *The Norton Anthology of American Literature.* Third Edition, Volume 1. Ed. Nina Baym, et al. New York: Norton, 1989.

Hesse, Herman. "*The Brothers Karamazov,* or the Downfall of Europe." 1922. Trans. Sydney Schiff. Ed. Richard A. Parker. Exploring Online Books. 8 August 2007. http://world.std.com/~raparker/exploring/books/hesse_hudson_ brothers.html.

_____. *Demian.* Trans. Michael Roloff and Michael Lebeck. New York: Harper & Row, 1965.

_____. *If the War Goes On....* Trans. Ralph Manheim. New York: Farrar, Straus, 1970.

_____. "On Recent German Poetry." Trans. F.S. Flint? 1922. Ed. Richard A. Parker. Exploring Online Books. 8 August 2007. http://world.std.com/~raparker/exploring/books/hesse_criterion_poetry.html.

_____. *Soul of the Age: Selected Letters of Herman Hesse, 1891–1962.* Trans. Mark Harman. Ed. Theodore Ziolkowski. New York: Farrar, Straus, 1991.

Hilton, Walter. *The Scale of Perfection.* London: John M. Watkins, 1948.

Hollander, P. Scott. *Tarot for Beginners: An Easy Guide to Understanding and Interpreting the Tarot.* St. Paul, Minn.: Llewellyn Publications, 2000.

Homer. *The Odyssey.* Trans. Robert Fitzgerald. New York: Farrar, Straus, 1961.

Howarth, Howard. *Notes on Some Figures behind T.S. Eliot.* Boston: Houghton Mifflin, 1964.

Hulme, T.E. *Selected Writings.* Ed. Patrick McGuinness. Manchester, U.K.: Carcanet, 1998.

Huxley, Aldous. *Crome Yellow.* New York: George H. Doran, 1922.

_____. *The Doors of Perception* and *Heaven and Hell.* New York: Perennial Library, 1990.

James, Henry. *The American. Novels 1871–1880.* New York: Library of America, 1983.

James, William. *Varieties of Religious Experience: A Study in Human Nature.* Charleston, S.C.: BiblioBazaar, 2007.

_____. *Hawthorne.* Project Gutenberg. 30 August 2007. http://www.gutenberg.org/etext/18566.

John of the Cross. *The Dark Night of the Soul* and *The Living Flame of Love.* London: Fount, 1995.

Julian of Norwich. *Showings (The Classics of Western Spirituality).* Trans. Edmund Colledge and James Walsh. New York: Paulist Press, 1978.

Jung, Carl. *Modern Man in Search of a Soul.* Trans. W.S. Dell and Cary F. Baynes. New York: Harcourt, 1933.

_____. *Psychology of the Unconscious.* Trans. Beatrice M. Hinkle. Mineola, N.Y.: Dover, 2002.

_____. *Word and Image.* Ed. Aniela Jaffe. Princeton: Princeton University Press, 1979.

Kaufmann, Walter. *From Shakespeare to Existentialism.* Garden City, N.Y.: Anchor, 1960.

Kenner, Hugh. *The Invisible Poet: T.S. Eliot.* New York: Ivan Obolensky, 1959.

Kirk, G.S., J.E. Raven, and M. Schofield. *The Presocratic Philosophers.* Second Edition. New York: Cambridge University Press, 1983.

Laforgue, Jules. *Selected Writings of Jules Laforgue.* Ed. and trans. William Jay Smith. New York: Grove, 1956.

Lovecraft, H.P. *Supernatural Horror in Literature.* 1927. Miskatonic University Press. 30 March 2007. http://www.yankeeclassic.com/miskatonic/library/stacks/literature/lovecraft/essays/supernat/supern00.htm.

Malory, Thomas. *Le Morte d'Arthur.* New York: Modern Library, 1999.

Mann, Thomas. "Goethe's *Faust.*" *Essays.* New York: Vintage, 1958.

Margolis, John D. *T.S. Eliot's Intellectual Development, 1922–1939.* Chicago: University of Chicago Press, 1972.

Matsunami, Kodo. *Introducing Buddhism.* Rutland, Vt.: Charles E. Tuttle, 1973.

Matthews, T.S. *Great Tom: Notes towards the Definition of T.S. Eliot.* New York: Harper & Row, 1973.

Matthiessen, F.O. *The Achievement of T.S. Eliot: An Essay on the Nature of Poetry.* Revised Edition. London: Oxford University Press, 1959.

_____. *American Renaissance: Art and Expression in the Age of Emerson and Whitman.* London: Oxford University Press, 1941.

Middleton, Thomas. *The Changeling.* Comp. Chris Cleary. The Tech Museum of Innovation. 27 February 2007. http://www.tech.org/~cleary/change.html.

_____. *Women Beware Women.* Edited by Charles Barber. Los Angeles: University of California Press, 1969.

Miller, James E., Jr. *T.S. Eliot: The Making of an American Poet.* University Park: Pennsylvania State University Press, 2005.

Morris, George L.K. "Marie, Marie, Hold On Tight." *T.S. Eliot: A Collection of Critical Essays.* Ed. Hugh Kenner. Englewood Cliffs, N.J.: Prentice-Hall, 1962.

Muller, Max, trans. *The Upanisads in Two Parts.* New York: Dover, 1962.

Nietzsche, Friedrich. *Basic Writings of Nietzsche.* Trans. and ed. Walter Kaufmann. New York: Modern Library, 2000.

_____. *Beyond Good and Evil: Prelude to a Philosophy of the Future.* Trans. and ed. Walter Kaufmann. New York: Random House, 1966.

_____. *The Portable Nietzsche.* Trans. and ed. Walter Kaufmann. New York: Viking, 1954.

Ovid. *Metamorphoses.* Trans. Charles Martin. New York: Norton, 2004.

Parsatharathy. A. *Choice Upanishads.* Mumbai, India: Vakil & Sons, 2001.

Plato. *Five Dialogues.* Trans. G.M.A. Grube. Indianapolis, Ind.: Hackett, 1981.

_____. *Great Dialogues of Plato.* Trans. W.H.D. Rouse. Ed. Eric H. Warmington and Philip G. Rouse. New York: Signet, 1999.

_____. *Plato's Republic.* Trans. G.M.A. Grube. Indianapolis, Ind.: Hackett, 1974.

_____. "The Republic." Trans. Paul Shorey. *The Collected Dialogues of Plato.* Ed. Edith Hamilton and Huntington Cairns. Princeton: Princeton University Press, 1961.

Plotinus. *The Essential Plotinus: Representative Treatises from The Enneads.* Trans. Elmer O'Brien. Indianapolis, Ind.: Hackett, 1964.

Poe, Edgar Allan. *The Collected Tales and Poems of Edgar Allan Poe.* New York: Modern Library, 1992.

Read, Herbert. "T.S.E. — A Memoir." *T.S. Eliot: The Man and His Work.* Ed. Allen Tate. New York: Penguin, 1966.

Reat, Noble Ross. *Buddhism: A History.* Berkeley, Calif.: Asian Humanities, 1994.

Riley, Gregory J. *One Jesus, Many Christs: How Jesus Inspired Not One True Christianity, but Many.* San Francisco: HarperSanFrancisco, 1997.

Rimbaud, Arthur. *Rimbaud Complete.* Trans. and ed. Wyatt Mason. New York: Modern Library, 2002.

Royce, Josiah. *The Problem of Christianity.* Chicago: University of Chicago Press, 1968.

Russell, Bertrand. *The Autobiography of Bertrand Russell, Vol. II.* Boston: Little, Brown, 1968.

_____. "Mysticism and Logic." *Mysticism and Logic Including A Free Man's Worship.* New York: Routledge, 2004.

Santayana, George. *The Philosophy of Santayana.* Ed. Irwin Edman. New York: Random House, 1942.

Schuchard, Ronald. *Eliot's Dark Angel: Intersections of Life and Art.* New York: Oxford University Press, 1999.

Scott, Henry Eliot. *The Family of William Greenleaf Eliot 1811–1887 and Abby Adams Eliot 1817–1908 (Fifth Edition).* [Wasilla, Alaska]: H.E. Scott: 1988.

Seltzer, Mark. *Serial Killers: Death and Life in America's Wound Culture.* New York: Routledge, 1988.

Seymour-Jones, Carole. *Painted Shadow: The Life of Vivienne Eliot, First Wife of T.S. Eliot.* New York: Anchor, 2001.

Shakespeare, William. *The Complete Works (Shakespeare Head Press Edition).* New York: Barnes & Noble, 1994.

Shelley, Percy Bysshe. "Alastor, or The Spirit of Solitude." *The Norton Anthology of American Literature (Third Edition, Volume 1).* Ed. Nina Baym, et al. New York: Norton, 1989.

Sigg, Eric. *The American T.S. Eliot: A Study of the Early Writings.* New York: Cambridge University Press, 1989.

Smith, Grover. *T.S. Eliot's Poetry and Plays: A Study in Sources and Meaning.* Chicago: University of Chicago Press, 1950.

Smith, William Jay. Introduction. *Selected Writings of Jules Laforgue.* New York: Grove, 1956.

Southam, B.C. *A Student's Guide to the Selected Poems of T.S. Eliot.* Fourth Edition. London: Faber, 1981.

Spender, Stephen. "Remembering Eliot." *T.S. Eliot: The Man and His Work.* Ed. Allen Tate. New York: Penguin, 1966.

Spengler, Oswald. *The Decline of the West, Volume I: Form and Actuality.* Trans. Charles Francis Atkinson. New York: Knopf, 1926.

Swinburne, Algernon Charles. "By the North Sea." Comp. George P. Landow. http://www.victorianweb.org/authors/swinburne/northsea.html. 15 December 2007.

Symons, Arthur. "Memoir [of Ernest Dowson]." Project Gutenberg. 8 August 2007. http://www.gutenberg.org/etext/8497.

_____. *The Symbolist Movement in Literature*. New York: E.P. Dutton, 1958.

Tennyson, Alfred. *Idylls of the King*. Ed. J.M. Gray. New York: Penguin, 1983.

Thomas, E.J., ed. and trans. *Buddhist Scriptures: A Selection Translated from the Pali*. London: John Murray, 1913.

Thomson, James. "The City of Dreadful Night." Comp. Mark Zimmerman. Encyclopedia of the Self. 7 October 2004. http://emotionalliteracy education.com/classic_books_online/ctdnt10.htm.

Thoreau, Henry David. *Walden and Other Writings*. New York: Barnes & Noble, 1993.

Underhill, Evelyn. *Mysticism (A Study in the Nature and Development of Man's Spiritual Consciousness)*. New York: New American Library, 1974.

Valéry, Paul. *Paul Valéry: An Anthology*. Ed. and trans. James R. Lawler. Princeton: Princeton University Press, 1977.

_____. *Le Serpent*. Trans. Mark Wardle. London: R. Cobden-Sanderson, 1924.

Van Dyke, John C. *The Desert*. Park City, Utah: Gibbs Smith, 1980.

Verlaine, Paul. *Selected Poems*. Trans. C.F. MacIntyre. Berkeley: University of California Press, 1948.

Virgil. *The Aeneid*. Trans. Patric Dickinson. Signet: New York, 1962.

Vittoz, Roger, and Christian H. Godefroy. *How to Control Your Brain at Will*. 2001. 21 June 2007. http://www.norom.com/ebooks/(ebook%20-%20english)%20How%20To%20Control%20Your%20Brain%20At%20Will.pdf.

Warren, Henry Clark. *Buddhism in Translations (Harvard Oriental Series)*. Vol. III. 1896. Comp. Christopher Weimer. The Internet Sacred Text Archive. 8 August 2007. http://www.sacred-texts.com/bud/bits/index.htm.

Watson, Peter. *The Modern Mind: An Intellectual History of the 20th Century*. New York: Harper, 2001.

Welsby, Paul A. *Lancelot Andrewes, 1555–1626*. London: S.P.C.K., 1958.

Wendell, Barrett. *A Literary History of America*. New York: Scribner, 1928.

Weston, Jessie. *From Ritual to Romance*. Garden City, N.Y.: Doubleday, 1957.

Whitman, Walt. "Leaves of Grass." *The Norton Anthology of American Literature*. Third Edition, Volume 1. Ed. Nina Baym, et al. New York: Norton, 1989.

Wilken, Robert L. *The Christians As the Romans Saw Them*. New Haven: Yale University Press, 1984.

Williams, Monier. *Indian Wisdom, or Examples of the Religious, Philosophical and Ethical Doctrines of the Hindus*. New Delhi, India: Rupa, 2001.

Wolters, Clifton, trans. *The Cloud of Unknowing and Other Works*. New York: Penguin, 1978.

Wordsworth, William. "Composed upon Westminster Bridge, September 3, 1802." *The Norton Anthology of American Literature*. Third Edition, Volume 1. Ed. Nina Baym, et al. New York: Norton, 1989.

_____. "Lines Composed a Few Miles Above Tintern Abbey." *The Norton Anthology of American Literature*. Third Edition, Volume 1. Ed. Nina Baym, et al. New York: Norton, 1989.

_____. "Ode: Intimations of Immortality from Recollections of Early Childhood." *The Norton Anthology of American Literature*. Third Edition, Volume 1. Ed. Nina Baym, et al. New York: Norton, 1989.

_____. "Preface to *Lyrical Ballads, with Pastoral and Other Poems*." *The Norton Anthology of American Literature*. Third Edition, Volume 1. Ed. Nina Baym, et al. New York: Norton, 1989.

_____. "The Two-Part Prelude." *The Norton Anthology of American Literature*. Third Edition, Volume 1. Ed. Nina Baym, et al. New York: Norton, 1989.

Yeats, W.B. "The Adoration of the Magi." 3 September 2007. http://www.HorrorMasters.com.

_____. "At Stratford-on-Avon." *Essays and Introductions*. New York: Collier, 1986.

_____. "The Autumn of the Body." *Essays and Introductions*. New York: Collier, 1986.

_____. *The Yeats Reader: A Portable Compendium of Poetry Drama and Prose (Revised Edition)*. Ed. Richard J. Finneran. New York: Scribner, 2002.

Index